Site of Governor Tryon's Residence (Russellboro) and Scene of Resistance to the Stamp Act

A History of New Hanover County

❖NORTH CAROLINA❖

and the

Lower Cape Fear Region

1723-1800

VOLUME I

Alfred Moore Waddell

HERITAGE BOOKS
2008

HERITAGE BOOKS
AN IMPRINT OF HERITAGE BOOKS, INC.

Books, CDs, and more—Worldwide

For our listing of thousands of titles see our website at
www.HeritageBooks.com

A Facsimile Reprint
Published 2008 by
HERITAGE BOOKS, INC.
Publishing Division
100 Railroad Ave. #104
Westminster, Maryland 21157

Originally published 1909

— Publisher's Notice —
In reprints such as this, it is often not possible to remove blemishes from the original. We feel the contents of this book warrant its reissue despite these blemishes and hope you will agree and read it with pleasure.

International Standard Book Numbers
Paperbound: 978-1-55613-268-1
Clothbound: 978-0-7884-7540-5

CONTENTS

CHAPTER I 7
Establishment of the precinct in 1729 (changed to county in 1738)—Its limits—Boundary line between North and South Carolina—The town of Brunswick and its history—History of St. Philip's Church—The Stamp Act troubles—Sons of Liberty.

CHAPTER II 38
The names of the earliest plantations, their location and their owners, with items of biography and incidents.

CHAPTER III 73
Under Martin's administration—Fire in Wilmington—A bold adventuress—The Scotch immigrants and Flora McDonald—Beginning of the Revolution—Help for Boston—Organization of Safety Committees.

CHAPTER IV 86
Proceedings of the Safety Committee of the town of Wilmington, with occasional minutes of joint meetings of the Committee of New Hanover County and the Committee of the District of Wilmington, in 1774, 1775 and 1776.

CHAPTER V 166
Burning of Fort Johnston and expulsion of Governor Martin—Vigilance of the Wilmington Committee—Movement of Scotch Highlanders — Battle of Moore's Creek Bridge — Colonel Moore's report—Letter of Colonel Purviance.

CHAPTER VI 175
Martin's and Parry's correspondence with the Committee—Clinton's Proclamation—Howe's plantation plundered—British abandon the Cape Fear until 1781—Craig comes in 1781—His operations.

CHAPTER VII 191
Wilmington from 1736 to 1800.

CHAPTER VIII 212
Fort Johnston and Smithville (now Southport).

CHAPTER IX 217
Interesting items from court minutes.

PREFACE

What is called the Lower Cape Fear Region of North Carolina has long been recognized by the writers of our history as the most interesting, and, as one of them designated it, "the most romantic" section of our State. Yet, up to this time, although partial sketches, historical and biographical, have appeared, no attempt at a regular history of it has been published, and, now such a history can not be written because of the destruction, by fires and otherwise, of a large part of the material requisite for the purpose. There was, perhaps, no part of the country where so many planters' residences with all their contents were lost by fire as on the Cape Fear and its tributaries, and it is well known among the descendants of those planters, some of whom were also members of the learned professions, that by these fires many manuscripts, family records, and documents of various kinds that would have been invaluable as material for the preparation of a local history, were lost. Besides these fires, the town of Wilmington was at an early period, as well as several times afterwards, nearly destroyed in the same way with the same results.

None of the ancient official records of the town of Brunswick were preserved, and a considerable part of the County records were destroyed by Northern soldiers when the town of Smithville (now Southport) was captured by them in 1865. Some of the town records of Wilmington of an early period have also disappeared.

There is enough material, however, for a fairly full history in the publications referred to, in the court records, and especially in the Colonial Records; and the writer of this book has undertaken the task of collating all the facts bearing upon the subject that are known. The volume covers only the period from 1723 to 1800. A second volume extending the work to the beginning of the war of 1861-65 may be published, if considered advisable. When this book was first projected William B. McKoy, Esq., of the Wilmington Bar, intended to unite with the author in preparing it as their joint work, but Mr. McKoy found it impossible to devote the necessary time to it, and reluctantly abandoned the enterprise. He, however, generously furnished some valuable material from his unequaled store of notes and memoranda on our local history, for which the author desires to make especial acknowledgment of his thanks. Mr. McKoy promises to publish at some early day a small work entitled "Chronicles of Wilmington."

The author is also under obligations to Messrs. Junius Davis, R. D. W. Connor, James Sprunt and J. Alves Walker, for various documents kindly loaned that have been helpful to him.

ALFRED MOORE WADDELL.

Wilmington, Nov. 5, 1909.

CHAPTER I

ESTABLISHMENT OF THE PRECINCT IN 1729 (CHANGED TO COUNTY IN 1738)—ITS LIMITS—BOUNDARY LINE BETWEEN NORTH AND SOUTH CAROLINA—THE TOWN OF BRUNSWICK AND ITS HISTORY—HISTORY OF ST. PHILIP'S CHURCH—THE STAMP ACT TROUBLES—SONS OF LIBERTY.

In the first subdivision of that part of the province of "Carolina" which has since the year 1729 been known as North Carolina, all the territory south of Albemarle and extending to the Cape Fear River was called Bath County, but its limits were undefined toward the South.* This southern part was, however, by an Act of Assembly, passed in July 1729, "erected into the precinct of New Hanover," the boundaries of which were prescribed to be "to the Northward by the Haule-over and Little Inlet, and to the Southward by the Southernmost bounds of the Province."

There were several places call the "Haulover" along the coast lower down than that named in the act. Little Inlet is marked on Wimble's map (1738), and was north of New River and between it and White Oak river, which identifies it with either Brown's, or Bear Inlet.

In 1734 an act was passed reciting that "as the precinct of New Hanover is now become very populous, and the extent thereof being found too incommodious to many of the inhabitants thereof, particularly those of New River and the upper part of the North West river," it was therefore enacted that a precinct be erected at New River by the name of Onslow precinct, and in the same Act "the upper part of the Northwest river" was "erected into a precinct by the name of Bladen precinct," the boundaries of each being prescribed.†

The southern boundary of New Hanover, named in the Act

---

* The territory south and west of the Cape Fear river, of which Yeamans was appointed governor in 1664, was named Clarendon county and extended to Florida. Albemarle and Clarendon were established in 1664, and Bath in 1669.

† Martin's Pub. Stat., 38

of 1729 was "the Southernmost bounds of the province," as already stated.

Where was this southernmost boundary line? For some time after the first settlements were made on the lower Cape Fear River that river was supposed to be the boundary line, and many grants for land south and west of the river were made by the Governors of the southern province (South Carolina) which then claimed and still claims the name "Carolina," but in the year 1729 the nominal division into North and South Carolina was generally recognized, and a start toward running the boundary line was made in 1734,* but it extended only a comparatively short distance, and the line continued to be a subject of doubt and uncertainty for half a century or more.

"This matter of boundary," says McCrady† in his History of South Carolina, "had not been of so much importance while the two colonies constituted but one province. But now that under his Majesty's government the territory was divided and distinct governments established, it became necessary that the limits of the two provinces, as they now were, should be definitely defined. In fact, however, this matter was not finally settled until 1815, and in the meanwhile was the subject of many disputes."

The original controversy over the boundary line arose out of the apparently conflicting instructions on the subject from the home government to Governor Burrington, of North Carolina, and Governor Johnson, of South Carolina, as to whether the line should be run from the mouth of Waccamaw River, or from a point thirty miles from the mouth of Cape Fear River, and continuing thence westwardly. Burrington displayed maps to the authorities in favor of the latter and his contention was sustained.

The line as finally run looks like a series of steps from the Atlantic toward the northwest for half its length, and an

---

* The commissioners on the part of North Carolina to run this line were Eleazer Allen, Edward Moseley, Robert Halton, Mathew Rowan, and Roger Moore.

† II, 110. In his Prefatory Chapter to the second volume of the Colonial Records, Colonel Saunders gives a very interesting summary of the history of this controversy.

irregular west line for the other half, and, like some other
State lines, is a geographical absurdity illustrative of the jealousy and land grabbing propensity of our race.

The Atlantic Ocean was the eastern boundary of New Hanover County, and the western boundary was "the South Seas,"
which was a term in common use, but conveyed no more
meaning in the then state of geographical knowledge than "the
land of sunset" would have done; but it was sufficient to embrace a territory of the width of the county indefinitely westward, which made it literally a boundless empire with a very
sparse population confined to the extreme eastern end.*

New Hanover precinct was alleged to have been unlawfully
established by Governor Everard and his council without the
concurrence of the Assembly in 1729, but John Swann and
John Porter were in that year elected representatives to the
Assembly, and Swann was admitted to his seat, although
Porter does not seem to have taken his. The act establishing
the precinct was part of an act for regulating vestries, which
act was repealed as to church matters, but not specifically
repealed as to the precinct.

It was a matter of controversy up to the time of Dobbs's
administration, and in 1760 Dobbs wrote to the Board of
Trade a full statement as to the legislation, justifying his
order for an election of representatives to the Assembly, and
that caused a final settlement of the matter.

New Hanover is now the smallest county in the State, containing, according to a United States survey, only about
122,752 acres, or approximately 192 square miles, in the shape
of a narrow triangle pointing southward, and is the southernmost county, except one (Brunswick) in the State.

In the treatment of his subject the author will confine himself chiefly to the territory generally called the lower Cape
Fear region, embracing the present county of New Hanover,
and the counties of Bladen, Brunswick, and Pender. He will

---

* Out of the territory of New Hanover the whole southern tier of counties of the State, including Onslow and Duplin, and thence westward, was carved. The dates of their respective formation may be found in Wheeler's History and other books.

not go back to the first attempts at colonization by the New England adventurers in 1660, and the Yeamans colony in 1664-65, for they were only temporary settlements and interesting incidents in our earliest history; but he begins with the first settlement at the town of Brunswick and along both branches of the river in the years 1723, 1724, and 1725. Contemporaneously with, and even prior to the settlement of the town, the larger part of the best lands on both branches of the river had been patented by the wealthier settlers.

OLD BRUNSWICK.

The history of this vanished town, of which the only remains are the four walls of its once imposing church, some tombstones, and the basements of some buildings covered by the mould of the surrounding forest, is both interesting and pathetic. It was laid out in 1725 on part of 320 acres of land given for the purpose by Col. Maurice Moore, second son of Governor James Moore of South Carolina, who had first come to the Albemarle country to aid in the suppression of the Indians in 1713, and, after making his home there for about ten years, removed to the Cape Fear, having induced his two brothers, Roger and Nathaniel, living in South Carolina, and other friends there and in Albemarle, to unite with him in founding the new settlement. A recital of some of the facts connected with the establishment of the town is contained in the preamble of an Act of Assembly passed in 1745, twenty years afterwards, entitled: "An Act to encourage persons to settle in the town of Brunswick on the southwest side of the Cape Fear River," which act also recites the conditions as to trade and navigation on the Cape Fear, and other facts, as good reasons to justify its passage.

At March term, 1727, of the General Court, held at Edenton, the following entry was made: "It being represented to this Court that it is highly necessary that a ferry should be settled over Cape Fear River, and that part of the province not being laid out into precincts, therefore it is by this Court ordered that the ferry be kept for that river by Cornelius Harnett from the place designed for a town on the west side of the river to a place called the haule-over*, and that he receive the sum of five shillings for a man and horse, and half a crown for each person, and that no person to keep any ferry within ten miles of the said place."

The Cornelius Harnett named in the order of the Court was the father of the distinguished man of that name, justly called "the pride of the Cape Fear," and was afterwards the innkeeper at Brunswick. He came from Albemarle, where he had married Mary,† daughter of Martin Holt (who succeeded him as inn-keeper and owner of the ferry), and he was afterwards the first sheriff of the county in 1739-41. His son and only child, above mentioned, married Mary, daughter of Joshua Grainger, Jr., and left no issue.‡

When established it was confidently believed that the town of Brunswick would grow into an important city, because of its situation near the mouth of the largest navigable river in the province, and because it was the only town in that region. It certainly seemed a reasonable belief, but, owing to various causes, the hope of its founders was never realized. However, during the half century of its existence it was the theater of stirring events, some of which are justly entitled to an honorable place on the page of history. It was the place of residence of three Colonial Governors—Johnston, Dobbs and Tryon—and three acting Governors—Rice, Rowan and Hasell—and the Assembly of the province convened there several times. It never reached larger proportions than those of a small town, having a white population of not more than four hundred, but there was not at that time, if ever since, a town on the continent

---

* This haulover was nearly opposite Brunswick, and the land there was conveyed by Maurice Moore to Col. Thomas Merrick April 21, 1736.

† Will of Mary Holt, mentioning C. Harnett, Jr., as grandson.—N. H. Records, C., p. 328.

‡ The name of Cornelius Harnett's wife was unknown, even on the Cape Fear, for nearly a hundred years, and until discovered by the present writer through references in wills and the fitting together of names and facts, which settled the question. Her sister was the mother of Judge Joshua Grainger Wright, and the ancestress of the prominent Wilmington family of that name. The four daughters of Joshua Grainger, Jr., Ann, Elizabeth, Mary, and Catherine, married Thos. Wright, Obadiah Holt, Cornelius Harnett, Jr., and Henry Young. Holt was Harnett's uncle and their wives were sisters.

of the same size that contained so many men who afterwards became equally distinguished in military and civil life, as an enumeration of some of them will show. First among them were Maj. Gen. Robert Howe and Cornelius Harnett, Jr., and Gen. John Ashe, and Gen. James Moore, and Judges Maurice and Alfred Moore, and Attorney-General Archibald MacLaine, and Chief Justices Allen, Hasell, and Smith, and others of whom further mention will be made when giving a list of the estates on the Cape Fear in the early days.

In laying out the town, lots were provided for a church, a market, and other public structures.*

THE PARISH AND CHURCH OF ST. PHILIP.

The history of the parish and church, which was the largest and handsomest one in the province, is as follows: In the year 1729, a year before there was any organized parish on the Cape Fear, the Rev. John LaPier, "a French Huguenot who had been ordained by the Bishop of London in 1708, and for many years had served a congregation of his own people in South Carolina, called St. Denis Parish," came into the region of the Cape Fear River upon the invitation of the people. He served for several years and removed to New Bern about 1735. He was succeeded by Rev. Richard Marsden, who had also been a minister in South Carolina from 1705 to 1709, but had removed to New Hanover and become a planter, trader, and ship owner. He died in 1742.† These two ministers served both St. Philip's at Brunswick and St. James's at Wilmington. Then in 1741 Rev. James Moir, also from South Carolina, came to St. James's first and then to St. Philip's, and served until about 1746, when, without notice, he went to Edgecombe on invitation of the

---

* At December Term, 1739, of the County Court, a poll tax of five shillings was laid to build a court-house and jail at Brunswick, but this tax was afterwards applied to build a court-house and jail at Wilmington, in pursuance of the determination of Governor Johnston and his faction to remove the seat of government to that place, and thus destroy the older town and the dominating influence of the Moores and their connections, who were designated as "The Family," and who had brought with them about twelve hundred slaves into the settlement.

† John Ellis, in an affidavit made at Brunswick September 17, 1747, stated that he sailed in June on the brigantine "John and William," Thomas Corbett, Master, and that she was captured by the Spanish privateer "St. Gabriel, the Conqueror," and sent to Hispaniola, but was retaken and sent to St. Simons, and that the brigantine belonged to Rev. Richard Marsden.

Ruins of St. Philip's Church, Brunswick—Exterior

people. He died at Suffolk, Va., in February, 1766, on the eve of returning to England.

In 1746, Rev. Christopher Bevis, who had been in the Cape Fear settlement since 1729, preached at the court-house in Wilmington, and was then called to the church at Brunswick, where, Governor Johnston in 1748 mentioned, he had been for two years, and that he had lived all these years as a layman in the province, was generally esteemed and respected for innocence of life and blameless conversation, and only within the last few years let it be known that he was in orders. He proved that he was ordained by the Bishop of Peterborough in 1711. The Governor recommended him to the "Society for the propagation of the Gospel" to fill the vacancy caused by Rev. James Moir, who had, without asking leave, left for the northern part of the colony. Mr. Bevis, in a letter, November 1, 1748, mentioned that he was born in Peterborough, Northamptonshire, and educated at the free school till 1703; then went to Edmund College, Cambridge, and abode there six years; took the degree of A.B., entered orders as a Deacon in the same Cathedral Church, afterwards served in the cure of Bannocks, Northamptonshire, for six or seven winters, then in the cure of Paston, then Wilby for five or six years, and in 1728 he gave up on account of hemorrhages, and in 1729 came to Cape Fear. Mr. Bevis was not able to attend long to his duties on account of ill health, and returned to his plantation, where he died in 1750. In his will, dated December 13, 1750, he left his estate to the church wardens of St. Philip's church for the use of the church, and appointed Richard Quince his executor.

In 1754, Rev. John McDowell became minister at Wilmington, which was then the largest town in the province. He had been put in orders upon the recommendation of Governor Dobbs, and spent the whole of his ministry in the parishes of St. James and St. Philip. April, 1760, he was made a missionary of the Society upon the recommendation of the vestry of St. Philip's church, and the approval of the Governor

(Dobbs). From 1754 to 1757 he was at St. James's church, and in the latter year took charge of both St. James's and St. Philip's. The church at Brunswick was expected soon to be finished. It was the largest and most pretentious in the province.* Richard Quince and John Davis were church wardens, with Robert Snow, Richard Eagles, Benjamin Davis, Thomas Neal, John Davis, Jr., James Murray, John Watters, Joseph Watters, and William Dry, vestrymen.

Governor Dobbs wrote to the Society, April 15, 1760, upon the petition of the vestry, and mentioned that St. Philip's was the parish where he resided, that the roof of the church was now being put on, and that he purposed when it was finished, to make it his Majesty's chapel in the government; that his Majesty was pleased to give the communion plate, surplice and furniture for the communion table and pulpit, with a Bible and Common Prayer books—"so that the service will be performed with decency," and that the church "is the largest and most complete in the province, and may be an exemplar for building other churches."

Mr. McDowell says that the walls are finished and the roof partly done, and to be finished in the summer, a parsons house to be actually built and a glebe provided, and that Colonel Dry, the Collector, and Mr. Richard Quince, merchant, deserve special mention for their zealous interest in the work. The Governor is to put up a pew for himself and the Council. He has a very good vestry.

In May, 1761, he says, the church is not done, the old chapel was repaired, and Mr. Dick, the carpenter, who had been working on the Governor's house, was to undertake the work.

In 1759 an act called the Lottery Act was passed for the benefit of St. James's and St. Philip's parishes, and in 1760 an act was passed appropriating the funds received from the sale of the effects of the Spanish pirates, whose attack on the town is hereinafter described, to the benefit of these churches.

---

* It was 76½ feet long by 54.8 in. in width, and the height of its walls, as they stand to-day, is 34.4. There are 11 windows which measure 15 by 7 feet each, 3 doors, and the thickness of the walls is 33 inches. It was floored with large square bricks, and fitted, as others of its kind, with large square pews. It is the most interesting ruin in the State.

RUINS OF ST. PHILIP'S CHURCH, BRUNSWICK—Interior

In April, 1760, the vestry and wardens of St. James parish—John Swann, John Lyon, ... Bishop, Christopher Dudley, and Jonathan Evans—send Mr. McDowell a certificate expressing their satisfaction with his services while in their parish, and Mrs. Allen, then in London, writes to Charleston in his behalf, mentions his singular temperance, his happy disposition, and strong and healthy constitution.

In November, 1760, he was bereft of wife and child, leaving with him an infant son twelve months old. With his home broken up and increasing responsibilities, he applied to the vestry for increase of salary, to which the vestry, then consisting of John Paine, James Murray, William Dry, Richard Eagles and Robert Snow, reply in a very sharp letter, reminding him that he ought to be able to support himself now with a diminished family on what he had before.

In July, 1760, just as the church was nearing its completion, in a severe thunder storm it was struck by lightning, and the roof, which had been just finished, all fell down. The chapel which was used is described as a miserable old building, 24 feet by 16 feet, which was drenched by every shower, and the wind blew through it.

Mr. McDowell became disheartened and visited Charleston, in hopes of finding a more desirable place, and was offered a parish by the Governor, but, apprehensive of the displeasure of the Society whose aid he was soliciting, returned to Brunswick. He was now 44 years of age, but the exposed life in this new country had impaired his strong constitution. There were 800 taxables in the parish, which included, (except white females) the white, black, and mixed blood over twelve years of age, and among these there were only fifteen communicants, two of whom were black.

In 1762, the Society at last made Mr. McDowell a missionary, which increased his salary. He had then been in the province nine years, but his ministry was near its close; the strong, vigorous and healthy man had succumbed, and the following year he died. In his will he directed that his body be buried at the east end of the church near the grave of his wife, Sarah; tradition says that he was buried within the church beneath the altar. He left his infant son to the care of the Governor and his uncle John Grange, and requested that he be brought up under Mr. Richard Quince and sons as a merchant.

In a letter to the Society announcing his death it was said he was a good man, faithful in his sacred office, and well deserved to be a missionary.

In 1764 Governor Dobbs wrote to England for a minister, and Rev. Mr. Barnett was sent out in 1765. In the meantime the Governor was in correspondence with Mr. Ichabod Camp, of Middletown, Conn., a missionary who was inclined to come to Carolina if encouraged, but would lose his mission if he should do so without the consent of the Society.

Mr. Barnett came after the death of Governor Dobbs, strongly recommended both in England and America, was appointed a missionary to officiate both in St. Philip's and St. James's, as his Excellency Governor Tryon might think proper to direct, and for the first year he resided in the parish of St. James. In 1766, he was removed to Brunswick, and, like his predecessors, extended his services to remote congregations.

The work on St. Philip's church was renewed with energy. Having suffered by fire in the attack of the Spanish pirates, and the roof having been torn off by a terrible hurricane in 1760, for the third time it was drawing near its completion. The glass and sash arrived in 1766 for the windows, and in June, 1768, it was advanced enough to hold service in.

On Whit Tuesday, 1768, Rev. Mr. Barnett, assisted by the Rev. Mr. Wills, of St. James's, dedicated the building. Not having a form of service for the occasion, he drew up one.

Mr. Barnett was desirous of being inducted into office by letters from the Governor, to secure some certainty of holding his station permanently, which now depended on an annual election by the vestry, but he discovered that the people were violently opposed to induction by the crown, and he shortly after resigned and removed to the interior where there was no opposition, and was inducted in a parish in Duplin County.

In 1768, a young comedian, Mr. Gifford, arrived in Brunswick, and won the respect of the people for his talents and ability. He was recommended to the Governor as a proper person to take orders, and open a school for the youth of the town.

The Governor, in his letter to the Bishop of London, expressed the opinion that he did not think that the Bishop would like to take an actor into the church, but if he did so it would be the taking off of the best player on the American stage. What became of him we do not know.

No history of St. Philip's parish would be complete if the name of William Hill should be omitted, for he was the only Lay Reader there, of whom we have any knowledge, and was, perhaps, the most exemplary member of the parish in the performance of his religious duties as the head of a family, and as an officer of the church. He was, consequently, highly esteemed by pious folk, and respected by all who knew him. He was commonly referred to as "the elegant gentleman from Boston." Josiah Quincy, when on his tour in 1773, mentions being his guest and hearing him read the service at St. Philip's, and characterizes him as "a most sensible, polite gentlemen, and, though a Crown officer, a man replete with sentiments of general liberty and warmly attached to the cause of American freedom"—a tribute fully justified by Mr. Hill's letter to the Safety Committee the next year in regard to the importation of tea, in which he asserted the doctrine that the safety of the people is the supreme law.*

Mr. Hill died August 23, 1783, and is buried in St. Philip's churchyard. He left four sons—John, an officer in the Revolution, Nathaniel, a graduate of Edinburgh, and distinguished physician, William Henry, member of Congress and first U. S. District Attorney for North Carolina, and Thomas, a planter, and cultured gentleman.

---
* See ch. IV, p. 3.

Many of the residents of Brunswick owned plantations in the surrounding country, on which they lived, but spent much of their time in the town. One of the first settlers was Col. John Porter who got a grant for 640 acres below the town, July 14, 1725, and the next year conveyed it to Governor Burrington. This tract on the oldest charts is called Governor's Point, and Sturgeon Point. Governor Burrington, who has been by most writers of North Carolina history unsparingly and bitterly criticised and denounced as possessing no worthy characteristics, was not quite as bad as he was painted, but he was quite an early bird in securing desirable lands, and was frequently engaged in broils with the planters about titles. He was first appointed Governor in 1724 under the Proprietary Government, but was succeeded by Sir Richard Everard in 1725, and then moved from Albemarle to the Cape Fear to look after his landed interests. He went to England in 1730, and the Crown having bought out seven of the eight Proprietors in 1729, he was appointed the first *royal* Governor in 1730, and came back to North Carolina in 1731. In 1732 he wrote to the Government as follows: "A multitude of people have come into this country to settle last winter. Some have very great American fortunes. I now think there are men here to make up a creditable Council."*

Having had a controversy with Col. Maurice Moore about the title to valuable lands at Rocky Point, which the Colonel was ready to settle with guns with which he had armed his retainers, Burrington in 1731, in a dispatch to the Colonial office, tried to square accounts with him by saying: "About 20 men are settled on the Cape Fear from South Carolina—among them are three brothers of a noted family whose name is Moore. These people were always troublesome where they came from, and will doubtless be so here".† He was justified from a Government standpoint in saying so, for only twelve

---

* Col. Rec., Vol. III, 344. He was always quarreling with and denouncing members of the Council, and indeed, did not hesitate to characterize as "villains" all who opposed him.

† Col. Rec., III, 338.

Orton House

years before that time, in 1719, Col. James Moore, the eldest brother of Col. Maurice Moore, led the revolution in South Carolina against the Proprietary Government and was made Governor, as his father had been in 1701, and he was also the grandson of the leader of the Irish rebellion in 1643—a rebellious tribe indeed. Burrington also recommended the establishment of a new town on the Cape Fear to supersede Moore's town of Brunswick, as Governor Johnston did later by the establishment of Wilmington in 1736.

Gabriel Johnston succeeded Burrington as Governor and took the oath of office at Brunswick on the 2d November, 1734. Under his administration the Colony generally, and the Cape Fear country especially, prospered. Many settlers came there from different places, bringing retainers and slaves, acquiring valuable lands and adding to the general culture, material and intellectual. They lived in ease, with abundance of rural comforts, and dispensed a generous hospitality.

As illustrative of this hospitality and the mode of life of these early settlers, a pamphlet published in the second volume of the Georgia Historical Collections, entitled "A New Voyage to Georgia," dated 1734, and written by a young English gentleman who had visited the Cape Fear settlement, says:

"We left Lockwood's Folly about eight the next morning, and by two reached the town of Brunswick, which is the chief town in Cape Fear, but with no more than two of the same horses which came with us out of South Carolina. We dined there that afternoon. Mr. Roger Moore, hearing we had come, was so kind as to send fresh horses for us to come up to his house,* which we did and were kindly received by him, he being the chief gentleman in all Cape Fear. His house is built of brick and exceedingly pleasantly situated about two miles from the town and about half a mile from the river, though there is a creek that comes up close to the door between two beautiful meadows about three miles in length. He has a prospect of the town of Brunswick, and of another beautiful

---

*Orton.

brick house,* a building about half a mile from him, belonging to Eleazer Allen, Esq., late speaker to the Commons House of Assembly in the province of South Carolina.

"There were several vessels lying before the town of Brunswick, but I shall forbear giving a description of that place; yet on the 20th June we left Mr. Roger Moore's, accompanied by his brother, Nathaniel Moore, Esq., to a plantation of his up the Northwest branch of the Cape Fear river. The river is wonderfully pleasant, being, next to Savannah, the finest on all the Continent.

"We reached the forks, as they call it, that same night, where the river divides into two very beautiful branches, called the Northeast and Northwest, passing by several pretty plantations on both sides. We lodged that night at one Mr. John Davis's, and the next morning proceeded up the Northwest branch; when we got about two miles from thence we came to a beautiful plantation, belonging to Captain Gabriel,† who is a great merchant there, where were two ships, two sloops, and a brigantine loading with lumber for the West Indies; it is about twenty-two miles from the bar. When we came about four miles higher up we saw an opening on the northwest side of us which is called Black River, on which there is a great deal of very good meadow land, but there is not any one settled on it. The next night we came to another plantation belonging to Mr. Roger Moore, called the Blue Banks, where he is going to build another very large brick house. This bluff is at least one hundred feet high, and has a beautiful prospect over a fine, large meadow on the opposite side of the river; the houses are all built on the west side of the river, it being for the most part high champaign land; the other side is very much subject to overflow, but I can not learn they have lost but one crop. I am creditably informed they have very commonly four score bushels of corn on an acre of their overflowed land. It very rarely overflows, but in the winter time when their crop is off. I must confess that I saw the finest

---

*Lilliput.   † Gabourel—Joshua Gabourel, who came from the Isle of Jersey.

corn growing there that ever I saw in my life, as likewise wheat and hemp. We lodged there that night at one Captain Gibbs's adjoining Mr. Moore's plantation, where we met with very good entertainment. The next morning we left his house and proceeded up the said river to a plantation belonging to Mr. John Davis, where we dined.

"The plantations on this river are all very much alike as to the situation, but there are many more improvements on some than others; this house is built after the Dutch fashion, and made to front both ways on the river and on the land. He has a beautiful avenue cut through the woods for above two miles, which is a great addition to the house. We left his house about two in the afternoon, and the same evening reached Mr. Nathaniel Moore's plantation, which is reckoned forty miles from Brunswick. It is likewise a very pleasant plantation on a bluff upwards of sixty feet high."

This traveler says he did not see "so much as one foot of bad land" after leaving Brunswick. With some of his hosts he visited Waccamaw Lake, of which he said he had heard much and wished to see, and pronounces it "the pleasantest place that ever I saw in my life." The quantity of game he saw on the trip—deer, turkeys, geese, and ducks—amazed him. After a visit to Rocky Point, which, he says, "is the finest place in all Cape Fear," and where he was entertained by the leading planters, he returned to South Carolina.

The Court of Common Pleas was held at Brunswick, and in 1738, according to the Records, it was presided over by Nathaniel Rice, afterwards acting Governor, Matthew Rowan also later the acting Governor, Eleazer Allen, afterwards Chief Justice, James Innes, a distinguished colonel in the French War, Col. Robert Halton, also a distinguished soldier, and Cornelius Harnett, Sr.

War having been declared between England and Spain in 1740, Governor Johnston was active in raising troops to invade the Spanish Colonies. On the 5th November, 1740, transports left Brunswick with four companies of troops for Florida, of which James Innes was a captain, and these troops formed a part of the regiment commanded by Colonel Gooch, of Virginia, in which Washington's brother Lawrence was an officer. They constituted a part of the expedition from Jamaica to Carthagena, in Central America, under Admiral Vernon, which failed of its object. All that we know of the record of the Cape Fear men engaged in it is that Innes, Lieutenant Benjamin Heron, and Robert Halton were among the officers, and that Heron returned by way of England.

In 1743 South Carolina asked help to resist the Spanish invasion from Cuba, and it was granted to the extent of 1,000 men, on condition that a North Carolina officer should command them, and Colonel Maurice Moore was chosen for that purpose.* November 8, 1748, an attack on the town was made by two pirate ships, whose captured property was divided between the parishes of St. Philip's at Brunswick and St. James's in Wilmington. A full account of this attack is given in the State Records† and in Ashe's History of North Carolina,‡ from which it appears that in July some of the Spanish ships lay in the harbor of the lower river, watched by a company of militia who then captured six of the Spaniards; that they returned in heavier force September 4th, and the militia again turned out, three of the companies alone containing over 300 troops, but the Spaniards took possession of Brunswick and for four days, from the 6th to the 10th, hostilities were active— that on the 10th one ship was blown up and the other was driven off; that Colonel Dry was employed all that day burying dead Spaniards, and two days later in bringing the spoils from the wreck, and that in addition to the killed and wounded 29 prisoners were taken. In this year the fort at the present town of Southport near the mouth of the Cape Fear, named after the Governor (Johnston), was completed, having been authorized by an Act of 1745. It was commanded in 1755 by Captain John Dalrymple, who was appointed by General Braddock, the ill-fated commander of the expedition against Fort DuQuesne in that year.

---

*Col. Rec., IV, 633.   † Vol. XXII, 286.   ‡ Vol. I, 270.

In 1758 it was commanded by Captain James Moore, and from 1766 to 1774 by Captain Robert Howe.

At the beginning of Johnston's administration, or perhaps before, the merchants of Brunswick found their business hampered by the refusal of raftsmen to carry their tar, timber, naval stores, and other freight down to Brunswick because of the open and exposed water in front of the town, and these merchants were compelled to go up the river to a place called the Dram Tree, about two miles below the present site of Wilmington, to do their trading for these commodities. This was one of the causes of the struggle between Brunswick and Wilmington, then called Newton, for supremacy, which culminated on the 25th February, 1740, when, at a meeting of the council, the bill passed in 1736, making Newton a township to be called Wilmington, was bitterly assailed by Allen, Rice, Moseley and Roger Moore, on the ground that by the Act of 1729 Brunswick was made a township, and empowered to build a court-house, jail and church, that good houses had been built there before Newton was established, and that the custom house, if moved from Brunswick, would be too far up the river, etc. They were opposed by Halton, Rowan, Murray,* and Wm. Smith, the last of whom, after voting as a member and making a tie, as presiding officer cast another vote to break the tie in favor of Wilmington, which was, perhaps, the first time in American history that such an event occurred. Governor Johnston, who had the Act of 1736 (changing the name of Newton to Wilmington) passed in honor of his patron, the Earl of Wilmington, was greatly pleased, and expressed the hope that all public business would be done there. Governor Johnston died in 1752 and was succeeded, first by Nathaniel Rice, President of the Council, who only lived a short time, and then by Matthew Rowan, President of the Council. In 1754 Arthur Dobbs was sent over to be Governor. He was an old gentleman whose previous his-

*Murray was made a member of the Council by Governor Johnston suddenly and to accomplish this purpose, as appears from Murray's own statement in a letter to Henry McCulloh, dated 30th January, 1739-40, and this was perhaps the most discreditable act of Governor Johnston during his long and otherwise creditable administration.

tory was honorable, but who was unfitted for the duties of his office by reason of his temper and his extravagant notions of the kingly prerogative, and of the duty of subjects of the Crown to submit loyally to all, royal decrees and Acts of Parliament. He remained in authority about ten years, but was in constant disagreement with the Assembly and the people, although he attempted a good many reforms, and tried to do his duty as he saw it. Of him, as of his predecessors and successors, it is not the purpose of this book to give a personal history, but only to state such facts as bear upon the history of New Hanover County under their several administrations.

Burrington, the first royal Governor, did not afflict his soul with anxiety about the spiritual condition of the colonists, but both Johnston and Dobbs did take a deep interest in the religious welfare of the people, and endeavored to awaken a livelier sense of their obligations in that respect than was prevalent among them. Such counsel and action were certainly needed, for there was a very general indifference to, if not a positive disbelief in the truth of Christianity among them at that time. One of Johnston's first appeals to the Legislature was in regard to the lack of religious worship, and also to the need of educational facilities in the province, and Dobbs was really troubled over it, as appears from his frequent references to the subject, and his anxiety to increase the number of ministers, churches and schools. Dobbs resided in Brunswick, but owned a plantation on Town Creek a few miles distant, where there was a large number of other settlers, among whom were the following names: Watters, Dalrymple, Rice, Lewis, Hill, Assup, Bigford, Jean, Ashe, Grange, Neale, Davis, and others.

The year 1761 was quite an eventful one in the history of Brunswick, although not to be compared with what happened there a few years later. It was in that year that the fearful hurricane* along the coast occurred, which did great damage,

---
* *London Magazine*, December, 1761, and Col. Rec., VI, 605.

throwing down many houses including the roof of the church, driving every ship in the river except one ashore, and forcing open New Inlet—which remained for a hundred years and until after the War between the States (when it was closed by a great engineering feat of the Government)—a chief entrance for ships going to and from Wilmington. At this entrance stood the celebrated Fort Fisher during that war.

At the beginning of the year, Friday, February 6, 1761, at Brunswick, George III was proclaimed King in the presence of the Governor (Dobbs), the Council, and a number of the principal planters and people, an account of which, and of the repetition of the ceremonies the next day at Wilmington, was given by the Governor in a letter to the Board of Trade, dated February 9th.* Nothing after this especially connected with the history of New Hanover County occurred until 1764, when the county of Brunswick was established out of the territory of New Hanover and Bladen, except that in October of that year, because of the continual complaints against the irritable old Governor, the British Ministry sent over Lt.-Col. Wm. Tryon of the Queen's Guards to be Lieutenant Governor, and he took the oaths of office at Wilmington.

In the latter part of the following March (1765) Governor Dobbs, as Tryon wrote, "retired from the strife and cares of this world," and Tryon succeeded him as Governor, and qualified on April 3d. It was, for him, an unfortunate time to take charge of the government, for more serious troubles were brewing in the Province than at any previous period—the first being the Stamp Act upheaval, and the next the Regulators War.

THE STAMP ACT.

It is pleasant to know that the part taken by the Cape Fear people in the Stamp Act matter, although for a long period preserved only in tradition, has, since the official records were obtained, become familiar history, and that the hoary custom of doubting or denying every creditable event in North Caro-

---
*Col. Rec., VI, 520.

lina history can no longer be justified, as to these events at least.

The facts developed by the indisputable records prove beyond the shadow of a doubt that the only people in America who resisted *with arms* the landing of the stamps on their soil, and the first who defied British power with guns in their hands more than ten years before the Declaration of Independence, were the people of the lower Cape Fear.

It is not my purpose to give an elaborate account of those proceedings, but rather to briefly epitomize the events in the exact order in which they occurred, as follows:

The Stamp Act was passed by the British Parliament in March, 1765, Tryon succeeded Dobbs on the 3d of April, and the first Assembly after his succession met the 3d of May. Immediately after its meeting, the news of the passage of the act arrived. This event had been anticipated, and Tryon, knowing the popular sentiment and desiring to find out what would be the probable action of the Assembly, in an interview with the speaker (Col. John Ashe) asked him the question, to which Ashe replied that the act would be resisted with arms—or as tradition has preserved his reply, "to blood and death." Thereupon Tryon on the 18th May prorogued the Assembly to meet at New Bern, November 30th. Then the pot began to boil, meetings were called and resolutions denouncing the act and expressing a determination to resist it were adopted, and these meetings occurred at intervals during the summer and early fall. Dr. Wm. Houston* was appointed to the position of Stamp Master by the Governor and Council. On the 25th October Tryon again prorogued the Assembly until the following March 12th, and this aggravated the situation because it prevented the election of delegates by the Assembly to the Stamp Act Congress, as it has always been called. On the 16th November the people went to Tryon's house in Wilmington and demanded Dr. Houston, the Stamp Master, and upon

---

*One of Dr. Houston's descendants, Capt. William Houston, a talented young lawyer was a captain of the 1st North Carolina Cavalry, C. S. A., killed in battle.

Tryon's refusal to surrender him, they prepared to burn his house. Tryon then requested Colonel Ashe to come in and talk with Houston, which he did, and Houston, realizing his danger, agreed to accompany Ashe to the street, and, escorted by a large crowd, they went to the court-house and there, in the presence of the mayor (Moses John DeRosset) and the public officers, took and subscribed an oath that he would never apply for, or receive any stamp-paper or exercise the duties of his office. Thereupon the crowd gave three cheers and dispersed.

On the 18th November, two days after this affair, about fifty of the merchants of New Hanover and Brunswick counties, upon invitation from Governor Tryon, dined with him, and he strenuously urged them to permit the circulation of the stamps, but received very cold comfort.

On the 20th Tryon opened and proclaimed his commission at Wilmington and consulted the Council if any measures could be proposed to induce the people to receive the stamps. "They were unanimously of the opinion that nothing further could be done than what I have already offered," he wrote to the Secretary of State in England.* Meantime the arrival of the stamps was daily expected at Brunswick, and preparation for their proper reception was made. Tryon was uneasy and anxious to conciliate the people whose good will he desired to cultivate, whose condition he knew to be depressed, and whose spirit he was obliged to respect. In the dispatch just referred to he informed the government that, although the courts had been regularly opened, no business was done, and all civil government was at a stand—that there was little or no specie in circulation, and that the Attorney-General had assured him that the stamp duties on the instruments used in the five Superior Courts alone would in one year require all the specie in the country, and that to these were to be added the instruments used in the twenty-nine inferior or County Courts, those in the hands of the sheriffs and other civil officers, in the Land

---

* Tryon to Conway, December 26.

Office, and many others used in the transaction of public business; and he declared his belief that the operation of the Stamp Act was for these reasons impracticable, and therefore he had made proposals for the ease and convenience of the people and tried to reconcile them to the act. There can be no doubt that Tryon regarded the act as outrageously oppressive on the people of the colonies, and would gladly have escaped any connection with it.

On the 28th November the sloop of war Diligence arrived at Brunswick with the stamps, and was greeted by an assemblage of citizens with guns in their hands. The stamps were not landed. Tryon afterwards wrote that the reason for not landing them was that after Houston resigned there was no distributor or other officer of the stamps in the country and they remained on board, but the true reason was that the gentlemen carrying the guns had "submitted a few broken remarks" concerning the state of heath of any one who should undertake to fetch that part of the cargo ashore.

The Diligence, either upon her arrival or not long afterwards, was accompanied by the Viper sloop of war, and both lay at anchor off Brunswick awaiting developments.

Nothing occurred, except the continued organization of the people in the surrounding country, until the 14th January, 1766, when two merchant vessels, the Dobbs and the Patience, arrived, when it was discovered that their clearance papers were not stamped, whereupon the captain of the Viper immediately seized both vessels, regardless of the assurance of their captains that it was impossible for them to comply with the law, for the reason that when they left Philadelphia and St. Christophers, from which ports respectively they had come, no stamps could be obtained.*

---

* Since this was written I have had the pleasure of inspecting the long lost and recently found Entry Book of the Port of Brunswick from 1765 to 1774, a very large and much mutilated and stained volume, now owned by Mr. James Sprunt, which contains the entries of the Dobbs and Patience at the custom house at that time, and several times afterward. They are both entered as "Plantation" built. The Dobbs was built in 1763, 40 tons and 4 men, owned by Richard Quince, Eleazer Callender, Master. The Patience, built in 1762, 20 tons and 4 men, owned by William Hawkins, Will Ward, Master. Both were sloops. The sloop Ruby, afterwards seized and released, was also "Plantation" built in 1762, 55 tons and 5 men, owned by Thos. Homer & Co., Thomas Homer, Master, trading to Philadelphia. We also note the "Plantation" built (1764) sloop Charming Peggy, 50 tons and 5 men, owned by *Cornelius Harnett*, John Cray, Master, and others owned by Cape Fear men.

And now the situation became serious indeed. The news of the seizure spread like wildfire and soon five hundred and eighty men with arms, and one hundred without, assembled and chose Col. Hugh Waddell as their commander. On the 16th of February Col. Wm. Dry, Collector of the port of Brunswick, received a letter from Wilmington dated the 15th, demanding his presence there, which he answered promising to be there the next day, but the weather prevented him from going.

"The next intelligence I received," says Tryon,* "was in the dusk of the evening of the 19th, soon after 6 o'clock, by letter delivered me by Mr. George Moore, and Mr. Cornelius Harnett, bearing date the 19th, and signed "John Ashe, Thomas Lloyd, Alexander Lillington."

This letter stirred Tryon to an interview with the captains of the men of war, because it notified him that the people were going to march to Brunswick "in hopes of obtaining in a peaceful manner a redress of their grievances from the commanding officer of his Majesty's ships," and at the same time assured the Governor of protection from insult to his person and property, and that if agreeable to him, a guard of gentlemen should be immediately detached for that purpose.

Tryon, who was a fearless soldier, told Messrs. Moore and Harnett that he wanted no guard, and that the gentlemen need not come to give protection where it was not necessary or required, and that he would answer them in writing next morning.

As soon as Moore and Harnett left, the house was surrounded by about one hundred and fifty armed men, who informed Tryon that they were looking for Captain Lobb, of the Viper, and on discovering that he was not there the majority of them went toward the town (Tryon's residence being a short distance from it), leaving a number of men to watch the avenues to it.

Armed men, as Tryon wrote, were continualy coming into

---
* Tryon to Conway, February 25.

Brunswick from different counties, for the whole Cape Fear region was roused.

On the 20th Pennington, the Comptroller, went to Tryon and told him there had been a search for him also, and Tryon invited him to remain with him, which he did.

The next morning, the 21st, Col. James Moore went for Pennington, and, being informed by Tryon that he "could not part with him," Colonel Moore went away, "and in five minutes afterwards," says Tryon, "I found the avenue to my house again shut up by different parties of armed men."

About 10 o'clock he observed a body of men in arms, estimated by him to be from 400 to 500, moving toward his house, the main body of which drew up in front about 300 yards distant, and a detachment of men advanced down the avenue headed by Harnett, who sent a message that he wished to speak to Pennington, and upon Tryon's statement that Pennington had sought refuge in his house and he would give him all the protection he could, Harnett told him the people were determined to take him out, although they did not intend to harm him. Thereupon Pennington concluded to go with him, but resigned his office to Tryon first. They and the armed citizens then went back to town where Pennington was required to take an oath similar to the one administered to Houston in Wilmington.

On the evening of the 19th (when George Moore and Harnett went to deliver the note from Ashe, Lloyd and Lillington) Lieutenant Calder, of the Viper, informed the commander of that ship "that a party of men, consisting of three or four hundred under the command of Colonel Waddell were on their march to Fort Johnston, in order to take possession of it," and thereupon Calder was sent in a boat with orders to spike the guns of the fort, which he did, having reached it before Waddell's column arrived.

In the meantime the people of Wilmington seized the boat of the contractor for supplies to the men of war at Brunswick, and put its crew in jail. The men of war had only one day's supply of provisions on hand, and the only source of supply being thus cut off, Tryon had to yield, and the vessels, which had been seized for the want of stamps on their clearances, were released.

And so ended this gallant episode in the early history of the lower Cape Fear.

We are not willing, however, to close this episode without reciting a ludicrous incident that has been embalmed in the history of that exciting period and may be found in the Colonial Records.*

The present age is supposed to be *par excellence* the era of what is called, in the slang of the day, "gall," but this was an instance of an almost sublime exhibition of it, and is given in a letter from the Rev. John Barnett, minister of St. Philip's church at Brunswick, to a Mr. Waring in London, dated at "Castle Tryon near Brunswick" (Tryon's residence, Russellboro), February 1, 1766, about the time Tryon was in the midst of the Stamp Act troubles.

Mr. Barnett was very much exercised over the performances of an individual whom he characterized as "one Stevens, a Scotch Presbyterian teacher" who, he said, was going in the vessel that carried his letter to apply to the Bishop of London for orders as a clergyman; that he had "illused the Governor, affronted all the King's Council (but one *Scotch* gentleman), most villainously abused me," and was going to apply for orders without any recommendation to the Bishop; that he "has several times preached here in a lawyer's old gown, given him at Wilmington," and "has baptized several children in the character of a clergyman of the Church of England, which, before I came, he had the impudence to assume," and that he had told him (Barnett) that he would make a genteel present to the Bishop and get an order to supersede him (Barnett) as Missionary, and had told some of the Council that "any one might get orders on making a Bishop a present of the price of a good beaver hat, which he intended doing";

---
*VI, 161.

that he "came to Brunswick a distressed stranger and the Governor had taken pity on him and given him 50 guineas, but had found him out and had forbidden him his presence."

Poor Tryon was certainly having a rough experience about that time, and brother Barnett was evidently sorely grieved in spirit at such a manifestation of wickedness and irreverence for church dignitaries—irrespective, of course, of any personal anxiety in regard to his own tenure of office.

The repeal of the Stamp Act and the generous proclamation of Governor Tryon announcing the fact and warning the public officers to refrain from further extortions upon the people, were acceptable to the conservative element who still cherished the hope of a satisfactory adjustment of affairs, but there was a feeling of unrest and distrust prevalent, and the enforcement of the Navigation Act, which forbade the carriage of anything to European ports north of Cape Finisterre, except the one article of rice, they felt was a discrimination against them like that against Ireland, and they naturally resented it. Soon after this the Regulators movement in the middle of the State began, and although the people of the Cape Fear regarded Governor Tryon as disposed to be tyrannical, they regarded the Regulators as the organizers of a mobocracy, and sustained the Governor as the representative of orderly government by contributing troops to aid him in his effort to suppress them. The history of the Regulators war is familiar to all, and therefore we give no further space to it, except to say that New Hanover County contributed a company of artillery under Col. James Moore and John B. Ashe. They had proved their devotion to liberty by their armed resistance to the Stamp Act, but with an intelligent appreciation of the difference between asserting their rights as British subjects, and countenancing lawlessness and anarchy, while reluctant to antagonize with arms their countrymen, they felt that it was their duty to stand for law and order and sustain even a government which was not acceptable to themselves against mob violence, and the domination of ignorant and fanatical demagogues.

The new town of Wilmington, from its establishment in 1736, had outgrown Brunswick, and at the time of the Stamp Act troubles contained more than twice as many inhabitants, and when the Revolution began had more than three times as many. It accordingly became the chief center of events after that time, while Brunswick continued to decline and soon ceased to exist as a town, although a good many of its former inhabitants continued to use the old church yard of St. Philip's for the burial of their dead. Most of the dead, however, were buried on the plantations, as required by the Act of 1741, which made it the duty of every planter to set apart a burying ground for dead Christians, free and bond.

Thus ended the history of the second settlement on the Cape Fear, which began with every promise of becoming both the permanent seat of government and the leading commercial mart of the Province of North Carolina. For nearly a hundred years after its abandonment, it remained a decayed and melancholy relic, hidden among the moss-draped pines and undergrowth that crowned the bluff on which it was built, and by which swept silently the wide, historic river, until the beginning of the War between the States in 1861, when a great earthwork fortification, Fort Anderson, was erected on the site, enclosing with one of its arms the walls of the old church, which, again as of old, was bombarded by a hostile fleet, and again, as if under divine protection, escaped destruction or serious injury, and still stands old and gray in a new-grown forest, and amid crumbling tombs.

SONS OF LIBERTY.

During the excitement over the Stamp Act in the fall of 1765 and before the arrival of the Diligence with the stamps, the people of the Cape Fear in common with the people every where throughout the country began to organize themselves under the name "Sons of Liberty," and that organization continued under that title until after the year 1770, but how long after that date we do not know, although it is probable that after the formation of Safety Committees in 1774, the name ceased to be used.

At a meeting held June 2, 1770, a general committee was appointed, as appears from the following extract from the *South Carolina Gazette* of July 5th:

"We hear that in consequence of a letter addressed to the Sons of Liberty in North Carolina, under cover to Col. James Moore, a meeting has been appointed, and held on the 2d of last month, where a number of gentlemen from the several southern counties in that Province were chosen as a committee to meet at Wilmington on this day, to consult upon such measures as may appear most eligible, for evincing their Patriotism and Loyalty in the Present critical situation of affairs; which committee are, Col. Thomas Lloyd, Cornelius Harnett, Frederick Gregg, William Campbell, Esq., Messrs. John Robinson and William Wilkinson, for the town of Wilmington— George Moore, Frederick Jones, Esqs., Col. James Moore, Messrs. Samuel Ashe and James Naran [Moran] for New Hanover County—Richard Quince, Sen., and Richard Quince, Jun., Esqrs., and Mr. Wilkinson, for the town of Brunswick— John and William Davis, Esqrs., Messrs. Samuel Watters, Thomas Davis, and Samuel Neal, for Brunswick County— Messrs. John and George Gibbs, and John Grange, Jun., for Bladen County—Col. James Sampson, and Felix Keenan [Kenan], Esq., for Duplin County—William Gray, Henry Roads [Rhodes], and Richard Ward, Esqrs., for Onslow County—and Walter Gibson, Farquhar Campbell, and Robert Rowan, Esqrs., for Cumberland County."

And again, on the 5th of July, according to a publication in the same paper of August 9th, there was a meeting of which the following account is given:

"At a meeting of the General Committee of the Sons of Liberty upon Cape Fear, in Wilmington the 5th of July, Cornelius Harnett, Esq., was chosen Chairman, and the following Resolutions unanimously agreed on, viz:

"I. Resolved, That the following answer to the letter received from the Sons of Liberty in South Carolina, of the 25th of April last, be signed by the Chairman and sent by the first conveyance:

To the Sons of Liberty in South Carolina.

GENTLEMEN:—Your favor of the 25th of April last was laid before the Sons of Liberty upon Cape Fear, at a general meeting in this town, on the second of last month, and received with the highest satisfaction.

We have the pleasure to inform you, that many of the principal inhabitants of six large and populous counties attended when it was unanimously agreed, to keep strictly to the non-importation agreement entered into last fall, and to cooperate with our sister colonies, in every legal measure for obtaining ample redress of the grievance so justly complained of.

Happy should we have thought ourselves, if our merchants in general, would have followed the disinterested and patriotic example of their brethren in the other colonies. We hope, however, their own interest will convince them of the necessity of importing such articles, *and such only,* as the planters will purchase.

We should have done ourselves the pleasure of answering your letter much sooner, but the gentlemen of the committee living at such a distance from each other prevented it.

We beg leave to assure you, that the inhabitants of those six counties, and we doubt not of every county in this colony, are convinced of the necessity of adhering strictly to their former resolutions, and you may depend they are as tenacious of their just rights as any of their brethren on the continent and firmly resolved to stand or fall with them in support of the common cause of American liberty.

Worthless men, as you very justly observe, are the production of every country, and we are also unhappy as to have a few among us "who have not virtue enough to resist the alurement of present gain." Yet we can venture to assert, that the people in general of this colony, will be spirited and steady in support of their rights as English subjects, and will not tamely submit to the yoke of oppression—"But, if by the iron hand of power," they are at last crushed, it is, however, their fixed resolution, either to fall with the same dignity and spirit you so justly mention, or transmit to their posterity entire, the inestimable blessings of our free Constitution.

The disinterested and public spirited behavior of the merchants and other inhabitants of your colony, justly merits the applause of every lover of liberty on the continent. The people of any colony who have not virtue enough to follow so glorious examples must be lost to every sense of freedom and consequently deserve to be slaves. We are, with great truth, gentlemen,

Your affectionate countrymen,

CORNELIUS HARNETT, Chairman.

Signed by order of the General Committee, Wilmington, Cape Fear, July 5th, 1770.

"II. Resolved, That we will strictly and inviolably adhere to the non-importation agreement entered into on the 30th day of September last, until the grievances therein mentioned are redressed.

"III. Resolved, That we will not, on any pretense whatever, have any dealings or connection with the inhabitants of the colony of Rhode Island, who contrary to their solemn and voluntary contract, have violated their faith pledged to the other colonies, and thereby shamefully deserted the common cause of American liberty, and if any of their vessels or merchants shall arrive in Cape Fear River, with intention to trade, we will to the utmost of our power by all legal ways and means prevent any person buying from, or selling to them, any goods or commodities whatever, unless they give full satisfaction to the colonies for their base and unworthy conduct.

"IV. Resolved, That the merchants of Newport, Rhode-Island, and all others on the continent of North America, who will not comply with the non-importation agreement are declared enemies to their country, and ought to be treated in the most contemptuous manner.

"V. Resolved, That we will not purchase any kind of goods or merchandise, whatever, from any merchant or other person who shall import or purchase goods for sale contrary to the spirit and intention of the said agreement, unless such goods be immediately re-shipped to the place they were imported from, or stored under the inspection and direction of the Committee.

"VI. Resolved, That the members of the committee for the several counties in the Wilmington District, and particularly those for the towns of Wilmington and Brunswick, do carefully inspect all importations of goods, and if any shall be imported contrary to the true intent and meaning of the said non-importation agreement, that they give public notice thereof in the *Cape Fear Mercury*, with the names of such importers or purchasers.

"VII. Resolved, That copies of these resolutions be immediately transitted to all the trading towns in this colony."

The Committee of the Sons of Liberty upon Cape Fear, appointed for the town of Wilmington to inspect into all goods imported, take this opportunity to inform the public, that Mr. Arthur Benning of Duplin County hath imported in the sloop Lancashire Witch from Virginia, a small assortment of goods, several articles of which are not allowed by the non-importation agreement. But it appears at the same time to the Committee, those goods were expected to arrive before the first day of January last, having been ordered by Mr. Benning some time in July last, his correspondent sent them to Virginia, where they have lain a considerable time since.

"We have the pleasure to inform the public, that Richard Quince, Esq., a member of the general committee, and who may with great propriety be deemed a principal merchant, hath joined heartily in the non-importation agreement. It will, no doubt, be looked upon as a very great misfortune to this country, that some merchants and others seem resolved not to follow so disinterested an example, but on the contrary, are daily purchasing wines and many other articles contrary to the said agreement. Should those gentlemen still persist in a practice so destructive in its tendency to the liberties of the people of this colony, they must not be surprised, if hereafter the names of the importers and purchasers should be published in *Cape Fear Mercury*. This is intended to serve as a friendly admonition. And, it is hoped will be received as such, and have its due effect."

CHAPTER II

THE NAMES OF THE EARLIEST PLANTATIONS, THEIR LOCATION
AND THEIR OWNERS, WITH ITEMS OF
BIOGRAPHY AND INCIDENTS.

As already stated, settlements were made on the Cape Fear River, and in its vicinity as early as 1723. A grant for 48,000 acres was made to Landgrave Thomas Smith* as early as 1713, but no attempt to settle on that grant (which included Bald Head at the mouth of the river and extended above Wilmington) was made for some years. These settlements were chiefly on the west side of the river below Wilmington, and in the locality known then and ever since as Rocky Point on the northeast branch above Wilmington, but some were on the sound and on the upper Northwest river. There were a few grants for land as far south and west of the river as Lockwood's Folly, but these were isolated places to which no historic interest attaches.

We will begin our account of these oldest plantations and their owners by first taking those farthest down the river and proceeding up it as high as Wilmington, and then take those above on both branches in the same order, and finally those on the sound.

And, as preliminary to the subject, it will be "news" to the present generation of Cape Fear people to learn that in the early days fine crops of wheat were raised in the Rocky Point neighborhood on the northeast branch of the river. In those days rice, indigo, corn, and tobacco were the principal crops, but there is contemporary evidence of the culture of wheat also in the region referred to, and probably in many other places. In a letter written by a lady from her residence near Castle Haynes to Mr. John Burgwin in London, in the year 1775 (August 25th), is this language: "We have prodigious crops of wheat this year—better never known in the memory of men. The corn will also be very fine if these deluges of rain do not spoil it."

---
*A recital in a deed (N. H. Records, C. 77) says this grant is in the Secretary's office of South Carolina.

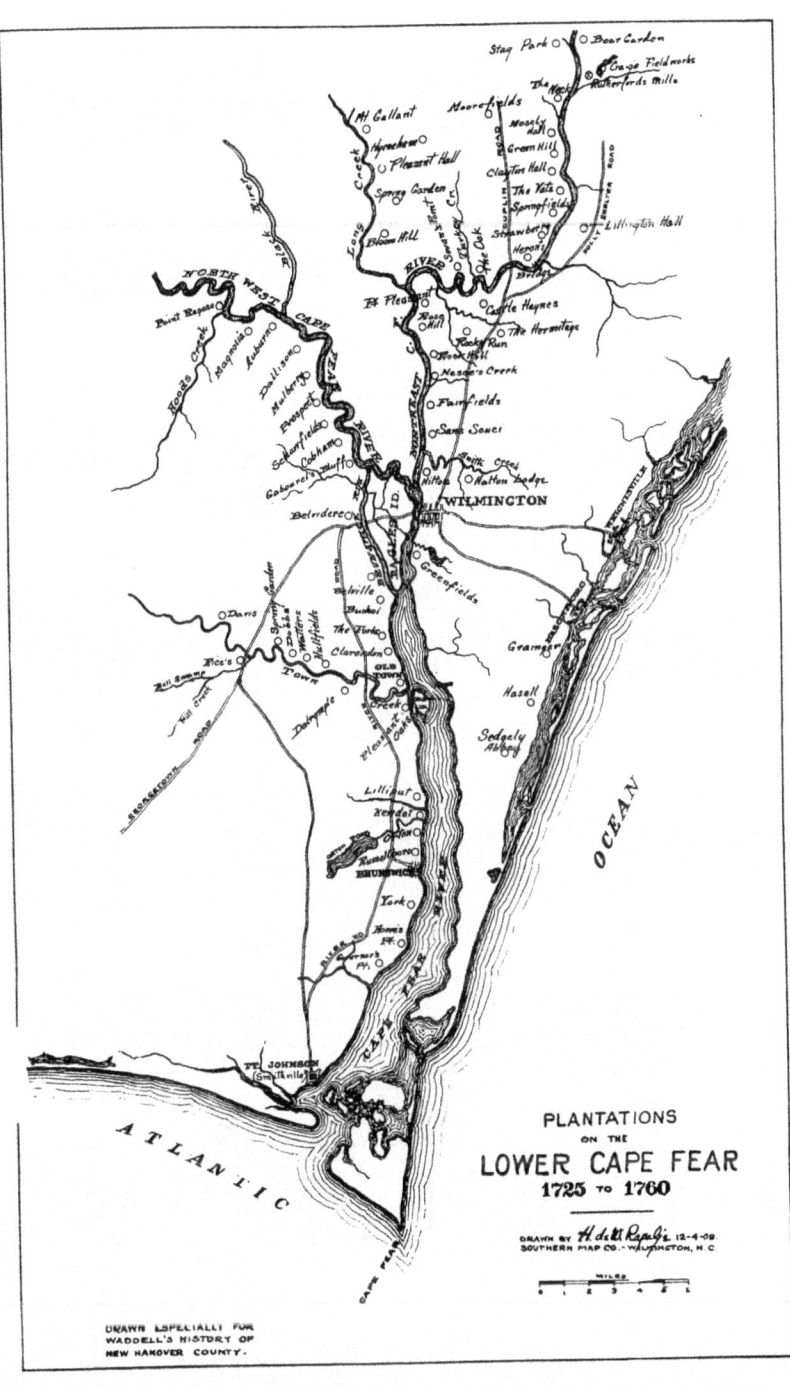

In speaking of the British troops grinding grain at Rutherford's mills, above Rocky Point in 1781, McRee* says: "With the exception of a small experiment by Dr. J. F. McRee on Rocky Point, wheat has not been cultivated in that region since the Revolution." The reason, or one of the reasons, probably was that after that time it was found to be cheaper to buy flour brought from the back country to Fayetteville, and thence by boat to Wilmington, than to raise the wheat and send it miles away to be ground on toll at the few mills that were equipped with proper stones for grinding that grain. It certainly was not because the land was not capable of producing fine wheat crops.

GOVERNOR'S POINT.

The southernmost estate on the river was called Governor's Point because Governor Burrington bought it from the first grantee, John Porter. John Porter came from the Albemarle region, where he had been for many years a leader of the people. He moved to the Cape Fear country in 1723 and died at Rocky Point in 1734. Members of his family intermarried with the Moores, Ashes, Lillingtons, and Moseleys.

In a lecture delivered before the Historical and Scientific Society of Wilmington, on the 26th of November, 1879, entitled "A Study in Colonial History," the Hon. George Davis overwhelmingly vindicated the memory of Porter from the grossly unjust attacks upon it by Dr. Hawks and other writers of our colonial history. Under his claim, clear and masterful analysis of the facts concerning the Cary rebellion and the characters connected with it—an analysis illuminated by flashes of satire and genial humor—the true character and valuable services of John Porter were portrayed, and his claim to the admiration and respect of posterity was triumphantly established. Like too many others who have lived in troublous times, and have taken an active part in public affairs, Porter was the victim of party rancor and the personal hostility of those in authority who used their power to defame him and destroy his influence and reputation, but it was almost worth

---
*Life and Correspondence of James Iredell, Vol. I, 526, *noto*.

undergoing the wrong and injustice to have received after many years such a splendid vindication as the lecturer pronounced.

HOWE'S POINT.

Job Howe, father of Gen. Robert Howe of Revolutionary fame, was the son of a prominent man of the same name in South Carolina, and was the grandson of Governor James Moore (the first) of that State. His residence at Howe's Point, the next place above Governor's Point, was in rear of an old colonial fort, built, according to tradition, for defense against pirates who infested the harbor and river, and the ruins of both his residence and the fort were visible until a comparatively recent period.

In his interesting little book, entitled "Tales and Traditions of the Lower Cape Fear," Mr. James Sprunt says: "Mr. Reynolds, the present intelligent owner and occupant of the Howe place behind the colonial fort, who took part in building Fort Anderson, says that his father and his grandfather informed him forty years ago that this fort was erected long before the War of the Revolution as a protection against buccaneers and pirates; that his great-grandfather lived with General Howe on this place during the war (Revolution) and took part in a defense of this fort against the British who drove the Americans out of it; that the latter retreated to Libery Pond, about a half mile in the rear, pursued by the British; that a stand was made at this pond, the Americans on the west and the enemy on the east side, and that the blood which flowed stained the margin of the beautiful sheet of water which still bears the name of Liberty Pond, and that the Americans again retreated as far as McKenzie's mill dam behind Kendall, where the British abandoned the pursuit and returned to their ships of war."

And Mr. Sprunt adds: "Since the foregoing was written Mr. Reynolds's statement with reference to General Howe's residence has been fully corroborated by the well-known Cape Fear skipper, Captain Sam Price, now eighty-six years old.

He remembers distinctly and has often visited the house known as General Howe's residence, which he says was a large three-story frame building, on a stone or brick foundation, on the spot already described just below Old Brunswick, and still known as Howe's Point." General Howe was one of the really brilliant officers of the Revolution, having been promoted to the rank of Major General in October, 1777, although his advancement had been most ungenerously obstructed by persons in South Carolina and Georgia. He was a man of much more than usual culture and ability, and who, by his intelligent activity in supporting the rights of the people against the unconstitutional aggression of King and Parliament before the Revolution broke out, had become so obnoxious to the Government that when pardon was offered to all who would abandon the American cause during the war, he and Harnett, who was his close friend and coadjutor, were specifically excepted from clemency, and his plantation was plundered by a British expedition. It would require a volume to adequately present his most valuable services to his country from early manhood to the day of his death, which occurred in December, 1786, at the residence of his friend and brother hero, Gen. Thomas Clark, at Point Repose, while on his way to attend the session of the Legislature, of which he was a member, then assembled at Fayetteville. We shall have occasion to refer again to this brave and gifted soldier and patriot, and therefore postpone further comment now.

YORK.

The place next above Howe's Point, and just below the town of Old Brunswick, belonged to Nathaniel Moore,* a brother of Col. Maurice Moore and "King" Roger Moore, but he owned several other plantations up the river and does not seem to have lived at York. There is, or recently was, a steamboat landing and post-office about forty miles farther up the river that has for more than a hundred years borne the name of "Nat Moore," but generally spelled Natmore.

---

* Nathaniel Moore married Sarah Grange April 13, 1720, in South Carolina, as we learn from the *Annals and Register of St. Thomas's and St. Denis's Parish, S. C.*, and after her death married a Miss Webb.

RUSSELLBORO.

Immediately north of the town of Brunswick was the historic place called Russellboro, a residence with 55 acres of land attached, which was bought from Roger Moore's estate by Captain Russell of the British navy,* and afterwards was sold to Governor Dobbs, whose son, Captain Edward Brice Dobbs, sold it to Governor Tryon in 1767.† It was at this residence that the Stamp Act patriots interviewed Tryon to his great indignation and humiliation. As in nearly every other instance of the places, there is nothing left of Russellboro but a few broken bricks.‡ It was a part of the Orton estate.

ORTON.

The first plantation above Brunswick, which from its first settlement to this day has been one of the largest and most beautiful estates on the Cape Fear River, is Orton. It was settled by "King" Roger Moore in 1725, and remained in his family for three generations, and then was bought by Richard Quince, a wealthy merchant, in whose family it remained for about thirty years, when Gen. (afterwards Governor) Benjamin Smith owned it. It was the southernmost *rice* plantation on the river.

KENDALL.

Adjoining Orton on the north is Kendall, where Governor Smith's brother James lived. He was the father of R. Barnwell Smith, who, with his brother, took the name of Rhett and moved to South Carolina. Kendall was first granted to Col. Maurice Moore in 1725, conveyed by him to his brother Roger Moore in 1726, and sold by the latter's son George to John Davis, Jr., in 1765.§ It was later owned by the McRee

---

* Captain Russell owned the land on which the town of Campbellton (adjoining Cross Creek, now Fayetteville) was built, which land descended to his sons John and William, who are named as the owners in the Act of 1762 establishing the town, and who were pensioned by the British government, and were Tories in the Revolution. Their father died prior to 1762, and Andrew J. Howell, Esq., of Wilmington, tells me he is one of his descendants. Captain Russell commanded the sloop of war Scorpion.

† Book B, 309, N. H.

‡ The North Carolina Society of Colonial Dames have erected, with the foundation stones of the building, a memorial structure, and have placed on it a large marble tablet reciting the history of the place.

§ Book E, 242.

family. The first of this family in North Carolina was Samuel McRee, who settled in Bladen County about the year 1740, having come from Ireland. His son, Griffith John McRee, born in Bladen February 1, 1758, was an enthusiastic patriot at the beginning of the Revolution, and was commissioned on the 16th of April, 1776, captain in the 6th Regiment, Continental Line of North Carolina. He was at the battle of Fort Moultrie, and afterwards at the battles of Brandywine, Germantown, and Monmouth. Being transferred in March, 1779, to the 1st Regiment, Continental Line, he marched in the next fall to South Carolina, and was at the long siege of Charleston, where he was made prisoner. After his exchange he joined Greene's army and fought at Guilford Court House, Hobkirk's Hill, and Eutaw Springs. In the last named fight his conduct secured his promotion to the rank of Major and Brevet Lieutenant Colonel. After the Revolution, in 1785, he married Miss Fergus, of Wilmington, and lived at Lilliput, next adjoining to Kendall. General Washington appointed him Captain of Engineers and Artillery in 1794, and while in command at Fort Johnston he was appointed, in 1798, collector of the port of Wilmington. He was a member of the Society of the Cincinnati and was distinguished for his exceptional Christian character. Only five of his children reached maturity, but of these, three were men of marked ability, viz: Col. Wm. McRee, who graduated at West Point in 1805 with the first honors, distinguished himself in the War of 1812, was made Chief of Engineers U. S. Army in 1814, Lieutenant Colonel of Engineers in 1818, resigned 1819, and died in 1833. Also Col. Sam McRee, who graduated at West Point, reached the rank of Lieutenant Colonel in the Mexican War as General Taylor's Chief Quartermaster, and died in 1849; and Dr. James Fergus McRee, perhaps the most learned, scholarly and accomplished physician and scientist ever reared on the Cape Fear. He was distinguished for his attainments in natural science as well as in the different branches of his profession and in general literature, and was a correspondent of the Royal Society and a friend of the celebrated Lyell, who with his wife once visited Dr. McRee at his Rocky Point plantation. He was an upright gentleman and devoted Christian, who, after a life of nearly seventy-five years crowned with honors, died in 1869 at his home in Wilmington. He had two sons who sustained the intellectual reputation of the family, viz: Dr. James F. McRee, Jr., a prominent physician and surgeon in the Confederate army, and Griffith J. McRee, author of the "Life and Correspondence of James Iredell," Justice of the Supreme Court of the United States.

LILLIPUT.

The plantation next north of Kendall was Lilliput, which was granted in 1725 to Eleazer Allen, an educated gentleman and native of Massachusetts, who had previously been a member of the Assembly in South Carolina, and a member of the Council there, and who came with the early settlers from there in 1734. He lived at Lilliput until his death in 1749, and, with his wife,* is buried on that place under two of the best preserved tombstones on the Cape Fear. The stone over his remains is inscribed "Chief Justice of North Carolina." He had also been a member of Council, Receiver-General, Judge of Oyer and Terminer, and Treasurer of New Hanover precinct. Lilliput was afterwards owned by the McRee family, as above stated.

PLEASANT OAKS.

Next above Lilliput was the plantation called Pleasant Oaks, granted to the widow of John Moore, (another brother of Maurice and Roger) in 1728, and from whom it is believed that the "Widow Moore's Creek," where the first victory of the Revolution (February 27, 1776) was won, took its name.†

OLD TOWN CREEK.

This list of the plantations brings us up to the mouth of Old Town Creek, on the western bank of the river, about eight

---

* A lady of culture, who had traveled in Europe, a daughter of Col. William Rhett, of South Carolina.
† She was, before marriage, Justina Smith, daughter of Landgrave Thomas Smith the second, and died in Philadelphia after a brief illness while on a visit to relatives in 1742. Her will is recorded in Philadelphia.

miles below Wilmington, where the colony of Sir John Yeamans settled the first Charlestown in this country, in 1664-65.

RICE'S PLANTATION.

Now, leaving the river and following up Old Town Creek, one of the plantations on the south side, was that of Nathaniel Rice, the remains of the fine residence there having been visible as late as the early youth of the late Hon. Geo. Davis, who said he had seen them.* Nathaniel Rice was the son-in-law of Col. Martin Bladen, one of the Lords of Trade and Plantations, and was a prominent man in the Province, having been first the Secretary of the Province and later a member of the Council and acting Governor for a short period, just before Matthew Rowan, the next senior member of the Council, who succeeded him until the arrival of Governor Dobbs in 1754.

The order in which the plantations up Old Town Creek came is not known, and we can only give the names of a few of them.

SPRING GARDEN.

In a deed from Maurice Moore to John Baptista Ashe, dated December 5, 1727, in which Moore is described as "of Bath County," he conveys 640 acres on the north side of Old Town Creek, "about five miles above ye Old Town, commonly known by the name of Spring Garden," granted to said Moore, June 20, 1725. The name of this place was afterwards changed by some of Mr. Ashe's successors to Grovely, by which name it has been known for more than a hundred years past. It was given, by the will of Ann R. Quince, to her cousin, A. D. Moore, son of Maj. A. D. Moore, and for sixty years or more last past has belonged to the estate of the late Dr. John D. Bellamy.

BELGRANGE.

Another plantation, on Old Town Creek, containing 2,500 acres, was owned by Chief Justice Hasell and was conveyed to James Murray, Trustee, in a marriage settlement between

---

* "An Episode in Cape Fear History," in *South Atlantic Magazine*, January, 1879.

Hasell's son, James Hasell, Jr., and Sarah Wright, February 20, 1750,* and this place was called Belgrange.

HULLFIELDS.

Next to Belgrange was Hullfields, owned by Schencking Moore, son of Nathaniel Moore, and sold by him to John McKenzie.

DAVIS PLANTATION.

Another place at the head of Old Town Creek, containing 750 acres, was sold by Eleazer Allen to John Davis, June 9, 1744.

DALYRMPLE PLACE.

Another place "on the north side of Old Town Creek, adjoining the land of the late John Baptista Ashe at Spring Garden," containing 550 acres, was sold by the executors of Joseph Watters to "John Dalrymple, Gent.,† September 12, 1744.‡

DOBBS PLACE.

Governor Dobbs owned a plantation on Old Town Creek, where he is supposed to have been buried, but its name and locality are unknown, and the same may be said of most of the plantations located there, of which there were a dozen or more.

The best known of these proprietors, except Dobbs, was John Baptista Ashe, who was the father of Col. John Ashe of Stamp Act fame, and of Governor Samuel Ashe. He went from South Carolina to the Albemarle country, where in 1719 he married the daughter of Samuel Swann, and afterwards removed with his relatives, Porter, Moseley, Moore, and Lillington, to the Cape Fear and took up his residence at Spring Garden in 1727, where he died in 1734.

---

* Book D, 188, N. H.

† Afterwards (in 1755) commander of Fort Johnston. His brother (?) Sir Wm. Dalrymple, married Miss Martha Watters, sister of Joseph Watters. Captain Dalrymple had trouble with Governor Dobbs, was removed from command of the fort, and was succeeded (1758) by Captain (afterwards general) James Moore.

‡ Book C, 32, N. H.

HISTORY OF NEW HANOVER COUNTY. 47

OLD TOWN.

Returning now to the mouth of Old Town Creek and proceeding north on the river, the first place is the site of the Old Town, which still retains its name of the Old Town plantation. In 1761 Judge Maurice Moore, son of Col. Maurice Moore, bought this plantation from his brother Gen. James Moore, and in 1768 sold it to John Ancrum, one of the early settlers and a prominent man, who was a leading merchant, chairman (after Harnett) of the Safety Committee, and one of its most active members from the start.

CLARENDON.

The place next north of Old Town was called Clarendon, and still retains the name. Who gave it the name we do not know, but it was owned by Mr. Campbell at an early period, and afterwards by Mr. Joseph Watters.

THE FORKS.

Next above Clarendon was the estate called the Forks, which was owned by Richard Eagles in 1736, and was afterwards bought by John Davis, Esq., and later by Mr. Joseph Eagles. Richard and Joseph Eagles were among the first settlers on the Cape Fear. Their descendants were prominent, but the family is now extinct. They came from Bristol, and it is a remarkable fact that this writer some years ago, being introduced to a Mr. Eagles living about 25 miles from Wilmington, upon inquiry discovered that he had come with the Northern army which captured Fort Fisher in 1865, had never heard of the Old Cape Fear family, was an Englishman, was from Bristol, and was named Richard!

BUCHOI.

The next place was Buchoi, owned by Judge Alfred Moore. The origin of this name puzzled the present writer because he knew that while there was a number of French names, then fashionable for estates, Judge Moore would not have written the name Buchoi (intending Beauchoix) but his puzzle was

48   HISTORY OF NEW HANOVER COUNTY.

solved when he discovered several years ago, that one of the old Moore estates on Goose Creek, S. C., bore an Indian name which was spelled in the records there Boo-Chawee, the spelling in both cases being according to the sound, or, in modern phrase, phonetic.

BELVILLE.

Adjoining Buchoi was Belville, owned by Mr. John Waddell,* son of Gen. Hugh Waddell, who also owned three other plantations farther up the river.

BELVIDERE.

Then came Belvidere, owned by Col. Wm. Dry, and later by Governor Ben Smith. This place is nearly opposite the City of Wilmington, but intervening is Eagles' Island, formed by the cut-off now called Brunswick River, but in the earliest period called the Northwest or main branch, which latter was then called the Thoroughfare.

This completes the list of places on the west side of the river from below Brunswick to the forks of the river at Wilmington, all of which except those on upper Old Town Creek, were rice plantations with large tracts of timber land adjoining them to the westward.

NEGRO HEAD POINT.

Between the forks of the river opposite Wilmington was the Negro Head Point plantation which at an early period belonged to Col. Peter Mallett, and from his time to the present has been called Point Peter.

The name of this place has long been erroneously supposed to have been given to it from the fact that a negro's head was

---

* Mr. Waddell used to tell of an incident that happened not far from this plantation during Craig's occupation of Wilmington. He was a little boy eleven years old at the time, and was being carried by his guardian, Mr. John Burgwin, to Charleston to be sent to school in England, where his two elder brothers were. A sentinel halted the vehicle and demanded Mr. Burgwin's pass, which he received and solemnly inspected and returned, saying it was all right. After passing, Mr. Burgwin began to laugh heartily, and the little boy asked the reason, to which he replied that the sentinel held the pass upside down while pretending to read it. Mr. Waddell also related that when the ship that carried him to England was entering the Thames a great ship, called the Royal George, hailed, and asked, "what news from America," to which the answer was shouted: "A great victory for His Majesty's troops at Guilford Court House." Mr. Waddell married Sarah, daughter of Gen. Francis Nash.

said to have been stuck up there at the time of the Nat Turner insurrection in 1831, but this is a mistake, for the point was called Negro Head Point in court records as early as the year 1764. How it originated is not known.

There is a similar error as to the name of the stream called Jumping Run, just below Wilmington, which has long been attributed to an alleged incident of the American Revolution, but that name also appears in court records more than ten years before the Revolution.

Now, beginning at Wilmington and going up the Northeast River, the first place was Hilton, owned by Cornelius Harnett, "the pride of the Cape Fear."

HILTON.

There has been much misinformation about this place. As early as June 3d, 1730, in a deed from John Gardner Squier* to John Maultsby for land on Smith's Creek, he described it as "adjoining Harnett's," showing that Cornelius Harnett, Senior, owned it at that time, for then the younger Harnett was only seven years old. About that time the elder Harnett had a ferry at Maultsby's Point. The land was called Maynard by Harnett, and the name Hilton was not given to it until the widow of C. Harnett, Jr., conveyed it to John Hill and he sold it to his brother, Wm. H. Hill, who says in his will that he named it Hilton after his family, although in doing so he left out one L, and thus gave color to the tradition that it was named after the first explorer in 1663, Captain Hilton.

HALTON LODGE.

Adjoining the Hilton estate on the east and fronting on Smith's Creek (which was named for Chief Justice Smith, who owned land at the head of it) was Halton Lodge, owned by Col. Robert Halton, one of the founders of Wilmington. This place was between where the county road and the present track

---

* A, B, 161. Squier got a grant for the Hilton tract November 5, 1728. It was conveyed by Wm. Moore to C. Harnett, Jr., (150 acres) May 3, 1753 ; so that the elder Harnett must have sold or mortgaged it before his son bought it from Wm. Moore.

of the A. C. L. R. R. cross the creek, and contained 640 acres. It subsequently bore several names.* It was sold under execution by Arthur Benning, Sheriff, on the 14th October, 1765, to satisfy a debt to Caleb Grainger, administrator of Joshua Grainger, and was bought by Cornelius Harnett, Jr., for nine pounds proclamation money. It was stated in the Sheriff's deed that the property was in possession of "John Rutherford, surviving administrator of Robert Halton."

Of the history of Colonel Halton prior to the year 1730 we have no knowledge. In that year Burrington recommended him for a seat in the council, and he served both under him and under Governor Johnston. He was also Provost Marshal (changed by the Act of 1738, Ch. 3, to Sheriff) of Bath County. Probably on the suggestion of Burrington, who had located patents there, he removed to the Cape Fear about 1734, and was one of the original settlers at Wilmington.† He was an officer of the troops that left the Cape Fear on the expedition to Carthagena in 1740.

SANS SOUCI.

The plantation next north of Hilton has for a hundred years borne the name Sans Souci, which was probably given it by one of the Hill family, but the original owner was Caleb Grainger, Sr.

Caleb Grainger, Sr., was the son of Joshua Grainger, one of the founders (1733) of Wilmington, then called Newtown. He early took an active and prominent part in public affairs, being a member of the Assembly in 1746, and Sheriff of the county in 1749. In the numerous deeds recorded in the county from him he signs himself as planter, inn-holder, and esquire.

He was Lieutenant Colonel of Innes's regiment on the expedition to Virginia in 1754, the other officers being Robt. Rowan, Major, and Thos. Arbuthnot, Edward Vail, Alex.

---

* D 488. It seems most probable that this was the "Poplar Grove" from which Harnett dated all his published letters. Poplar Grove was certainly not the same as Hilton (called *Maynard* by Harnett), for Harnett applied for permission for his "negro man Jack to carry a gun on his two plantations, Maynard and Poplar Grove."

† Colonel Halton owned Eagles' Island, opposite Wilmington, and sold half of it to Roger Moore December 13, 1737.

HISTORY OF NEW HANOVER COUNTY. 51

Woodrow, Hugh Waddell, Thos. McManus, and Moses John DeRosset, Captains. Upon the reorganization of the regiment after Braddock's defeat (1755) he went on the expedition to New York (1756) as a Captain under Major Dobbs, son of the Governor, and for some years afterwards was prominent in civil life.

He was a large landholder and was described by Governor Dobbs as a "gentleman of good fortune in the province." He was a prominent Mason, and having bought from George Moore the land on which Masonboro was settled, is believed to have given it that name, as the first deed in which the name is mentioned was made by his widow and executrix. He died in 1769 or 1770.

ROCK HILL.

Then came Rock Hill, the residence of John Davis, Esq., who also owned the Mulberry plantation on the Northwest River, or main branch.

ROSE HILL.

Then came Rose Hill, the residence of Mr. Quince, a member of one of the oldest families on the Cape Fear. They came from Ramsgate, England.

ROCKY RUN.

Next to Rose Hill was Rocky Run, the home of Maurice Jones, Esq., and later of his son-in-law, Dr. Nat. Hill, a distinguished physician and graduate of Edinburgh.

CEDAR GROVE.

Near Rocky Run was Cedar Grove, owned by the DeRosset family, of the earlier generations of which we give the following biographical notes. The "Annals" of this family have been recently published in a beautiful volume:

About 1735 there arrived in Wilmington from England a gentleman with his wife and two sons, whose name from that time to the present has been an honored one on the Cape Fear, Dr. Armand DeRosset. He was descended from three noble families of France and was a distinguished graduate of the University of Basle, Switzerland, from which he received his medical diploma in 1720; but being a Huguenot and son of an exile he neither assumed nor claimed any right to consideration on that account. He practiced his profession with modesty and diligence, and because of his charity and benevolence was beloved by the people among whom he had cast his fortune. He was recognized from the start as a leading and public-spirited man, and was assigned to positions of trust and honor in the community. He was a devoted member of the Church of England, and he and his sons exerted themselves to establish the parish and church of St. James, so much so as to be called the founders thereof.

His two sons, Louis Henry and Moses John DeRosset, inherited his virtues, and each attained distinction in the Colony. The elder one, Louis Henry, in 1751 represented Wilmington in the Assembly at New Bern, was Justice of the Peace, appointed by the Council, was a member of the Council under Governor Johnston in 1752, and continued in that position until the Revolution; was Commissioner to issue bills of credit, and Receiver General of quit rents in the Province, was Adjutant General on the staff of General Waddell in the Regulators War, and Lieutenant General under Tryon. He was a merchant and planter and accumulated what was in those days regarded as a large fortune. Being an intense loyalist, he did not, like his brother and nearly all his family connections and friends, take the American side when the Revolution began, but adhered to his convictions and followed Governor Josiah Martin, the last of the Royal Governors of the Province, when the latter was driven out of North Carolina.

In 1779 he "was banished by the Province on pain of death if he returned." "There is," says one of a later generation* of his family, "an element of tender pathos in the story of this good man's life. Exiled in early childhood from his native Province (in France) with loss of all worldly possessions, his

---

* "Annals of the DeRosset Family," by Mrs. C. DeR. Meares.

later years saddened by war and strife and banishment, losing again home and kindred and fortune, his life was ever tempest-tossed. * * * Through all his life, so full of trial, trouble and temptation, his integrity was always his preeminent characteristic."

After the Revolution the French Government offered to restore to him the family titles and estates on condition that he would return to France, and to the Roman Catholic church, but the offer was refused, and he died in London February 22, 1786.

His younger brother, Moses John DeRosset, who succeeded his father as a doctor of medicine, soon became prominent, not only in his profession, but in military and civil life. When Col. James Innes, in 1754, took his regiment to Virginia to fight the French and Indians, DeRosset was commissioned as one of the captains of that regiment. Afterwards he held prominent offices, and in the troublous time of the Stamp Act was Mayor of Wilmington, and wrote a letter to Governor Tryon, containing the celebrated sentence "Moderation ceases to be a virtue when the liberty of the British subject is in danger." He wholly differed with his elder brother on the rights of the colonies, and if he had lived until the Revolution would have been prominent in it, but he died in 1767.

THE HERMITAGE.

The next place was the Hermitage, owned by Mr. John Burgwin, a noted seat of generous hospitality. Mr. Burgwin was a leading merchant of Wilmington and for some time the Treasurer of the southern half of the Province before the Revolution. The Hermitage is still owned by one of his descendants, a resident of Pennsylvania.

CASTLE HAYNES.

Adjoining the Hermitage on the north was Castle Haynes, named for the owner, Capt. Roger Haynes, who married the daughter of Rev. Richard Marsden, who owned both these places. Captain Haynes's two daughters married Mr. Burgwin and Gen. Hugh Waddell, and General Waddell's wife's brother gave* her Castle Haynes, where both she and the General were buried. He died before the Revolution in April 1773, and was the ranking officer of the Province, having been almost continuously in service in the French and Indian Wars for nearly twenty years, and dying in his 39th year. His biography was written by one of his descendants and was published in 1891.†

POINT PLEASANT.

At a sharp bend of the Northeast River to the west of Castle Haynes was Point Pleasant, the residence of Col. James Innes, a distinguished colonial officer, who came to the Province of North Carolina prior to 1735, was captain in the expedition to Carthagena in 1740, Colonel in the expedition to Virginia in 1754, a member of the Council from 1750 to 1759, agent for Lord Carteret and Colonel of the New Hanover Militia. He died in 1759, "a good and true man, who died a childless benefactor of the children of his poorer fellow-citizens"‡ by leaving the bulk of his estate for their education, the first known instance of this kind in the history of the State.

THE OAK.

We have now reached the point where the Northeast River makes a bend to the eastward and where the lower end of the Rocky Point neighborhood near the mouth of Turkey Creek began on the opposite side; and the first place to mention was The Oak, the residence of Speaker Samuel Swann, a distinguished lawyer who, in conjunction with Edward Moseley, compiled the first Revisal of the Laws of the Province of North Carolina, (called the Yellow Jacket from the color of the binding) which was the first book printed in the Province. His residence was the finest on the Cape Fear.‡

---

* Will of Mrs. Waddell, registered in Bladen County.
† "A Colonial Officer," etc., by A. M. Waddell.   ‡ The same, 52-53.
‡ A gentleman who visited the ruins of this house more than fifty years ago, in a private letter to the writer of these pages, says: "It must have been one of the finest residences in America. * * * The stairs were mahogany. * * * The elegance one could trace in the ruins amazed me." There is nothing left of this mansion now except the broken fragments of its brick foundation. During the Revolution intrenchments for defense against the British were erected near it, and again in 1865 on the same ground, the Confederates, retreating from Wilmington, erected breastworks and delayed the enemy.

HISTORY OF NEW HANOVER COUNTY. 55

He began life as a surveyor, and was one of the party appointed to run the dividing line between North Carolina and Virginia in 1729, being then 25 years old, and was the first white man that ever crossed the Dismal Swamp, a terrible undertaking from which he emerged to the great relief of his associates, who passed around it and were ready to give him up after waiting for him several days. He was a member of the Assembly for many years and became Speaker in 1742, and was most influential in shaping public affairs throughout his career. He had one son, Maj. Sam Swann, an officer in the Revolution, who was killed in a duel with Mr. Bradley at Wilmington some years after the close of that war (July 11, 1787).

SWANN POINT.

Not far west of The Oak was Swann Point, the home of John Swann, called "Lawyer" John, which was also one of the finest residences on Rocky Point.

SPRING GARDEN, MT. GALLANT, PLEASANT HALL.

A short distance to the northwest of Swann Point was Spring Garden, the home of Frederic Jones, Esq., a prominent planter. Near it was Mt. Gallant, owned by Col. John Pugh Williams, who was Colonel of the 9th Regiment, Continental Line; and at a short distance from this place was Pleasant Hall, the residence of Wm. Davis, Esq., who also owned a place on Turkey Creek called Bloom Hill in 1809.*

HYRNEHAM.

Above the last two places and farthest west from the river was Hyrneham, owned by Capt. Edward Hyrne, which was convey to him by Col. Maurice Moore, October 10th, 1736,† as a gift (as Hyrne declared in his will) ‡ and which Hyrne devised to his son, Henry Hyrne, who in turn by his will gave it to his nephew, Harry Hyrne Watters, a minor, who after-

---
* A, 189.   † E, 230.   ‡ D, 142.

wards married the daughter of Wm. Hooper, the signer of the Declaration of Independence.

Col. Le Hansyus De Keyser, a Virginian by birth, but of French and Swiss ancestry,* who had been adjutant of the 1st Regiment, Continental Line of North Carolina, occupied Hyrneham as an inn after the Revolution, and tradition says that he there trained the fastest horse then in America, which belonged to a club of young men, sons of the neighboring planters. Colonel De Keyser left descendants who were among the most respectable people of the upper Cape Fear, one of whom was the mother of Hon. Warren Winslow, and others of the Belden and Gilliam families. Hyrneham was burned, like the Oaks and other places, but much later.

SPRINGFIELD, STRAWBERRY, AND THE VATS.

And now we reach the center of the Rocky Point settlement, the first three plantations on the south end of which—Springfield, Strawberry† and The Vats—having been embraced in the original grant to Col. Maurice Moore in 1725.‡ This was the place, where Governor Burrington and Col. Maurice Moore met each other with their respective surveying parties, and came near engaging in personal combat over their respective claims to the land. Moore kept possession, and, according to tradition, told Burrington he would find as good land higher up at Stag Park, which he did. At the Vats is the ruined vault in which the body of Colonel Moore and those of his two sons, Judge Maurice and Gen. James Moore, and others of his family were entombed. The plantation was bought by Mr. Ezekiel Lane, whose son, Levin Lane, inherited it.

CLAYTON HALL.

Next above the Vats came Clayton Hall, the residence of Francis Clayton, a prominent citizen, who, after being a Whig

---

* Letter from Robert Belden, his grandson, to Louis S. Belden, of Wilmington, kindly loaned to the writer.
† Near Strawberry (or possibly the same tract) was The Mulberry, the residence of Thomas Hooper, younger brother of the signer, who was a merchant in Wilmington and Charleston, and a loyalist. There was also a plantation called Mulberry on the Northwest river, owned first by the Watters family.
‡ D, 278, called Rocky Point, from a point of rocks at the sharp bend of the river there.

leader, became a loyalist. This place was bought from the executors of Clayton by Col. Sam Ashe, son of Governor Sam Ashe, and was one of the most interesting localities on Rocky Point. Colonel Ashe was universally beloved and revered as the last noble specimen of the ancient Cape Fear gentleman and soldier, having lived until 1836. He was the grandfather of Capt. S. A. Ashe, author of the latest (and best) history of North Carolina, issued in 1908.* Clayton also owned the plantation on the Sound previously owned by Cornelius Harnett, containing 800 acres.

GREEN HILL.

Next above Clayton Hall was Green Hill, the home of General John Ashe, of Stamp Act and Revolutionary fame. His family graveyard is there, although he himself was buried under an oak on Col. Jno. Sampson's farm near the town of Clinton in Sampson County.

MOSELEY HALL.

Next above Green Hill was Moseley Hall, owned by Col. Sampson Moseley, son of the distinguished Edward Moseley, whose career in the early history of North Carolina marks him as perhaps the most accomplished man of his era, as well as the ablest.

THE NECK.

A short distance above these last named places was The Neck, the residence of Governor Sam Ashe, who with his family is buried there. His son, John Baptista Ashe, was also elected Governor, but died before taking his seat.

MOOREFIELDS.

At some distance west of the last three places was Moorefields, the home of George Moore, a rich planter, who seems

---

* The advertisement of this estate for sale was published in the *North Carolina Chronicle* or *Fayetteville Gazette* of October 25, 1790, and it was described by the executors, Archibald Maclaine, Henry Urquhart, and Henry Toomer, as follows: "That well-known valuable plantation and parcel of land, called *Rocky Point* on the Northeast river, in New-Hanover county, containing, by original grants, 1920 acres, with a large brick house and other buildings—one hundred and ninety acres of this has been under crop this year, and is enclosed with new fence; and there are several hundred acres clear, and fit for immediate cultivation. These lands are some of the best in the State, both for tillage and pasture."

to have made a brave effort to rival old King Priam in the number of his offspring, having been the father of 28 children by his two wives. He left two other evidences of his industry in the form of an immense long ditch and embankment called to this day the Devil's Ditch, because, tradition says, the rapidity of the work was so astonishing—one story being that it was done in a night—that the Devil must have had a hand in it. The other was the construction of a perfectly straight road from Moorefields to his summer place on Masonboro Sound, a distance of about 15 miles, which he did with his own slaves. The road is still known as the "George Moore Road," and according to tradition his method of changing his residence from the one place to the other was to call up fifty or more negroes and, distributing his household effects for summer use among them, chairs, tables, bedsteads, etc., to start the procession afoot along this road, and thus make the change in one day, his family accompanying them on horseback.

STAG PARK.

The last and uppermost estate on the west side of Northeast River was Stag Park, a name given by the first explorers under Hilton and preserved to the present. This place was granted to Governor Burrington, or rather he located there an old "Blank Patent" issued in 1711, and which (it was alleged) he altered from 640 acres to 5,000 acres. He afterwards conveyed it to Mr. Strudwick, together with the Hawfields in Orange County.

BOWLANDS.

In this neighborhood, but exactly where is not known, was Bowlands, a plantation owned by John Rutherford, for many years a prominent man in the Province. He also owned two other plantations, Stoney Creek and Bear Garden,* in New Hanover, and lands in Bladen and Duplin Counties. John Rutherford was brought out to North Carolina by his cousin, James Murray, in 1741, when a very young man, and began

---

* County Court records, 1772.

life under his care. Murray provided a home for him in his own house in Wilmington, and put him to work in his store; where he learned to keep accounts and sell goods. He does not seem to have enjoyed any educational advantages prior to coming to America, but he was taught by his cousin, who was a fairly educated man, and it was not very long before he began to get the benefit of Murray's influence with Governor Johnston and others in authority, and to be advanced to official position. He was appointed Recorder of Quit Rents in 1750 and in 1756 was a member of the Council, but having displeased Governor Dobbs by not agreeing with that disputatious and obstinate old gentleman, was removed from the latter position in 1757, and again restored to it by the Crown in 1763. He owned lands in Bladen as well as in New Hanover, and in the latter county he established mills at his plantation, Stoney Creek, which were known first as Rutherford's mills and afterwards as Ashe's mills. At these mills, during Craig's occupation of Wilmington in 1781, the British erected a field work, the remains of which were plainly visible fifty years ago, and used the mills to grind the grain robbed from the neighboring fields. Rutherford married Governor Johnston's widow, Frances, and their ante-nuptial settlement, dated May 6, 1764, is on record.*

LILLINGTON HALL.

On the opposite side of the river, (the east side) and about four miles above the Vats, was Lillington Hall, the residence of Gen. Alexander Lillington, hero of the battle of Moore's Creek Bridge, who with his command first arrived on the field, held the first line of battle, fought splendidly, and saw Caswell receive the chief honors. Lillington was a noble old patriot and soldier, who, after this first victory of the Revolution, February 27, 1776, rendered other valuable service, military and civil, to his country, and after the war dispensed a most generous hospitality at Lillington Hall. There were no valuable

---
* Book F, p. 1.

farm lands on that side of the river, at least in comparison with those on the west side, or Rocky Point proper, but below Lillington Hall Colonel Merrick owned a place, and there was another called Porter's Bluff, which was described in a deed made in 1751 as "the property of the late John Porter."

We have now given a complete list of all the old places on the Northeast River, and will now take up those on the Northwest or main branch, above Wilmington, and in all cases we confine ourselves, both as to names of the estates and of their owners, to the Colonial and Revolutionary periods. In a few instances these places remained for one or two generations in the hands of the descendants of the first owners, but there is not one now so owned, except the Hermitage. The houses on all were burned.

THE BLUFF.

The first place above Wilmington on the Northwest River, situate about four miles distant, was originally called Gabourel's Bluff, being named for its owner, Captain Gabourel, where the English traveler from South Carolina in 1734 found the flourishing shipping point mentioned in the first chapter.

There was in the early days a ferry from there to Newton, as Wilmington was then called. This ferry was operated by James Campbell in 1736, and by Cornelius Harnett, Sr., in 1739, who qualified as Sheriff in that year, and the records of the County Court show that there was much rivalry in securing the ferry privileges and some annoyance to the Court over it. After Gabourel's time the place was called Maclaine's Bluff, it then being the property of Archibald Maclaine, the great lawyer. It is now the site of the Navassa Guano Company's works, and if the enemies of Maclaine, who so often felt the fierceness of his invective, were now alive they would probably regard it as appropriate that his body should lie, as it does, under the acid chamber of that factory.*

---

* "He was of sanguine temperament and irritable passions. The slightest spark sufficed to kindle into flame his combustible nature. The explosions of his wrath were sudden and terrific, and his fiery denunciations and heated satire seethed and scorched as burning lava."—McRee's "Iredell," Vol. I, 370. Maclaine married Elizabeth Rowan, daughter of Jerome Rowan by his wife Elizabeth, who afterwards married Matthew Rowan.

COBHAM.

There were several plantations in close proximity above the Bluff, the first of which was Cobham, owned by Dr. Thos. Cobham, a leading physician at an early period. He and Dr. Haslin (who married Governor Nash's daughter) were the surgeons of Tryon's army at Alamance in 1771.

PROSPECT.

The next place was Prospect, the original owner of which is not known, but was probably one of the Moore family. In the early part of the last century it was owned by Maj. John Walker, nephew of Maj. "Jack" Walker, of the Revolution.

SCHAWFIELDS.

Next to Prospect was Schawfields, owned by Robert Schaw, partner in the leading mercantile firm of Ancrum, Brice, and Schaw, which firm was established some years before the Revolution, and did a very large business until about 1780. In Tryon's expedition in 1771 Schaw was Colonel of Artillery under General Waddell.

MULBERRY.

The next place was Mulberry, which, in his will,* made in 1751, Wm. Watters said was left to him by his father. In 1788 it was the property of John Davis, as appears by his will of that date,† and later it belonged to the Hall family.

There was another Mulberry on the Northeast River in the Rocky Point settlement, owned by Thos. Hooper, brother of Wm. Hooper.

DALLISON.

Next came Dallison, which, as we learn from a recital in a deed from Maurice Moore, was "the property of Col. John Dallison, deceased." Of Colonel Dallison we know nothing.

AUBURN AND MAGNOLIA.

The next two places were Auburn and Magnolia, which belonged to the Watters and Hall families.

---
* C, 323—Wills.   † C, 80—Wills.

POINT REPOSE.

Then came a place located between Hood's Creek and the river, that has an interesting history and still bears the name given to it by its first purchaser—Point Repose. It was bought in 1735 and settled in 1739 by James Murray, a young Scotchman of an excellent family, who came as a merchant and trader first to Charleston, S. C., and then to Brunswick. Very soon after his arrival here he bought Point Repose and a lot in Wilmington, situated about where the present Orton Hotel stands. He was in a little while afterwards made clerk of the Crown and Secretary of the Council, and was for many years afterwards a member of the Council and an especial favorite of Governor Johnston. He was a man of high character, apparently, but was, as the editors of his letters say,* "although public spirited, never a true American," having been, from his arrival in the Province until he left it and removed to Boston in 1765, an unwavering Loyalist. His property was all confiscated and sold by commissioners appointed for the purpose in 1783,† and the deed is recorded in New Hanover County. It was all bought by his nephew, Gen. Thomas Clark, a gallant Revolutionary officer, who was his largest creditor, and General Clark took up his residence at Point Repose.

There is something pathetic in Murray's case, as in all others of like kind. His adherence to King and Parliament was not dictated by the sordid and vindictive spirit that animated those who sought to make it the means of self-advancement and the gratification of personal revenge, but was inspired by a sincere conviction of the righteousness of such a course and of an honest belief that rebellion would be equally as disastrous to the colonies as to the Crown, and therefore although he erred in judgment to his own financial ruin, his motives were honorable and worthy of respect.

---

* Letters of James Murray, Loyalist, 65.

† Petition of Thomas Clark, John Innis Clark, and Anne Hooper, wife of Wm. Hooper, asking appointment of commissioners (*Martin's Priv. Stat.*, 103). Report of com. (same, 113). The commissioners were Sam. Ashe, Alfred Moore, Thomas Craike, John Lillington, Caleb Grainger, John Moore, and James Gillespie.

He took no part in the Revolution, but merely got out of the trouble and sought a peaceful home elsewhere. No intelligent and fair-minded person now denounces indiscriminately those who were Tories in the Revolution. Some of them, like David Fanning and his followers in North Carolina, and "bloody Cunningham" and his crew in South Carolina, were lawless murderers and robbers, who wreaked their vengeance on their Whig neighbors and their families, and were inspired by no reverence or affection for royalty or the British Constitution; but there were others who were gentlemen of high character who venerated both, and were honestly afraid of popular government, and they acted according to their conscientious convictions of duty.

Gen. Thomas Clark's father, Thos. Clark, Sr., married James Murray's sister Barbara in 1737, and in 1741 was made Sheriff of New Hanover County for two years, and was also appointed Collector of the Port of Wilmington, in place of Samuel Woodward, deceased, by Dinwiddie, Surveyor General of the colonies. He died in 1748 or 1749.

His son, Gen. Thos. Clark, was born about the middle of August, 1741, in Wilmington. He was sent to England and there learned the watchmaker's trade, which, on his return, he practiced for a time in Boston, but abandoned it in 1767 and came back to the Cape Fear to take charge of his uncle James Murray's estate, of which his elder brother James had previously been manager. He seems to have been a favorite of his uncle because of his unusual intellectual capacity.

When the Revolution began Clark was appointed Major of the 1st Regiment, Continental Line, and afterwards was promoted Lieutenant Colonel and Colonel, succeeding Gen. Francis Nash in the last two positions, and was later, by resolution of the Continental Congress, September, 1783, brevetted Brigadier General. He was a gallant officer throughout the war, particularly distinguishing himself in the repulse of the attack on Sullivan's Island by the British in 1776; and yet, perhaps, no other officer of equal rank and valuable services has occupied so small a space in the pages of our history. There does not seem to have been any design in this neglect to do him honor, but he has been strangely overlooked. General Nash, having been killed at the battle of Germantown, Pa., October 4, 1777, Clark, his associate and successor in rank, married his widow in 1782, and they lived at Point Repose, where both died and were buried.* They left no issue.

In a letter written from Point Repose under date of 31st December, 1787, by Wm. Hooper (Clark's brother-in-law) to Judge Iredell, he says:† "Immediately upon my arrival at Wilmington it was announced to me that my son William at midnight had left his uncle George Hooper's house to visit General Clark, who had been attacked with a violent disorder in his head, which had utterly deprived him of his senses and left him (stone blind) to the care or inattention of nearly 40 slaves, without a white person on his plantation to attend to his distresses. * * * I found the General ill indeed. He consented that I should send for his sister, proof positive that he thought himself near his dissolution. Mr. Clark is in a recovering state of health, his sight is, however, very bad, and I suppose will never be better. Mrs. Hooper and I are here, she waiting his consent to return, I preparing to leave this, tomorrow or next day."

And again on March 1st, Mr. Hooper,‡ writing from Hillsborough to Judge Iredell, says: "I have just now returned from the most painful visit that I ever paid in my life. Your old friend General Clark is struck with blindness. He went to bed in perfect good health; rose after the accustomed hour; opened his window shutters; the yard of the house appeared to be in an undulating motion, black and yellow spots floating upon the surface of the earth; the floor of his chamber covered with dry brush, which he atempted to kick away; complained

---
* Tradition says Mrs. Clark's body was afterwards removed, although the stone over he grave remained on the ground.
† McRee's "Iredell," II, 184.   ‡ The same, 158.

to his servants that the day was dark and cloudy, who informed him that the sun shone with remarkable brightness; bound up his eyes, and the next morning awakened stone blind. My hand was in his without his knowing me, my voice helped him to the discovery. His firmness is beyond all description. Thus he tells me, he reasoned when he was first attacked: 'Shall I blow my brains out? It will be pusillanimity. I can do it. But to dare to be blind for life will be an effort that will discover real resolution.' Not a single complaint or repining. He is now on his plantation without a single white person. It is a school to which I would recommend youth to learn philosophy and to bear misfortune. I always loved the man, I reverence him blind, he is something more than man."

Hooper's estimate of Clark was corroborated by Judge Iredell, who, in a letter to his wife August 29, 1781, speaking of him, says: "His conduct, perseverance and losses as an officer must highly endear him to every friend of American liberty and virtue"; and again says: "His worth is so great everybody ought to be eager to testify their sense of it."

Such tributes from such sources are not only remarkable but establish for General Clark a high claim to the veneration of his countrymen for all time.

It was at Point Repose, as already stated, that Gen. Robert Howe died while on his way to attend the session of the Legislature at Fayetteville in November, 1786. Both of these heroes and patriots sleep in unknown and unmarked graves—Howe being buried a few miles from Point Repose on Grange farm, named for his wife's family, without a stone to mark the spot, and Clark's grave hidden by a tangled mass of vines and shrubbery—and the name of the historic home where both died has been corrupted by the river men and others who never heard of either of them, from Point Repose into Piney Poles!

And just here the sad reflection forces itself upon us that within a radius of twenty miles from Wilmington lie the remains of at least a dozen men, who were worthy of perpetual remembrance for their splendid services to the cause of patriotism, liberty and humanity, and yet their deeds, their homes, and their last resting places are unknown to more than perhaps one per cent of the present population. It is the same old, sad story. Although a part of a comedy, one of the most pathetic utterances that ever fell from human lips was the sentence as rendered by Joseph Jefferson in the play of Rip Van Winkle: "How soon we are forgotten when we are gone." It was the exclamation of a common vagabond returning twenty years after his supposed death to his native village, and finding there no remembrance of himself. Even he felt the force of the thought and was humiliated by it.

OAKLAND.

Farther up the river in Bladen County was Oakland, owned by Gen. Thos. Brown, a Colonial and Revolutionary officer of distinction, and commander of a division of North Carolina troops at Norfolk in the War of 1812. He married first, Sarah Bartram, niece of the distinguished botanist, Wm. Bartram, and second, Miss Bradley, of Wilmington. General Brown also owned a place called Ashwood, where he lived.

BELFONT.

Belfont,* the residence of Gen. Hugh Waddell, which he made his home, although he owned several, and is buried at Castle Haynes on the Northeast River, in New Hanover County.

OWEN HILL.

Owen Hill, the home of Col. Thomas Owen, a hero of the battle of Camden and father of Governor John Owen, (who succeeded him as the owner) and of Gen. James Owen. Colonel Owen married Eleanor Porterfield, sister of Major Porterfield, killed at Camden. Governor John Owen married Gen. Thos. Brown's daughter Elizabeth.

---

*On this plantation the body of Lieutenant-Colonel Webster, Cornwallis's favorite officer who was mortally wounded at Guilford Court House, was buried.

LAURENS.

Col. James Morehead, another hero of the Revolution and a leader in the assault and capture of Elizabethtown, owned a place called Laurens near that town. He was "a tall, thin man," married the widow of John Owen, brother of Col. Thos. Owen, and left two daughters, one of whom married Hinton James, the first student at the University of North Carolina, and the other, Isaac Wright. Colonel Morehead died November 11th, 1807, and was buried at Owen Hill.

BROMPTON.

Brompton was owned by Governor Gabriel Johnston, whose brother, Gilbert Johnston, lived there, and to whose two sons the Governor devised it. It was at Brompton that Gen. Francis Marion, Huger, the Horrys and others met to reorganize Marion's men, a large proportion of whom were North Carolinians from Bladen and Brunswick counties. It would seem, from a letter written by James Murray, that Governor Johnston intended to make Brompton his home, but, if so, he changed his intention.

This list of places in Bladen does not include all that were owned by prominent men there, but only some of those nearest the river. Col. Thos. Robeson, a gallant soldier for whom Robeson County was named, owned large estates there, his residence being called Walnut Grove, and was always a leader of the people. He married Mary Bartram, sister of General Brown's wife.*

On the east side of the river, below Wilmington, and between the river and the sound, there were only a few estates, as the land, except on one or two small creeks, was not suitable for profitable cultivation. Rev. Christopher Bevis, referred to in the first chapter as one of the early ministers of St. Philip's church at Brunswick, owned a place two or three miles below Wilmington on the east side of the river, which by his will, made in 1750, he devised to the church wardens for the benefit

---

*For further items about Colonel Robeson, see note Chapter V.

of that church; and Dr. Samuel Green owned Greenfields, about a mile below Wilmington, which still retains its name. There were also one or two places on Barnum's Creek, lower down, the early names of which, if they had any, are unknown.

SEDGELY ABBEY.

Now, beginning on the east, or sound side of the lower river, there was a place nearly opposite Brunswick caled Sedgely Abbey, of some pretensions to unusual elegance of structure and equipment, according to tradition, but there is no record by which the tradition may be corroborated.

That there was a place so named is certain, and that its owner's name was John Guerard is equally so. He is buried at Brunswick, and the inscription on his tomb says he died April 25, 1789, and had been "for many years an inhabitant of Cape Fear." His widow married Peter Maxwell, who came from Glasgow, and died at Wilmington, September 23, 1812, she having died two years previously.

Thus the tradition that the place belonged to "an Englishman named Maxwell" who lived in great state, had a private race track on it, and so forth, is accounted for. It was not a plantation, as the land there is all a sandy plain, thinly covered by pines and scrub oaks, but was doubtless a summer residence, where the sea breeze made life comfortable. A large number of the planters on the west side of the river made their summer homes on the sound, and among them James Hasell, Chief Justice, who owned Belgrange on Town Creek.

HASELL'S PLACE.

Judge Hasell's place was next north of Sedgely Abbey. These places were just above the present summer resort called Carolina Beach, the head of the sound, and opposite the inlet then called Cabbage Inlet. James Hasell was a very prominent man for forty years, having been first a Justice of the inferior court and afterwards Chief Justice of the Colony, member of the Council, President of the Council and acting Governor of the Province. When the Revolution broke out he remained a loyalist, but kept quiet, and continued to live at his home until his death in 1786. His estate was confiscated, but afterwards restored to his family by an Act of 1802.

PROSPECT HALL.

Next above Hasell's was Prospect Hall, owned by Maj. "Jack" Walker, who was one of the remarkable characters of the Cape Fear, but in a different way from others. He was an Englishman, born December 10, 1741, at Wooler, county of Northumberland, of a family of land-holding farmers, one of whom was steward of the estates of the Duke of Northumberland, and came to North Carolina in early manhood (1761). He was a man of powerful frame and tireless energy, and in a comparatively short time accumulated a large fortune. He early took an active part in the troubles preceding the Revolution and was a Captain in Tryon's expedition against the Regulators in 1771. At the beginning of the Revolution he was appointed Captain in the 1st Regiment, Continental Line, September 1, 1775.* brevetted Major at the battle of Brandywine, April 25, 1777, and was an aide with rank of Lieutenant-Colonel on Washington's staff. He was afterwards Colonel of New Hanover County, where he reorganized the militia at Washington's request, and so continued to the end of the war.

He cherished an intense hostility to the Tories after the war, which caused much feeling between him and those who, like Hooper and Maclaine, favored a more forgiving spirit toward them. In the gift of vituperation he excelled, and if he and Maclaine ever "locked horns" in that way the atmosphere must have been very blue while the contest continued. He was uncultured and unrefined, and a great fighter, but good natured and a great practical joker, who never seriously injured an antagonist, although a tradition (preserved in McRee's "Iredell") says that when greatly angered the revenge in which he took the greatest delight was to pull one of the

---

* He raised and equipped his company from his own private means.

teeth of his prostrate antagonist, forceps for which purpose he generally carried in his pocket, and regarded it as a good joke. And McRee also gives the following anecdote about him, viz: that a mad bull on one occasion rushed through the streets to the great terror of the people, and as he tore by, Maj. Walker seized him by the horns, threw himself on his back, and to the great horror and astonishment of the people rode him around several squares.

Major Walker, being a bachelor, brought over from England two of his nephews, Carlton Walker in 1797, and John Walker, his namesake, in 1803. Both of these gentlemen served with the rank of major in the war of 1812, the former on the staff of General Gaines, and both had plantations on Rocky Point. Upon his death at Wilmington in 1813, Major Walker left his large estate to his namesake, Maj. John Walker, and it is an interesting fact in this connection that the latter, who went several times to Europe, was within less than fifty miles of Waterloo when that famous battle occurred.

Maj. John Walker, Jr., married the daughter of Col. Thos. Davis, of Fayetteville, and died in 1862, leaving a large family. Maj. Carlton Walker married three times, but had children only by his third wife, who was the daughter of Col. Peter Mallett. He died at Hillsborough in 1839.

PURVIANCE.

Above Hasell's place on the creek then called Purviance's Creek, and in recent times by the intoxicating name of Whiskey Creek, lived Col. William Purviance, an active patriot and member of the Safety Committee, and a useful officer of the militia, who rendered valuable service during the Revolution, as appears by his letter, hereinafter published.

MASONBORO.

Then came the settlement called Masonboro, which still bears that name, in which, among others, the following distinguished characters had summer residences, viz: Hooper, Harnett, Lillington, and Maclaine.

Mr. Hooper named his place Finian, and there he dispensed a delightful hospitality. Judge Iredell described in a letter* the reception he met with at that place from Mrs. Hooper during the absence of her husband, whom he expected to meet there, which is a charming picture of the hospitality characteristic of the people of that day, and a fine tribute to the remarkable gifts of that lady, who was the sister of Gen. Thos. Clark.†

It is unnecessary at this late day to pay a tribute to Wm. Hooper, and we will not attempt it.

It is equally needless to discuss Cornelius Harnett, with whose name and fame every school child in North Carolina is familiar.

Of Archibald Maclaine, Attorney-General, member of the Safety Committee in 1776, of the Congress at Hillsboro in 1775, and of the Convention there in 1778, we have spoken elsewhere, and the services of General Lillington have also been briefly referred to.

To the northward of Masonboro and across Deep Inlet Creek, as it was called, there were fewer residents but larger tracts. The creek took its name from the inlet opposite to its mouth, but when that inlet was closed by the restless sea the creek was called McKenzie's, and for many years past, Hewlett's Creek. On the north side of it, on a tract patented in 1737, lived Wm. Nichols, whose descendants lived there for

---

*McRee's Life and Correspondence of James Iredell, I, 393.

†In regard to the social life and hospitality of the people of the Cape Fear in the early days, the following quotation from a work published some years ago presents a truthful picture:

"It was a life given to hospitality, and, though marked by some features which appear rude and unattractive to modern eyes, was characterized by others which might be imitated with profit by the present generation. The respect for authority, the deference paid to age, to parents, and to women, and the sense of personal honor among men which prevailed, would be regarded as quite fantastic in this age of superior enlightenment; but they are, after all, the truest signs of real civilization, and the safest guarantees of good government."

And again, speaking of the social life of the people, is this passage:

"Some of them had town residences, but most of them lived on their plantations, and they were not the thriftless characters that by some means it became fashionable to assume that all southern planters were. There was much gayety and festivity among them, and some of them rode hard to hounds, but as a general rule they looked after their estates and kept themselves as well informed in regard to what was going on in the world as the limited means of communication allowed. There was little display, but in almost every house could be found valuable plate, and in some excellent libraries."—*A Colonial Officer and His Times*, 188.

72   HISTORY OF NEW HANOVER COUNTY.

nearly a century, and near the mouth of that creek was the summer residence of George Moore, of Moorefields, heretofore spoken of as both the Priam and the road-builder of his age.

Next north of this place and extending to Lee's Creek, now called Bradley's Creek, the land was owned by Martin Holt, the maternal grandfather of Harnett and father of Obadiah Holt, Sheriff of the County. After Martin Holt's death both Harnett and Obadiah Holt moved from Brunswick to Wilmington and the sound.

North and east of Lee's Creek and embracing the front of what is now Wrightsville, the land was owned by Governor Gabriel Johnston, to whom it was conveyed by Thos. Clark, the father of General Clark, in 1738, as part of the Ogden patent; and beyond Wrightsville to the northward Job Howe owned a place which he called Howe's Point, after the old Howe place below Brunswick. Beyond this was the residence of Mr. Bridgen, whose sister was the second wife of the first Dr. Armand DeRosset (1751), and this place bore four different names at different times, according to a deed recorded, being called Royal Oak Point, Bridgen's Pastime, Bridgen's Hall, and Ludlow Hall.*

Beyond the Bridgen place, up the coast, the next place of which we have any knowledge was Porter's Neck, the property of John Porter, the third of that name. It was afterwards owned by Dr. Corbin, Governor Sam Ashe, and others, the original tract having been divided into two or three.†

There were other places beyond that up to Sloop Point, of which we have no early history, except that the latter was owned by Mr. Whitfield about the time of the Revolution, and has been owned by his descendants, the McMillans, ever since.

---
* D, p. 490.
† The last owner, prior to 1861, of Porter's Neck was N. N. Nixon, Esq., whose peanut crop for 1860 netted him over twenty thousand dollars.

Cornelius Harnett Monument
Fourth and Market Streets, Wilmington, N. C.

CHAPTER III

UNDER MARTIN'S ADMINISTRATION—FIRE IN WILMINGTON—
A BOLD ADVENTURESS—THE SCOTCH IMMIGRANTS—FLORA
MCDONALD—BEGINNING OF THE REVOLUTION—HELP FOR
BOSTON—ORGANIZATION OF THE SAFETY COMMITTEE.

Governor Tryon left North Carolina June 30, 1771, to take the governorship of New York, and the next day James Hasell, the senior member of the Council, took charge of the government until August 11, when Josiah Martin, the newly appointed Governor, arrived and took the oaths of office at New Bern.

In January prior to his arrival there was a disastrous fire in Wilmington, and the first Assembly under his administration, in November, 1771, passed an act in which provision was made for better protection against fires there.*

In the following winter the prominent people of Wilmington were victimized and made ridiculous, as the Governor himself and many gentlemen in Virginia had been, by one of the most audacious female impostors that ever lived. In Martin's History of North Carolina,† the following account of this bold and accomplished person is given:

"In the course of the winter a female adventuress passed through the province and attracted great notice. She had assumed the name of Lady Susanna Carolina Matilda, sister to the Queen of Great Britain, and had traveled through the province of Virginia from one gentleman's house to another under those pretensions. She made astonishing impressions in many places, affecting the manners of royalty so inimitably that many had the honor of kissing her hand.

"To some she promised governments, to others regiments, or promotions of different kinds in the treasury, army, and navy; in short, she acted her part so adroitly as to levy heavy contri-

---
* The title of this act is given in Martin's Public Statutes, but the act itself is not contained in his Private Statutes. It is, however, in the Colonial Records.
† Vol. II, 292.

butions upon some persons of the highest rank. She received the marked attention of Governor Martin and his lady whilst in New Bern; and proceeded thence to Wilmington, where she was also received with great marks of distinction. At last, after remaining some days in Charleston, she was detected and apprehended. Her real name was Sarah Wilson.

"Having been taken into the service of one of the maids of honor to the Queen, she found access into one of the royal apartments, and, breaking open a cabinet, rifled it of many valuable jewels, for which she was apprehended, tried, and condemned to die, but through the interposition of her mistress, her sentence was softened into transportation. She had accordingly been landed in the preceding fall in Maryland, where she was purchased by a Mr. W. Duval, of Bush Creek, Frederick County. After a short residence there she effected her escape into Virginia, and, when at a prudent distance, assumed the name and character of the queen's sister, having brought with her from England, clothes that served to favor the deception and a part of the jewels, together with her Majesty's picture, which had proved so fatal to her."

The immigration of the Scotch Highlanders which had begun as early as 1736, under Johnston's administration, and was supplemented in 1739 by several hundred more, was in 1749 again increased by about five hundred, and in 1754 and several times afterwards up to 1775, was again increased, until a very large proportion of the population of the country above Wilmington consisted of these immigrants. Among the last arrivals in the winter of 1774-5 were the McDonalds with their glorious heroine, Flora, the wife of Allan McDonald, whose fame for her noble conduct in saving Prince Charles Edward, the Pretender, was world-wide. Upon the arrival of the heroine in Wilmington there was a general turnout of the people, and she and her daughter were treated with great distinction. A great ball was given in her honor, and tradition says that she was especially pleased by the attentions paid to her daughter by the gentlemen of the town.* The Highlanders themselves, being about to separate for their different destinations, kept up a frolic for two days and nights, and many pathetic scenes were witnessed among them.†

When Flora arrived at Fayetteville, where there were hundreds of her countrymen who had preceded her and had made that region their home for years, she was greeted by a great throng with manifestations of joy and was welcomed with the wild notes of the bagpipes. She lived for a short time in Fayetteville and then at Cameron Hill, and finally, early in January, 1776, her husband bought a farm on the borders of Richmond and Montgomery counties, which he named Killegray, where two of their children died and were buried.‡ And then came the battle of Moore's Creek Bridge (February 27, 1776), which was the final blow to their hopes.

It was the intention of Governor Martin to make Allan McDonald Commander-in-Chief of the Scotch Highlanders and Tories, but General Gage, whose authority in military matters was superior to his, had sent Gen. Donald McDonald, accompanied by Capt. Alexander McLeod, out on a secret mission with a Commission as Brigadier General to take command, which he did and led their movement to Moore's Creek, although, because of illness, he was not present in that engagement.

Annie, the daughter of Flora McDonald, was married to Capt. Alexander McLeod, the gallant officer who led the charge there and received twenty bullets in his body. An article published in the *University Magazine* in 1853, and quoted by Ashe,§ states that McLeod left his bride at the altar to go on the march to Moore's Creek, and to his death, and tells of a dispute between him and Major McLean the night before the battle as to whether the Americans ought to be assaulted in

---
* Address of James Banks, 1857.
† A tradition received by the present writer many years ago from his father, who said it was received by him in his early life from one or more eye-witnesses.
‡ Banks.
§ Vol. I, 503-504.

their intrenchments or avoided by making a detour—McLeod doubting and McLean insisting on the assault—and that McLean, who survived the fight, was saddened by McLeod's death for the rest of his life.

After the battle, Allan McDonald, Flora's husband, being captured, was confined in Halifax jail, and after a few days was released on parole within the town limits for about two months, and was then sent to Reading, Pa., where he was confined.

In 1779, Flora sailed from Charleston to Scotland, and, upon his release later, he joined her there and they lived in Skye. He died prior to 1790, and she on the 5th March of that year. Sir Walter Scott said that he possessed her marriage certificate, and that she signed her name to it "Flory."

Before Martin's administration had half expired the first clouds that presaged the storm of the Revolution were gathering, and one of the occurrences that aided in their concentration on the Cape Fear was the visit of Josiah Quincy, of Massachusetts, to Wilmington, on his tour to the South for the purpose of securing united action among the colonies by a plan of correspondence between the leaders of the people. He arrived in Wilmington early in 1773 and, after dining with a number of gentlemen at Mr. Hooper's house, spent the night at Harnett's residence with others, of whom he says, in his diary, that Howe, Harnett and himself were "the social triumvirate of the evening," and that the plan of correspondence was heartily endorsed. In the month of November of that year, the Assembly appointed a Committee of Correspondence.

There was as yet no talk and no general desire of independence, although Hooper (the man that Jefferson afterwards, in a private letter, accused of being a Tory), as early as April 26th, 1774, in a letter to Iredell,* said: "The colonies are striding fast to independence, and ere long will build an empire upon the ruins of Great Britain." But while any inten-

---
*McRee, 1, 197.

tion to separate from the mother country was disclaimed, even by Washington, the march of events was steadily to that goal.

On the 4th of June, 1774, the port of Boston was closed by Act of Parliament, passed the previous winter, and among the expressions of sympathy for its inhabitants, which were universal throughout the country, none were more cordial or generous than those of the people of the Cape Fear. The *Massachusetts Gazette* of September 2d contains extracts from two letters from Wilmington, dated, respectively, August 2d, and August 3d. The first told of the great success of a subscription for the relief of the poor of Boston, which had "produced enough to load the vessel by which this letter comes." The other said: "You will receive this by Mr. Parker Quince, who generously made an offer of his vessel to carry a load of provisions to Boston, freight free, and what redounds to the honour of the tars, the master and mariners navigate her without receiving one farthing wages (truly Patriotick)."

The following is the official communication of the action of the Wilmington people, taken at a meeting held on the 21st of July, and is addressed to Messrs. John Hancock, John Rowe and Samuel Adams.* It will be observed that the name of Cornelius Harnett does not appear among the signers of this letter, nor was he present at the Convention held on the 25th August, a month later, at New Bern. The reason for this was that he had gone North to confer with the committees of the other colonies, and did not return until December, on the 17th of which month he first appeared at the meeting of the Safety Committee, of which he was the recognized leader:

Gentlemen:

We most heartily sympathize with the distressed inhabitants of the town of Boston, and take the earliest opportunity to assure them that we consider ourselves as deeply involved in the misfortunes of that brave people. We view the attack made by the Minister upon the Colony of the Massachusetts Bay, to be intended to pave the way to a general subversion of the constitutional rights of North America. It becomes,

---

*Mass. Hist. Soc. Collections, 4th Series, Vol. IV, pages 22-24.

therefore, the duty of every American, who is not an apostate to his country, to pursue every justifiable method that may have a tendency to avert this impending calamity. The enclosed Resolves* speak the sentiments of the inhabitants of Cape Fear, and, we are well assured, of this Province in general. As a testimony of the sincerity of our professions and good wishes in behalf of your Town, we have loaded a sloop with provisions, which we have taken the freedom to address to your care; and we request that you will apply them to the support of the indigent inhabitants of Boston, who, by the late oppressive Acts of Parliament, are now deprived of the means of procuring their subsistence by their daily labor and honest industry. Although inconsiderable in its value, yet we flatter ourselves that, when it is viewed as a testimony of the heartfelt share we take in the calamity of that Town, and as an earnest of our zealous endeavors to encourage them to persist, with prudent and manly firmness, in the cause in which they now suffer, it will not be thought altogether unworthy of their acceptance.

In behalf of the inhabitants of Cape Fear, North Carolina, permit us to subscribe ourselves, Gentlemen, your most obedient servants.

JAMES MOORE.
GEO. HOOPER.
R. HOWE.
A. MACLAINE.
WILL. HOOPER.
JNO. ANCRUM.
ROBT. HOGG.
FRANCIS CLAYTON.

To John Hancock, John Rowe, and Samuel Adams, Esquires.

The contribution forwarded to Boston was not the only one sent by the people of the Cape Fear, and the ladies were as active in the work as the men. Mr. Parker Quince, who furnished the vessel and went on it, was a member of the long established firm of Richard Quince & Sons, who were leading merchants and ship-owners, and among the most patriotic and liberal inhabitants.

The circular letter of the Wilmington Committee of Correspondence to the committees in the other counties was warmly endorsed by them, and soon the whole province was fairly seething with indigination at the Boston Port Bill and other legislation of the British Parliament, the result of which was

---

*Adopted July 21, 1774, at a general meeting, Mr. Hooper, Chairman, held at Wilmington to appoint a committee to issue a circular letter to the counties, and endorsing the proposition to hold a Continental Congress on the 30th September.

a provincial Congress which met at New Bern, August 25th, and appointed three delegates—Hooper, Hewes and Caswell—to the Continental Congress at Philadelphia. In accordance with the resolutions of both these Congresses, permanent committees, called Committees of Safety, were organized, to whose hands the control of affairs was willingly transferred by the people.

These committees were elected by the freeholders, and the Wilmington Committee held its first meeting on the 23d of November. As only partial accounts of these meetings have been published, and as a full and accurate history of them should be preserved, with the names of members present at each, we present in the next chapter a complete record of them, from which it will appear that among other things they "put a stop to horse-racing, to parties of entertainment, to the importation of negroes, requiring them to be returned to the countries from which they had been shipped; forbade any increase in the price of goods, sold the cargoes of merchandise that were imported, paying the profit for the benefit of the Boston sufferers, and particularly took action to secure a supply of powder. Its leading spirit was Cornelius Harnett, but with him were associated most of the merchants of the town.

"The merchants refused to receive any more tea shipped to them; locked up their stock, never to be sold, and one even threw his stock into the river. Nor were the women indifferent spectators of passing events. They sympathized with the ardor of their fathers, husbands and brothers, and were willing to make every sacrifice the situation demanded."*

From this general summary and from the details of the proceedings of the Committee of Safety, it will be seen that they exercised absolute control of all matters, public and private, which in their judgment affected in any way the welfare of the people; and their administration of affairs, despotic, but never unjust, was approved and submitted to by every patriotic man and woman.

---

* Ashe, History of North Carolina, Vol. I, 427.

TOUCHING THE MECKLENBURG DECLARATION.

It seems appropriate, and may be interesting, before giving the record of the Wilmington Safety Committee, to call attention to some facts in that record which appear to throw light on a subject of long-standing controversy, and which have never before attracted attention. They were first published by this writer in the *Charlotte Observer,* as an extract from this book, as follows:

In all the discussion of the Mecklenburg Declaration of Independence, which has proceeded intermittently for nearly a hundred years, there has never been the slightest allusion, so far as we have observed—and we have read most of the literature on the subject—to certain facts which seem to corroborate the evidence that there was a meeting in Charlotte, May 20, 1775.

These facts do not in any way affect the genuineness or the falsity of the Declaration so long accepted as having been framed on that day, nor do they indicate the action, if any, taken by the meeting on that day.

They are to be considered solely in connection with the question: Was there a meeting on that day in Charlotte?

It is not pretended that these facts are conclusive of the question, but that, taken in connection with the direct affirmative evidence, they raise a strong probability in its favor. Some writers not only deny the actuality of the Declaration alleged to have been made on the 20th, but deny that there was any meeting on that day; others deny that the alleged contemporary evidence in support of the meeting on the 31st of May, and of the allegation that the witnesses for the 20th confused dates, is sufficient or that purpose; but all admit that on some day in May, 1775, there was a meeting at which there was action amounting to a declaration of independence.

The facts to which we refer prove that for several months prior to May there was correspondence and concerted action between the town, county and district safety committees of the province, which originated with the Wilmington committee on the 4th of January, 1775, when that committee, after the freeholders of New Hanover County had also met and appointed a county committee to cooperate with the town committee, passed the following resolutions:

'Then the committee resolved to have monthly stated meetings, and that the first monthly meeting be in Wilmington on the 20th day of January, inst., and be continued the 20th day of every succeeding month.'

These monthly stated meetings on the 20th continued regularly until January 20th, 1776—that is for a year.

On the 8th of May the messenger bearing the news of the battle of Lexington and communications from the committees by whom it was forwarded, arrived in Wilmington at 3 o'clock p. m., and Cornelius Harnett, chairman of the committee, at 4 o'clock, forwarded the papers to Richard Quince, Sr., at Brunswick, with the following note:

Dear Sir: I take the liberty of forwarding by express the enclosed papers which were received at 3 o'clock this afternoon. If you would be at a loss for a horse, or a man, the bearer will proceed as far as the Boundary House.

You will please direct it to Mr. Marion or any other gentleman to forward the packet southward with greatest possible dispatch.

I am, Sir, &c, CORNELIUS HARNETT.
Wilmington, May 8th, 1775.

P. S.—For God's sake send the man with the least delay and write Mr. Marion to forward it by night and by day.

At 9 o'clock that evening Mr. Quince forwarded the papers with the following note:

BRUNSWICK, May 8, 1775.
9 o'clock in the Evening.

To Mr. Isaac Marion:

Sir: I take the liberty to forward by express the enclosed papers, which I just received from Wilmington and I must entreat you to forward them to your committee at Georgetown to be conveyed to Charleston from yours with speed. Enclosed is the newspaper giving the account of the beginning of the battle and a letter of what happened after. Pray don't neglect a moment in forwarding it.

I am your humble servant,
RICHARD QUINCE.

The news came to Wilmington via Edenton, where it arrived on the 4th, thence to New Bern on the 6th, New River on the 7th, and Wilmington the 8th, thus taking five days to come from Edenton. (Colonial Records IX, 1238). The distance from Edenton to Wilmington is nearly the same as from Halifax to Charlotte, which is supposed to have been the route of the messenger to the latter place, who arrived just before a meeting there, according to all accounts. Why there should have been such a difference in the time consumed in travel, we do not know. The message could have been sent even from Wilmington to Charlotte after it reached Wilmington, in six days, and that would have left five days before the 20th, and it would have been stale news by the 31st—news nearly three weeks old.

This would certainly seem to support the evidence of the various witnesses who certified that they attended a meeting on the 20th at which the news of the battle of Lexington was received, especially when the alleged Declaration of the 20th expressly refers to the battle of Lexington, while the Resolutions of the 31st make no allusion to it.

On the 20th of May, among other proceedings, the following resolutions were adopted in Wilmington:

"Resolved, That the committees of the respective counties in this district be invited to meet in Wilmington on the 20th of June next in order to deliberate on several matters of importance that will be laid before them respecting the general cause of America.

"Resolved, A paper containing the reasons of the magistrates of Chatham county for not signing the association presented to them by one Doctor Piles, is highly approved of by this committee, and is ordered to be published in the *Cape Fear Mercury.*"

On the 20th of June there was "a general meeting of the several committees of the district," as provided for at the May meeting, at the court-house in Wilmington, at which representatives from New Hanover, Brunswick, Bladen, Onslow and Duplin were present, and a letter from the committee of Cross Creek (Fayetteville) was read, and an answer was ordered to be written by the chairman, Mr. Quince. There was also a committee appointed to answer the proclamation of the royal Governor, Martin; and Cornelius Harnett was appointed to write a letter to the committee of Cumberland county to secure the gunpowder there for the public.

At this June meeting of the several committees of the district an "association," as it was called, was adopted, which is declared to have been "formerly agreed by the committee of New Hanover county." This association, or statement of facts justifying an appeal to arms and announcing that the subscribers were united "under every tie of religion and honor," and "associated as a band in defense of an injured country," was identical in language (except one or two words) with the Liberty Point resolutions adopted at the Cross Creek (Fayetteville) meeting on the same day, 20th of June.

Thus it appears that after correspondence between the committees of the six counties, New Hanover, Brunswick, Bladen, Onslow, Duplin and Cumberland, a common day (the 20th) for meetings, and a common form of association, were adopted, and that correspondence with the magistrates of Chatham county (who probably acted as the committee there) had been going on.

Now, while the Mecklenburg Declaration, whether made on the 20th or 31st of May (a question not before us) far surpassed the "association" of these counties, or any other part of the country, and was wholly different from, and not the result of concerted action as theirs was, still the fact that long before either date—that is to say, more than four months before—the 20th day of the month had been agreed on by these counties as the time for their regular monthly stated meetings, and that "occasional meetings" were held on the call of the chairman; and while it is admitted on all sides that "in March and April there were many meetings of the safety committee of Mecklenburg" (Ashe, 454) and that Gen. Joseph Graham said: "During the winter and spring preceding that event (the Declaration) several popular meetings of the people were held in Charlotte, two of which I attended," it would seem that the positive evidence of a meeting on the 20th is supported by the probabilities of the case.

There is no record of a meeting, made at the time of the meeting, either on the 20th or 31st. The meetings in Mecklenburg were popular meetings; those on the Cape Fear were meetings of the Safety Committee, to whom all government, in public and even in social life affecting the community, was entrusted by the people, and their proceedings were faithfully recorded and are preserved in their integrity. They were published in the *Cape Fear Mercury*, which was the nearest Whig paper to Charlotte, and it is reasonable to suppose that the resolution of the 4th of January, appointing the 20th of the month as the day for the monthly meetings, in which the other counties of the district united, was well known to the Mecklenburg committee, and that they had also appointed that day and provided, as did the Wilmington committee, for "occasional" meetings between times. Some very important matters were attended to at these occasional meetings as well as at the monthly meetings.

There is no reason for assuming that there was not a meeting on the 20th in the absence of evidence to sustain it. The fact, if it is a fact, that there was a meeting on the 31st does not disprove it. There may have been meetings on both days.

If it be said that the meeting was called not on the 20th, but on the 19th, and was continued on the 20th, the answer is that that meeting was not a safety committee meeting, but a popular meeting which discussed the situation, and the next day heard and endorsed the resolutions already prepared by the Safety Committee, just as was done at the June meeting of the district committees at Wilmington above mentioned. It is at least worthy of notice that meetings were held on the 20th of May, not only in the Cape Fear country, but in Pitt county and elsewhere in the province of North Carolina. They may have been mere coincidences, of course, and not the result (except in the Cape Fear counties) of a mutual understanding, but the latter is the more probable.

Disclaiming again any intention to express in this book an opinion on the main question, although we entertain one, we will merely add the following observations:

There are those who speak as members of "the modern school of historical writers"—a term more high sounding than self-explanatory—and some of them, in their zeal to establish the fact that the Resolutions of May 31st were the only ones adopted at Charlotte, deny that there was a meeting held there on the 20th.

If by the term "modern school" is meant those who have discovered or used new facts, the title is a misnomer; if it means those who use a new method in dealing with facts, old or new, we would like to know the method, but in either case we adhere to the opinion that in dealing with evidence and arguing probabilities there is no necessity for a modern school, as the rules applicable to the process have been well established for centuries.

CHAPTER IV

PROCEEDINGS OF THE SAFETY COMMITTEE OF THE TOWN OF WILMINGTON, WITH OCCASIONAL MINUTES OF JOINT MEETINGS OF THE COMMITTEE OF NEW HANOVER COUNTY AND THE COMMITTEE OF THE DISTRICT OF WILMINGTON, IN 1774, 1775, AND 1776.

WILMINGTON, November 23, 1774.

At a Meeting of the freeholders in the Court House at Wilmington, for the purpose of choosing a Committee for said town, to carry more effectually into execution the Resolves of the late Congress held at Philadelphia, the following names were proposed and universally assented to.

Cornelius Harnett, John Quince, Francis Clayton, William Hooper, Robert Hogg, John Ancrum, Archibald McLain, John Robeson, James Walker.

The Committee then adjourned until 6 o'clock that evening.

WILMINGTON, November 23, 6 o'clock p. m.

Present: Archibald McLain, John Quince, John Ancrum, Francis Clayton, James Walker.

It being then moved that Ancrum, Forster and Brice and others, having imported quantities of tea in the brig "Sally," Captain Innes not knowing how to dispose of them, had by the interposition of Captain Forster informed the Committee thereof, in the Court House immediately after the election craving their advice: It was Resolved—that though this application did not come properly under the cognizance of a committee chosen to inspect the conduct of the inhabitants of this town, regarding certain resolves entered into by the Continental Congress—yet as Capt. Forster and the other gentlemen concerned, chose to walk hand in hand with their approbation, the following letter to Mr. Hill* was agreed to:

WILMINGTON, November 23, 1774.

Mr. Hill: Sir: This day, at a very numerous meeting of the freeholders of this town, for the purpose of appointing a committee, to carry more effectually into execution the Resolutions of the late Continental Congress, the subscribers of this letter were chosen and compose a majority thereof. The first article presented to our notice being a quantity of teas imported by yourself and others, in your brig "Sally," Capt. Innes; we inquire of you and beg your immediate answer, whether said tea may not be regularly remitted by the vessel, and whether the Custom House will in that case have any right to demand the duty or refuse clearing her out.

WILMINGTON, November 25, 1774.

The Committee met according to adjournment.

Present: Archibald McLain, John Ancrum, Robert Hogg, James Walker, John Quince, Francis Clayton.† When Mr. Hill's answer being produced was read as follows:

BRUNSWICK, November 24, 1774.

Gentlemen: I can not take upon me to answer your inquiries concerning the tea brought into this port by the "Sally." The Collector and Comptroller, I hear, will be at Wilmington to morrow or next day. The management of the King's duty is particularly their department, and they will determine whether the tea may regularly be remitted by the vessel, or whether the duty is to be paid; or whether they will clear it out.

The safety of the people is, or ought to be, the Supreme Law; the gentlemen of the Committee will judge whether this law, or an Act of Parliament should at this particular time, operate in North Caro-

---

* Mr. William Hill, merchant at Brunswick and justice of the peace, was a man of prominence, of high character and well connected, having married Margaret, daughter of Nathaniel Moore. He was a native of Boston. His grandfather was Henry Hill, of Boston, who died in 1726, and who owned all of South street and large distilleries near Essex street. John Hill, his son, by will dated March 16, 1773, bequeathed his estate to his daughters, and "only son William, now living in Brunswick, Cape Feare, North Carolina." Mr. Hill's tomb is in St. Philip's churchyard. He died August 23, 1783. His descendants are very numerous, and several of them have been distinguished in both civil and military life.

† For notices of the above-named committee, except Walker and Hogg, see Chapter II. James Walker was a merchant and planter, and Robert Hogg a merchant. Each afterwards became so "neutral" in the Revolution as to lose the confidence of the Whigs.

lina. I believe every tea importer will cheerfully submit to their determination. I can answer for, gentlemen, your most obedient.
(Signed) W. HILL.

It was agreed by a majority, after the point had been maturely reasoned, that the subject was not in the extent of the Committee's inspection, and that it ought to be recommended to those concerned to conduct themselves with discretion and for the good of the country.

The Committee then adjourned to the 26th inst.

WILMINGTON, November 26, 1774.

The Committee met according to adjournment.

Present: Francis Clayton, Robert Hogg, John Ancrum, John Quince, James Walker, and Archibald McLain.

The Committee, finding that several gentlemen intended to start horses, which they have had for some time in keeping, for the Wilmington subscription purse on Monday the 28th inst., and the general Congress having particularly condemned horse racing as an expensive diversion, the Committee thought proper to send the following admonitory circular letter to the several gentlemen who had kept horses for the race, to wit:

WILMINGTON, November 26, 1774.

Sir: The Continental Congress,* lately held at Philadelphia, representing the several American colonies, from Nova Scotia to Georgia, associated and agreed among other things, for themselves and their constituents, to "discountenance and discourage every species of extravagance and dissipation, and especially all horse racing, and all kinds of gaming, cock-fighting, exhibitions of shows and plays and other expensive diversions and entertainments," and we being the majority of the committee, chosen by the freeholders of Wilmington to observe the conduct of all persons touching the association of the said Congress,

---

*The Continental Congress, which met in Carpenter's Hall, Philadelphia, following the precedent of the Association of the Sons of Liberty, drew up a Declaration of Rights, pledged themselves to break off all commercial intercourse with England and to forego all the luxuries of life. William Hooper, with Caswell and Hewes, were the representaivess from North Carolina. Mr. Hooper is noticed elsewhere. He was a truly loyal Whig, active and energetic, reserved, except with friends ; was not popular, but won respect by his culture and devotion to his duties ; was on several important committees and aided in drawing up the celebrated report of the committee on the "rights of the colonies in general." He did not deserve the aspersions of Mr. Jefferson.

think it our indispensable duty to inform you that in our opinion the avowed intention of running horses for the subscription purse near this town on the 28th inst., if carried into execution, will be subversive to the said association, and a breach of the resolves of the general Congress; and that if the gentlemen who intended to enter horses for said purse (of whom we understand you are one) persist in running the race, we shall be under the disagreeable necessity of bearing public testimony against a proceeding which immediately strikes at the ground of the association and resolves, by disuniting the people.

You must be sensible, Sir, that the Americans have not the most distant prospect of being restored to their former rights or of succeeding in their attempts to defeat a venal and corrupt ministry and Parliament, but by an unanimous adherence to the resolutions and advice of their representatives in the late general Congress; and as a friend to your country, we have no doubt but you will readily relinquish an amusement that however laudable in other respects, is certainly attended with considerable expense, and even destruction to many individuals; and may very justly be condemned at a time when frugality should be one of our leading virtues.

We shall only add that nothing will so effectually tend to convince the British Parliament that we are in earnest in our opposition to their measures, as a voluntary relinquishment of our favorite amusements. Those who will take the trouble of making observations on mankind must soon be convinced that the people who abandon their pleasures for the public good are not to be biased by any other consideration. Many will cheerfully give up their property to secure the remainder. He only is the determined patriot who willingly sacrifices his pleasures on the altar of freedom.

We are, &c.

which was signed by all of the committee present. The committee then adjourned to the 10th of December.

WILMINGTON, December 10, 1774.

The Committee met according to adjournment.

Mr. John Slingsby* & Co. inform the Committee that they have imported in the brig "Diana," Capt. Authven, master from Glasgow, since the first instant, a cargo of goods for their

---

* Slingsby afterwards turned loyalist, and commanded the Tories at the battle of Elizabethtown, August 29, 1781, where he was defeated and killed. He was an Englishman by birth, and a brother-in-law of John DuBois, another member of the Safety Committee.—Maclaine to Iredell (McRee, I, 549.)

store in this town, amounting to £1916.7s.2 2-3 sterling, and another cargo for their store at Cross Creek, amounting to £1018.13s.9 3-4 sterling, and delivered the same with the invoices thereof into the hands of the committee, requesting that they may be sold agreeable to the association of the general Congress.

Resolved therefore, that the sale of the said goods, be on Wednesday the 14th inst. and that public notice thereof be given immediately.

The Committee adjourned to the 14th inst.

WILMINGTON, Wednesday, December 14, 1774.

The cargoes of goods imported by John Slingsby & Co. and put into the hands of the committee the 10th inst., were put up to public sale at the Court-house pursuant to notice when the importers became the last and highest bidders for the said goods, that is to say for the several goods imported for their store in Wilmington, the sum of nineteen hundred and twenty-three pounds (£1923) ster. and for the several goods imported for their store at Cross-creek the sum of one thousand and twenty pounds (£1020) like money.

Exclusive of the amount of the several goods in the two invoices as mentioned in the proceedings of the 10th inst., there was gunpowder for the Wilmington store to the amount of £11.10s sterling, and for the Cross-creek store to the amount of £6.18s sterling, which as appears to the committee, never came to the hands of the said John Slingsby & Co., not having been shipped on board the said brigantine.

The committee met at 6 o'clock p. m. Mr. Herold Blackmore, informed that he had imported since the first instant, in the Sloop Mary and the Brig ———, five negro slaves, and craved advice how to proceed, as he had given orders for the purchasing and shipping said slaves, previous to the resolutions of the provincial Congress. The committee desired that Mr. Blackmore, would not sell, or send them out of town, but be accountable for them at the next meeting—then adjourned to December the 17th, 1774.

WILMINGTON, Saturday, December 17, 1774.

The Committee met according to adjournment.

Present: Cornelius Harnett, John Ancrum, Robt. Hogg, John Quince, Archibald M'Lain, James Walker and John Robeson.*

The committee finding upon inquiry that one of the slaves imported by Herold Blackmore, was ordered after the publication of the resolves of the provincial convention of this province, and in contradiction thereto, and that he had at that time an opportunity to contradict the orders he had given for the other slaves, and he now confessing that he sent a copy of the provincial resolves to Granada: it is the opinion of the committee that the said slaves be reshipped. And the committee do resolve, that all slaves imported since the first day of this instant, or which may be imported shall be reshipped from this province. Upon a suggestion to the committee that Mr. Arthur Mabson hath imported in his schooner from the West Indies, some slaves which are now at his plantation near this town: it is ordered that the sense of this committee relative thereto be made known to Mr. Mabson, and that Mr. McLain write to him for that purpose, which he hath done as follows, to-wit:

WILMINGTON, Dec. 17, 1774.

Sir: The committee for the town, chosen to observe the conduct of all persons touching the association of the General Congress, have resolved that all slaves imported into this river, since the first day of December, instant, shall be re-shipped to the place from whence they came as soon as possible, and being informed that you have, contrary to the express letter of the said association, imported slaves from the West Indies, which you have now at your plantation, it is expected that you will give a particular account of the number thereof, and take such

---

*Merchant and planter.

steps as may satisfy the committee that you intend, on your part, to adhere strictly to the regulations laid down by your representatives.
I am, Sir, your obd't servant,
(Signed) ARCHIBALD M'LAINE.
Mr. Mabson.

Capt. John Dean from Glasgow presented to the committee an invoice of goods amounting to (15) fifteen pound sterling, which he requested might be sold agreeable to the association and resolves of the General Congress, and the said goods are accordingly ordered to be sold on Monday the 19th inst.

Upon the complaints of divers persons that the proprietors of the distillery* in this town have advanced the price of their rum from 2s 8d to 3s currency, per gallon: Mr. Wilkerson the acting partner was summoned and attended, and having alleged in his justification that Molasses is now at a higher price than formally, that what he hath imported lately was purchased at an advanced price, and was of inferior quality, and that the cargoes sent out to purchase it sold lower than usual, it is the opinion of this committee that they can not interfere, unless the purchasers make it appear, that the proprietors of the distillery sell their spirits for greater profits than they have usually done.

The committee came to the same resolutions with respect to the complaints against some merchants for raising the price of goods, particularly gun-powder, it appearing that that article is extremely scarce, and that a merchant in this town, hath offered 4s per pound for a quantity to supply his country stores, and could not produce it at four shillings and sixpence.

The committee adjourned till Monday the 19th inst.

Monday, December, 19, 1774.

The committee met according to adjournment.
Present: [No names inserted in the manuscript.]
The goods of Capt. John Dean were exposed to sale, pursuant to notice, and sold for the sum of £——— sterling.
The committee adjourned till further notice.

* Harnett and Wilkerson.

December 30, 1774.

The committee met.

Present: John Quince, James Walker, Archibald McLaine, Fr's Clayton, John Hogg, Wm. Hooper.

Alexander Hostler & Co., produced invoices of goods amounting to twelve hundred and sixty pounds, seven shillings and ninepence sterling; five hundred and seventy-seven pounds, twelve shillings one and a half pence sterling; sixty-one pounds, nine shillings and ten and three quarters pence, and fifty two pounds, nine shillings and ten and a half pence sterling; in the whole nineteen hundred and fifty-one pounds, nineteen shillings seven and three quarter pence, imported in the Thetis from Glasgow, which they delivered into the hands of the committee and requested that the same might be sold pursuant to the resolves of the general Congress.

Hogg and Campbell, produced invoice of one hundred and thirty tons of salt, imported in the North Star, Capt. Saunderson, from Lymington, amounting to two hundred and twenty-five pounds, thirteen shillings and five pence sterling, which he delivered and requested to be sold, etc.

Abraham Hunter produced invoice of anchors, cables, canvas, rigging, cabin furniture and other articles, imported for a new vessel now on the stocks in this river, amounting to five hundred and sixty one pounds, seventeen shillings three and a quarter pence sterling, delivered the same, and requested that they be sold &c.

Hanna, M'Clintock & Co., produced invoices of goods imported in the Thetis from Glasgow amounting to two thousand six hundred and seventy one pounds, fourteen shillings eleven and a half pence sterling, delivered the same to the committee, and requested to have them sold &c.

John Cruden & Co., produced invoice of two bales of Osnaburgs, imported in the Thetis from Glasgow amounting to fifty-two pounds fifteen shillings sterling, which they delivered to the committee, and requested to have them sold &c.

Resolved that all the above mentioned goods be sold to-morrow, the 31st instant.

The committee adjourned till to-morrow.

Saturday, December 31, 1774.

Present: The last mentioned members.

The goods of Alexander Hostler & Co.; Hogg and Campbell, Abraham Hunter, Hanna, M'Clintock & Co., and John Cruden & Co., were exposed to sale according to notice, and sold as follows:

130 tons of salt, imported by Hogg & Campbell at £225.-13s 5d.

Anchors, canvas, cables, &c., by Abraham Hunter £561.

Sundry goods in 4 invoices by Alex. Hostler & Co., £1952 8s 8d.

2 bales of Osnaburgs, by J. Cruden & Co., £53.

Sundry goods by Hanna M'Clintock & Co., £2672.

Invoices of goods imported by Thomas Orr, amounting to seven hundred and sixty-three pounds, twelve shillings and two pence, and twenty-two pounds, nineteen shillings and seven pence sterling, were produced and the said goods delivered, and requesting that they be sold.

The committee adjourned to the 3d of January next.

January 3, 1775.

The committee met according to adjournment, when Mr. Orr's goods, mentioned in two invoices, were sold for seven hundred and eighty-seven pounds sterling.

Adjourned to the 4th inst.

Wednesday, January 4, 1775.

The committee met at the Court house.

Present: Cornelius Harnett, Archibald M'Laine, John Ancrum, William Hooper and John Robeson.

At the same time, the free holders of New Hanover county assembled to choose a committee for the county* to join and cooperate with the committee of the town; which the members present agreed to; then the freeholders present, having Cornelius Harnett in the chair, unanimously chose George Moore, John Ashe, Samuel Ashe, James Moore, Frederick Jones, Alex. Lillington, Sampson Moseley, Samuel Swann, George Merrick, esquires; and Messrs. John Hollingsworth, Samuel Collier, Samuel Marshal, William Jones, Thomas Bloodworth, James Wright, Wm. Jones, John Larkins, Joel Parish, John Devane, Timothy Bloodworth, Thomas Devane, John Marshall, John Colvin, Bishop Dudley, and William Robeson, esqrs. were unanimously chosen a committee to join the committee of Wilmington.

The freeholders at the same time nominated John Ashe, and William Hooper esq., as delegates for the said county, to attend at Newbern, with the delegates from the other counties and towns to choose representatives to attend the ensuing Congress at Philadelphia.

Then the committee resolved to have monthly stated meetings, and that the first monthly meeting be in Wilmington, on the 20th day of January, inst., and be continued the 20th day of every succeeding month.†

The committee adjourned till to-morrow.

Thursday, January 5, 1775.

The committee met according to adjournment, and chose Cornelius Harnett Esq., chairman and Mr. Francis Clayton, deputy chairman.

Present: Cornelius Harnett, chairman, Francis Clayton, deputy chairman.

Sampson Moseley, John Ashe, John Quince, George Moore,

---

* There was also a district Committee formed later.
† Was this action known in Mecklenburg prior to May?

William Jones, L. C.,* William Jones, W. T.,† John Ancrum, Wm. Robeson, F. Jones, Samuel Swann, Thos. Devane, John Marshall, Samuel Ashe, Wm. Hooper, Archibald M'Laine, Robt. Hogg.

Resolved that the following notice be sent to the merchants of Wilmington, by Mr. Swann and Mr. Robeson, to wit:

> To the merchants of the town of Wilmington, Masters of Vessels & Traders. The Committee of the County of New Hanover and Town of Wilmington, united and met for the important purpose of carrying into execution the resolves of the Continental Congress, earnestly request of you, as well wishers to the common cause of America, in which we are all embarked, to signify to them by the bearers of this, if you have any gunpowder on hand, and what quantity, that this committee may, in consequence of that information, take the most prudent steps to guard against the melancholy effects which may result from this part of the province, being left in a state totally deficient from the want of ammunition. It is likewise requested that you would cease to make further sales thereof, until informed by the committee.
>
> (Signed)   CORNELIUS HARNETT,
>   Chairman.

Mr. Owen Kenan, as holder of two notes of hand, of one hundred and fifty pounds each, from Jesse Barfield to Lehansius Kekeyser, and from the said Dekeyser to the said Barfield, and of two other notes of hand, for one hundred pounds, Virginia currency, each, from Alexander Outlaw, William Robeson and Wm. Jones, to John Lawson, and from the said Lawson and John Ashe, to Alexander Outlaw, for two races to be run between the several parties, was summoned to appear and compelled to deliver up the said notes, and the agreements made for running the said races, and the committee unanimously resolved to indemnify the said Owen Kenan for all damages he may hereafter sustain by the delivery of the said notes and agreement.

Mr. Swann, and Mr. Robeson, returned an account of the gunpowder in Wilmington, 1,434 lbs. in the hands of the several merchants applied to.

Mr. Thomas Craike, was requested by the committee, to act as secretary, which he readily agreed to.

---

* Long Creek.   † Welsh tract.

The committee sent the papers of the following tenor, to the persons within named by Mr. Swann and Mr. Robeson.

Fr. John Burgwin, John Robeson, Mr. McTier, Ancrum, Foster and Brice, Thomas Orr, George and Thomas Hooper, Hogg and Campbell, George Doherty, and Charles Jewkes.

The King's proclamation prohibiting the further exportation of gunpowder from Great Britain, renders it highly necessary, that some expedient should be adopted to prevent the melancholy consequences which to a province in respect to its inhabitants, circumstanced as this is, may in future arise from a total want of that article. We, therefore, gentlemen, assure ourselves, that you, animated with the same liberal sentiments that we feel, will contribute what at present falls to your particular department for the promotion of the public good.

The quantity of gunpowder which is at present in the town is very inconsiderable, and it is absolutely necessary that what there is should be reserved for any future emergencies, that we may be prepared for every, the worst contingencies.

We therefore, gentlemen, entreat you by the ties of honor and virtue, and love for your country, as you prize the regard of your fellow-citizens, as you wish to avoid the censure of this committee, and those whom they represent, that you would not within thirty days from this time, remove out of this town, or make sale of any of the gunpowder which you have reported to this committee as the stock you have upon hand, before the expiration of which time, this committee will endeavor to collect by subscription, and they doubt not of success, a sum sufficient to purchase and pay you for the whole of it at the reasonable price of three shillings per pound, which some of your well-disposed brethren have consented to take. And as it is intended to be made use of as much for your security as of the rest of the inhabitants of this part of the province, we address you with a certainty of succeeding in this application, which should it appear to you to carry with it anything uncommon, will find an ample vindication in the present critical circumstances of this province.

(Signed)   CORNELIUS HARNETT,
Chairman.

Mr. Swann and Mr. Robeson made report to the committee, that all the persons applied to had complied with the request of the committee, except Mr. Burgwin, whose answers appeared to be evasive, as he neither specified the quantity of powder he could spare nor absolutely fixed the price he would take for it. Therefore,

Resolved unanimously, that Mr. Burgwin's answer is unsatisfactory, and deserves the censure of this committee, and that he have notice thereof.

The committee then adjourned until 9 o'clock the next day.

Friday, January 6, 9 o'clock.

The committee met according to adjournment.

Present: Cornelius Harnett, chairman, Francis Clayton, deputy chairman.

Wm. Hooper, Samuel Ashe, George Merrick, James Moore, Bishop Dudley, Alexander Lillington, Thos. Devane, Samuel Marshall, William Jones, L. C.,* Wm. Jones, W. T.,† Frederick Jones, James Walker, Archibald M'Laine, Wm. Robeson, Samuel Swann, John Robeson.

Mr. Burgwin's letter to the chairman was produced and read, and ordered to be copied as follows:

Friday Morning.

DEAR SIR:—By what I hear passed in the Committee last evening, I imagine some misapprehension has taken place, as surely it can not be supposed I intended an insult to a set of gentlemen, for whom, individually, I have a high respect.

I was quite unacquainted with the quantity of powder we had on hand, and I told the gentlemen who came to me, that my powder cost seven shillings per hundred more than any in town, being made by a particular sample I had sent home for the purpose, and I thought we ought to have two shillings a pound more for it; however, we should not disagree about trifles, and that I would give orders none of it should be sold, but reserved as requested.

On the second application of Mr. Swann and Mr. Robeson, I think I told them with respect to two half barrels of Mrs. W's, as it was her property, should she send for it, I must deliver it to her order, but that I had no doubt of her acceptance of the price, and that I should write to her by the first opportunity.

Thus far, I have repeated if not the very words, the substance of what passed on this subject, and should be extremely sorry to act in any respect contrary to the true interest of my country, or give offence to any individual in it. Had I reflected a moment, I should have referred the Gentlemen to Mr. Graham, who is empowered to transact

---

* Long Creek.   † Welsh tract.

Mrs. Waddell's business, and could have answered for her at once, and to whom I now beg it to be referred.

Dear Sir, your most obd't servant,

(Signed) JOHN BURGWIN.

The committee on hearing the above letter read, ordered the following answer to be sent him by the Chairman.

Sir:—Your letter to me, respecting the message sent to you about your gunpowder, has been read to the committee, and they have desired me to acquaint you, that they are satisfied with it.

I am sir, Yours &c.

(Signed) CORNELIUS HARNETT.

The committee requested of Mr. Ancrum and Mr. Quince, that they would inspect the Custom House books at Brunswick, and report accordingly, which they agreed to do on Monday next.

The committee then adjourned until the 20th inst.

Friday, January 20.

Present: Cornelius Harnett, chairman, Francis Clayton, deputy chairman.

Samuel Swann, Timothy Bloodworth,[*] John Quince, John Ancrum, Archibald McLaine, Samuel Ashe, Wm. Jones, L. C., James Walker, Wm. Hooper.

Mr. Quince and Mr. Ancrum, reported to the committee, their return of the vessels entered at the Custom House since the 5th day of November, 1774, to the 4th January, 1775, which was ordered to be filed.

James Grant was appointed messenger to the committee, who agreed to act in that capacity.

The committee then adjourned until 10 o'clock the next day.

---

[*] Timothy Bloodworth, who was, *par excellence*, the representative of the "bone and sinew" element of the people during and after the Revolution, by his energy and activity acquired great popularity and high position, although his want of education was sadly manifest in all of his public utterances. He possessed a practical knowledge of various trades, being, says McRee, "preacher, farmer, doctor, watchmaker, wheelwright and politician," but he had been a brave soldier, and what is called a clever fellow and a good story teller. He was an intensely radical partisan of the extreme democratic type, and after holding various positions was a member of the Convention of 1788 at Hillsborough, which refused to adopt the Federal Constitution. He was the only representative from the Cape Fear country who voted to make Raleigh and not Fayetteville the capital of the State, and was rewarded for it by a seat in the United States Senate, which he held for one term.

10 o'clock, Saturday, Jan. 21, 1775.

The committee met according to adjournment.

Present: Cornelius Harnett, chairman, Francis Clayton, deputy chairman.

Samuel Ashe, Timothy Bloodworth, Wm. Jones, L. C., Sampson Moseley, John Quince, John Robeson, John Ancrum, John Ashe, Joel Parish, Wm. Hooper, Samuel Swann.

Messrs. George and Thomas Hooper, H. Blackmore, Arthur Mabson and Peter Mallett, reported sundry negroes imported by them since the 1st day of December last.

Resolved, That notices be sent to Messrs. George and Thomas Hooper, Herold Blackmore, Arthur Mabson, and Peter Mallett, to re-ship by the first opportunity, the sundry negroes they have imported since the 1st day of December last. It being the opinion of this committee that such importations are contrary to the resolves of the Continental Congress, and a particular resolve of this committee.

Resolved, that it is the opinion of this committee, a meeting of the merchants and traders of the town is necessary, in order to agree about the rates of goods they have for sale, to prevent, as far as possible, any advantage being taken from the present situation of this province, with America in general, rating goods higher than they were formerly sold at.

The committee then adjourned until 3 o'clock.

---

3 o'clock.

The committee met according to adjournment, and entered into the following resolves.

Present: Cornelius Harnett, chairman, Francis Clayton, deputy chairman.

William Hooper, John Ancrum, Samuel Ashe, John Quince, John Robeson, James Walker, Samuel Swann, Samuel Marshall, Robert Hogg, Timothy Bloodworth, Wm. Jones, L. C.

Resolved. That any quantity of salt, not exceeding 5 bushels, be sold, at not more than three shillings and six pence, any other quantity not higher than three shillings and four pence per bushel.

Resolved, That dry goods for ready pay, be sold not higher than two shillings and 2d, for one on the sterling cost, excepting small articles that are perishable, and not exceeding seven shillings and six pence profit, to be sold as usual, and all dry goods sold on credit at the same rates they have been sold at for 12 months past.

Resolved, That the permission of billiard tables, in this town, is repugnant to the resolves of the General Congress, and that the proprietors of them have notice thereof. They were accordingly served with such notice, and appeared at the committee, and declared their acquiescence in the resolves.

The committee then adjourned until the 28th of January.

Saturday, January 28, 1775.

At an occasional meeting of the committee:

Present: Cornelius Harnett, chairman, Francis Clayton, deputy chairman. John Ancrum, James Walker, Robt. Hogg, John Robeson.

Resolved, That balls and dancing at public houses, are contrary to the resolves of the General Congress. It is the opinion of this committee, that every tavern keeper in this town, have notice given them not to suffer any balls, or public dancing at their houses as they wish to avoid the censure of the people.

Mr. W. Campbell, and Mr. John McDonnel reported sundry dry goods, imported by them in the Brigantine Carolina Packet, Malcolm M'Neil, commander, and delivered up their invoices to the committee, to have the said goods disposed of agreeable to the resolves of the General Congress.

Ordered, That the said goods be advertised to be sold at public vendue, at 11 o'clock, on Monday, the 30th inst.

Ordered, That application be made to Capt. Bethune, of the schooner ———, from St. Augustine, to know whether the said schooner, is owned either in St. Augustine, or Georgia, and Mr. Clayton is requested by the committee, to make such inquiry, and report to the committee, on their next meeting.

The committee then adjourned to the meeting of course.

Monday, January 30, 1775.

At an occasional meeting of the committee.

Present: Cornelius Harnett, chairman, Francis Clayton, deputy chairman. Robert Hogg, James Walker, Archibald M'Laine, John Quince.

Mr. Adam Boyd, having applied for encouragement to his newspaper (some time ago laid aside,) it was resolved that the committee so far as their influence extended would support him on the following terms:

That he Mr. Boyd, should weekly continue a newspaper denominated the *Cape Fear Mercury,* of 21 inches wide, 17 inches long, 3 columns on a page, and of the small pica or long primer letter, and in return receive his payments at the following periods, viz: ten shillings at the delivery of the first number, ten shillings at the expiration of the year, and to be paid ten shillings at the end of every succeeding six months thereafter.

The committee then adjourned to the meeting of course.

Thursday, February 2, 1775.

The committee met as by adjournment.

Present: Archibald M'Laine, Wm. Hooper, Jas. Walker, John Robeson, John Quince, Robt. Hogg, J. Ancrum.

William Campbell's goods were set up at vendue, and sold for	£760 00 0
Amount of his invoice.......................	754 11 0
	£005 19 1

John Slingsby's goods sold £118 05 0
Amount of his invoice 117 18 3
                                            ─────────
                                            £000 06 9

Friday, February 3, 1775.
At an occasional meeting.
Present: Archibald McLain, James Walker, John Quince, John Robeson, John Ancrum.

John M'Donnel's goods were sold at vendue for sterling £725 13 06
To Wm. Purviance.
Amount of his invoice £717 13 04
                                            ─────────
To be received of Wm. P £008 00 02
William Campbell having delivered his invoice to the committee, at this meeting, his salt was put up at public vendue, and sold for £225 10 00
Amount of his invoice 218 08 04
                                            ─────────
To be paid by Wm. C. Sher £003 01 08

Monday, February 13, 1775.
At an occasional meeting.
Present: Cornelius Harnett, chairman, Francis Clayton, deputy chairman. Archibald M'Laine, Robt. Hogg, John Quince, Alexander Lillington, James Walker.

Information was made against Jona Dunbibin, for taking four shillings per bushel for salt, contrary to the resolves of this committee, he being sent for, waited on the committee, confessed it was a mistake, and promised to return the money so exacted, which the committee were satisfied with.

The committee then adjourned to the next occasional meeting.

Monday, February 20, 1775.

The committee met according to adjournment on the 13th of February last.

Present: Francis Clayton, deputy chairman, Robt. Hogg, James Walker, John Ancrum, Wm. Hooper, Samuel Marshall, Wm. Jones, L. C. John Devane, Timothy Bloodworth, Thos. Bloodworth.

It was proposed by Mr. Wm. Hooper, that as there was not a majority of the joint committee, that a message be sent to each member to meet on Monday the 6th of March next, which was agreed to, and the following message, ordered to be printed, and sent to each member:

Sir:—As a member of the committee appointed for the purpose of carrying into execution within the county of New Hanover, the Resolves of the General Continental Congress, you are requested to meet at the house of Lehansius DeKeyser, on Monday the 6th day of March next, then and there to consult of business of the utmost consequence to the patriotic support of the cause of British America.

By the order of the Committee,

(Signed) THOS. CRAIKE, Secretary.

Ordered, that the absentees of the committee be mulcted agreeable to the resolve of this committee.

Mr. Clayton, as deputy chairman, was requested by the committee, to write to Mr. James Kenan, chairman of the Duplin committee, which he did as follows:

Monday, February 20, 1775.

Sir—At a meeting of the joint committees for the town of Wilmington and county of New Hanover, on this day, it was among other matters proposed and agreed to. That for the better communication of intelligence and production of a similarity of conduct in your and our counties; we would send two members from our joint committees, on any day you should appoint, after the 6th of March, next, giving us twenty days notice thereof and as on that day, there would be several matters of much concern to American welfare, agitated, will be happy to see two of your members at our meeting. Sir, &c.

(Signed) F. CLAYTON.

Tuesday, February 21, 1775.

At an occasional meeting of the committee,

Present: Cornelius Harnett, chairman, Francis Clayton, deputy chairman, Robert Hogg, John Ancrum, Archibald M'Laine, James Walker.

Mr. Crowther presented to the committee, two invoices of European goods, imported since the 1st day of December last, to be disposed of agreeable to the resolves of the General Congress, which were ordered to be sold at vendue, as directed by the resolves.

Sales on 1st invoice	£204	13	1½
Sales on 2nd invoice	044	05	11
	£199	11	2½
Amount of the 1st invoice	£202	08	01½
Amount of the 2nd invoice	044	00	11
	£246	09	0½
	£002	10	00
Difference on 20 bushels of potatoes that were sold	£000	10	00
	£002	11	00

Wednesday, March 1, 1775.

At an occasional meeting of the committee.

Present: Cornelius Harnett, chairman, Francis Clayton, deputy chairman, Robt. Hogg, John Ancrum, James Walker, John Robeson.

The committee being informed of a Public Ball, to be given by sundry persons, under the denomination of the gentlemen of Wilmington, at the house of Mrs. Austin this evening, and as all public balls and dances are contrary to the resolves of the General Continental Congress, and a particular resolve of this committee:

106   HISTORY OF NEW HANOVER COUNTY.

Ordered, That the following letter be sent to Mrs. Austin, to forewarn her from suffering such public ball and dancing at her house.

Madam: The committee appointed to see the resolves of the Continental Congress put in execution, in this town, acquaint you, that the ball intended to be given at your house, this evening, is contrary to the said resolves; we therefore warn you to decline it, and acquaint the parties concerned, that your house can not be at their service, consistent with the good of your country.
By order of the committee.   (Signed)   THOS. CRAIKE.

Monday, March 6, 1775.
The committee met according to adjournment.

Present: Cornelius Harnett, chairman, Francis Clayton, deputy chairman, Archibald M'Laine, Alex. Lillington, James Moore, John Robeson, Sampson Moseley, Joel Parish, Timothy Bloodworth, Thos. Bloodworth, James Wright, John Hollingsworth, Samuel Marshall, F. Jones, John Ancrum, James Walker, Wm. Hooper, Samuel Collier.

The following association was agreed on by the committee, and annexed to the resolves of the General Congress, to be handed to every person in this county and recommended to the committees of the adjacent counties, that those who acceded to the said resolves, may subscribe their names thereto.

We, the subscribers, in testimony of our sincere approbation of the proceedings of the late Continental Congress, to this annexed, have hereunto set our hands, and we do most solemnly engage by the most sacred ties of honor, virtue and love of our country, that we will ourselves strictly observe every part of the association recommended by the Continental Congress, as the most probable means to bring about a reconciliation between Great Britain and her colonies and we will use every method in our power to endeavor to influence others to the observation of it by persuasion, and such other methods as shall be consistent with the peace and good order, and the laws of this Province, and we do solemnly intend to express our utter detestation of all such as shall endeavor to defeat the purpose of the said Congress, and will concur to hold forth such characters to public contempt.

William Wilkinson, reported sundry dry goods imported in the schooner ————, Yelverton Fowkes, master, from Charles Town, directed to his care by Joseph Robeson, of Deep river, to have their opinion whether the said goods could be landed agreeable to the general resolves.

The committee, after examining Mr. Wilkinson and Capt. Fowkes and such papers as they could produce,

Resolved, That the said goods can not be disposed of by the said Robeson, or his factor, till further proof of their having been imported or disposed of agreeable to the general resolves, and that William Wilkinson, be allowed six weeks from this time, to procure from the committee of Charles Town, such certificates as shall be satisfactory to this committee; and the said Wm. Wilkinson, is to store the goods, and deliver the key to Mr. James Walker, one of this committee.

The committee then adjourned till 3 o'clock this afternoon.

3 o'clock, the committee met according to adjournment.

Present: Cornelius Harnett, chairman, Francis Clayton, deputy chairman, John Robeson, Samuel Swann, A. Lillington, George Moore, Sampson Moseley, Wm. Jones, L. C., John Colvin, Samuel Marshall, William Jones, W. T., Thos. Bloodworth, Archibald M'Laine, John Ancrum, James Walker, James Wright, Timothy Bloodworth, Samuel Collier, John Hollingsworth, Joel Parish, John Devane, George Merrick, Wm. Hooper, James Moore, Frederick Jones.

Mr. James Kenan, chairman of the Duplin committee, pursuant to letter from this committee at their last meeting attended.

Resolved, That all the members of the committee now present go in body and wait on all housekeepers in town, with the association before mentioned, and request their signing it, or declare their reasons for refusing it, that such Enemies to their Country may be set forth to public view and treated with the contempt they merit.

Resolved, That it is the opinion of this committee, that all dances private as well as public, are contrary to the spirit of the 8th article in the association of the Continental Congress, and that as such they ought to be discouraged, and that all persons concerned in any dances for the future should be properly stigmatized.

Mr. Harnett desired the opinion of the committee respecting a negro fellow he bought in Rhode Island (a native of that place) in the month of October last, whom he designed to have brought with him to this province, but the said negro ran away at the time of his sailing from Rhode Island.

The question was put whether Mr. Harnett may import the said negro from Rhode Island.

Resolved, Unanimously, That Mr. Harnett may import the said negro from Rhode Island, and it is the opinion of this committee that under the above circumstances, such importation will not be any infringement of the article of the resolves of the General Congress.

Ordered, that Mr. Grant, Messenger to this committee, be paid for his attendance on .... committee, 10 days, (including to-morrow) at the rate of 8s. per day.

The committee then adjourned till 9 o'clock to-morrow morning.

Tuesday, March 7th, 1775.

The committee met according to adjournment.

Present: Cornelius Harnett, chairman, Francis Clayton, deputy chairman, John Ancrum, Geo. Moore, Wm. Hooper, Samuel Swann, James Moore, Sampson Moseley, Wm. Jones, W. T., Thos. Bloodworth, Alexander Lillington, F. Jones, Geo. Merrick, J. Robeson, John Devane, Jno. Colvin, Timothy Bloodworth, Wm. Jones, L. C., Joel Parish, Jno. Hollingsworth, Jas. Wright, Archibald McLaine.

Resolved, That three members of this committee attend the meeting of the committee at Duplin, on the 18th inst. Mr. Samuel Ashe, Mr. Sampson Moseley, and Mr. Timothy Bloodworth were accordingly nominated to attend the said committee.

The committee sent for Mr. John McDonnell, an importer and purchaser of sundry dry goods, as appears by the Journal of this committee, the 3d February last, to demand the sum of £ 8. o. 2 sterling money, which he became liable for to the committee. The said John McDonnell having made it appear to the satisfaction of the committee, that the goods he purchased were damaged in such a manner as not to be worth the first cost and charges: it is the opinion of this committee that the aforesaid sale is void, and that the said Jno. McDonnell be excused from paying the above sum.

Doctor Thomas Cobham, Messrs. Jno. McDonnell, Jno. Walker, Jr., Jno. Slingsby, Thomas Orr, Jno. Cruden, Wm. McTier, and Wm. McLeod, merchants, Wm. Whitfield, planter, and Kenneth McKenzie, and Dougal McNight, tailors, all of the town of Wilmington, appeared before the committee, and having refused or declined, under various pretences, to sign the association of the Continental Congress—

Resolved and agreed, That we will have no trade, commerce, dealings, or intercourse whatsoever, with the above mentioned persons or any others connected with them, or with any person or persons who shall hereafter violate the association, or refuse to subscribe hereto; but will hold them as unworthy of the rights of freemen, and as inimical to the liberties of their country, and we recommend it to the people of this colony in particular, and to the Americans in general, to pursue the same conduct.

Resolved, That a copy of the above resolve be given to Adam Boyd, to print in handbills and distributed through this province.

The committee being informed that a vessel arrived in the river from Glasgow, with bale goods, desired the chairman to write the following letter to Richard Quince, Esq., chairman of the Brunswick Committee:

110   HISTORY OF NEW HANOVER COUNTY.

Sir: From the captain of a vessel from Hispaniola, just come to town, we learn that a Snow has arrived from Glasgow, laden with bale goods, bricks, wines, &c.; you are sensible, Sir, that these goods, agreeable to the articles of Association, ought to be returned; and take this very early opportunity of putting you in mind that she is a subject of your attention, having committed a breach of said Association within your limits.

The names of the captain and vessel are not known, but supposed to be the Snow Relief, Dougal McGregor master. You will please communicate the procedure of your committee in this affair, I am, &c.

(Signed)   CORNELIUS HARNETT.

The committee then adjourned till afternoon.

Tuesday, 4 o'clock.

The committee met according to adjournment.

Present: Cornelius Harnett, chairman, Francis Clayton, deputy chairman, Jno. Quince, Jno. Devane, Thomas Bloodworth, Timothy Bloodworth, Wm. Jones, W. T., Wm. Hooper, John Ancrum, James Moore, F. Jones, Archibald McLaine, Wm. Jones, L. C.

Resolved, unanimously, That as the measures which this committee must be under an absolute necessity to adopt, in case any persons should mark themselves as objects of distinction, in opposition to the general American cause, must be greatly detrimental in their present operation and future consequence to them; We, therefore, in order to give full opportunity to those who have not yet subscribed their names as a testimony of their concurrence in the continental Association have thought fit to delay till Monday next, carrying into execution those signal marks of contempt which the Continental Congress have thought fit to consign those who are so far lost to public virtue, as to oppose the measures which that body proposed as a cement of allegiance to our sovereign, and as having a tendency to promote a constitutional attachment to our mother country.

Resolved, unanimously, Also, that if any person who, upon application having been made to him, to sign the association, has hitherto refused, if he shall make known that he has altered his Resolution, and shall be desirous to set his name to the said association, he will find it in the hands of the chairman, deputy chairman or secretary of this committee, till Monday next, before or at which time he may apply and save the dangerous consequence that may ensue from a longer neglect.

Account of money received by the secretary for the committee, to be disposed of agreeable to the resolves.

From Arch. McLaine, Corn'l Harnett, Al. Lillington, Sam'l Swann, Samp. Moseley, Fred'k Jones, G. Moore, Wm. Jones, Joel Parish, Jno. Devane, Jno. Robeson, at 8s. each, for not attending the committee as sum'd.............	£ 4	8s 0d.
From Mr. Crowther, for sale of goods, on the 21st Feby, 1775	4	8s 9d.
From Alexander Hostler, for sale of goods, on the 31st Dec. 1774........................	3	0s 0d.
From John Slingsby for sale of goods, at sundry times	14	10s 0d.
From Wm. McTier, for sale of goods, 31st Dec. 1774	2	0s 0d.
From John Cruden, for sale of goods, 31st Dec. 1774 :		8s 8d.
From Thos. Orr, for sale of goods, 31st Dec. 1774		15s 0d.
From J. McDonnel, a gift to the Bostonians....	3	0s 0d.
	£31	10s 0d.

Account of money paid by order of the committee.

To James Grant, messenger to the committee for his attendance 10 days including to-day at 8s. per day.	£4	0 0
To Owen Kenan for Dickson in full for the balance due him by the committee appointed to receive donations for the Bostonians, for carrying expresses to the Northern counties......................	£5	0 0
	£9	0 0

The committee adjourned to the next occasional meeting.

At a meeting of the Freeholders of Wilmington this day, Wm. Purviance, Esq., Messrs. R'd. Player, James Blyth, And'w Ronaldson, Wm. Ewins and Henry Young, were unanimously chosen an addition to the Wilmington committee.

Monday, March 13, 1775.

At an occasional meeting of the committee.

Present: Corn'l Harnett, chairman, Fran's Clayton, deputy chairman, Arch'd Maclaine, Rob. Hogg, Jno. Quince, Wm. Purviance, Jas. Walker, R'd Player, James Blyth, Wm. Ewins, And'w Ronaldson, Jno. Ancrum and Jno. Ashe.

Since the resolve passed the 6th of this inst. to make public, the names of the persons who refused to sign the Continental Association, the underwritten persons who had refused, have subscribed their names within the time limited.

John Cruden, Thos. Orr, Wm. McLeod, John Slingsby, Wm. Whitfield, Thos. Cobham, John Walker, Jr., and Wm. Mactier.

Rec'd this day from Mr. Harnett his subscription to the committee, for purchasing gunpowder.................... £25

Monday, March 20, 1775.

At a general meeting of the committee.

Present: Cornelius Harnett, chairman, James Moore, Samuel Ashe, Samuel Swann, Robt. Hogg, James Walker, Wm. Hooper, Alex. Ronaldson, Jno. Hollingsworth, Frederick Jones, Jno. Ancrum, Samuel Marshall, Arch. McLaine.

Resolved, That the Importers of negroes since 1st of December last, be called upon at the next general meeting of this committee on the 20th of April next, to produce bills of loading, or other sufficient proof to the committee, that they have reshipped the said negroes agreeable to the resolves of the general Congress as directed by this committee. Paid for paper, 2s. 8d.

The committee then adjourned to the next occasional meeting.

Tuesday, March 24, 1775.

At an occasional meeting of the committee.

Present: Robert Hogg, Jas. Walker, Jno. Robeson, Wm. Ewins, Jno. Ancrum, Wm. Purviance, Timothy Bloodworth, A. Ronaldson, James Blyth, Thos. Devane.

Messrs. George and Thos. Hooper, reported sundry dry goods of the Peggy, Graham, commander, from Leith, shipped to their address which they desired the committee to take into consideration and direct what should be done with the dry goods.

Ordered, That the said goods be not landed, but sent back to Great Britain, as directed by the 10th article of the General Association, and Mr. John Robeson is desired (as a member of this committee) to go on board the said vessel, and take an account of the goods on board, with their marks and numbers, and on her being ready to sail for Great Britain to examine the said goods with his account before taken.

Capt. Oldfield reported two negroes shipped to his address on the schooner Bedford, Capt. Benny, which were ordered to be re-shipped, and was complied with by Capt. Oldfield.

Wednesday, April 4.

At an occasional meeting of the committee.

Present: Arch'd Maclaine, Jno. Robeson, Wm. Purviance, Tim'y Bloodworth, James Walker, Alex. Ronaldson, Wm. Ewins, Jno. Ancrum.

Mr. Alexander Hostler applied to the committee to have their advice concerning a ship called the Clemantine, that was coming to his address from London, commanded by Dick Weir, which is lost on the middle ground near the bar of the river. At the same time Mr. Hostler delivered to the committee, an invoice, of sundry stationery goods shipped on board the said vessel, which he requested the committee to take also into consideration and direct him what may be done with the said ship, stores and materials and stationery goods.

Ordered, That it is the opinion of this committee that the vessel, with her stores and materials may be legally sold without any breach being made in the General Association, but as the stationery goods are landed at Brunswick, this committee think they don't come under their direction.

Thursday, April 20, 1775.

The committee met agreeable to adjournment.

Present: Cornelius Harnett, chairman, Robert Hogg, James Walker, Alex. Lillington, Timothy Bloodworth, Andrew Ronaldson, John Colvin, Francis Clayton, James Blyth, Sam. Marshall, Jno. Robinson, Wm. Purviance, Sampson Moseley, George Moore, Jno. Ancrum, Wm. Evans, Frederick Jones.

Mr. Wm. Wilkinson, appeared and produced a certificate for the proper landing of a parcel of goods consigned to him from Charlestown, in the schooner ———, Yelverton Fawkes, master, which being read, was deemed satisfactory by the committee.

Application was then made by Mr. Cruden, in behalf of a Mr. Elliott, setting forth that he had purchased the real and personal estate of Marmaduke Jones, Esq., both of the province, and praying to have leave to import some of his house servants (negroes) now in Jamaica; the articles in the above association respecting the importation of slaves being read, and the subject fully debated, it was determined that said servants could not be imported.

The committee then adjourned to May 20th.

Saturday, May 20, 1775.

The committee met according to adjournment.

Present: Corn'l Harnett, chairman, Fran's Clayton, deputy

chairman, George Moore, John Ashe, Sam'l Marshall, John Devane, John Colvin, Sampson Moseley, James Wright, Robert Hogg, John Hollingsworth, James Blythe, And'w Ronaldson, John Robeson, Thos. Bloodworth, Samuel Ashe, Fred'k Jones, Arch'd Maclaine, James Moore, William Robeson, William Ewins, William Jones, Sam'l Collier, Timothy Bloodworth, Alexander Lillington, James Walker, Jno. Ancrum, Jno. Quince.

Ordered, That this committee meet at 11 o'clock, in the forenoon, on the 20th day of month, otherwise to be subject to the fine agreed to be paid by absentees.

Resolved, That the committees of the respective counties in this district be invited to meet in Wilmington on the 20th of June next, in order to deliberate on several matters of importance that will be laid before them, respecting the general cause of America.

Ordered, That the Resolve entered on the journals of this committee on the last meeting, respecting the application to the committee for liberty to Mr. Elliott to import his house servants, be rescinded.

Resolved, A paper containing the reasons of the Magistrates of Chatham county for not signing the Association, presented to them by one Doctor Piles, is highly approved of by this committee, and is ordered to be published in the *Cape Fear Mercury*.

Account of money paid and received for the use of the committee this meeting.

Received from Jno. Ashe, 15s. Jno. Hollingsworth, 8s. Francis Clayton, 8s. Wm. Robeson, 8s. Wm. Jones, 8s. Jno. Quince, 16s for being absent, £3 3s 0d. Paid, to Wm. Mactier for 200 lbs. gunpowder, at 3s. 30. To James Harper's boy, at twice in part of two expresses, one to the Southward, and the other to the Northward, £1 10s. To James Grant in full to this meeting, £2 8s. To expenses for paper, 2s 8d. Total, £37 3s 8d.

The committee then adjourned to next meeting.

Tuesday, June 7, 1775.

At an occasional meeting of the committee.

Present: Cornelius Harnett, chairman. Arch. McLaine, Jno. Quince, James Walker, Jno. Ancrum, Wm. Purviance, Jno. Robeson, Andrew Ronaldson, James Blythe, William Ewins, Robt. Hogg.

Whereas, the Continental Congress, did resolve, in the words, following, viz: And we further agree and associate, that we will have no trade, commerce, dealings, or intercourse whatever, with any colony or province in North America, which shall not accede to, or shall hereafter violate this association, and whereas, the Parliament of Great Britain in pursuance of their plan for subjugating and distressing the colonies, have passed a bill for depriving our Brethren in New England, of the benefit of fishing on their own coasts. Therefore, resolved, that all exportations from this town and county, for the army and navy, in America, Newfoundland, or to the Northern colonies, from whence any supply of provisions can be had for those purposes, ought in the opinion of this committee, immediately to be suspended, and that it be accordingly recommended to every merchant, immediately to suspend all exportation to those places, until the Continental Congress shall give further orders thereon.

Paid to James Harper his account for two expresses sent by him to Brunswick and New River £4 0s. 0d.

The committee then adjourned to the next meeting.

At a general meeting of the several committees of the district of Wilmington, held at the court house in Wilmington, Tuesday the 20th of June, 1775.

For the county of New Hanover. Present: Cornelius Harnett, Francis Clayton, George Moore, sen., Jno. Ashe, Jno. Quince, Wm. Ewins, James Walker, James Blythe, John Devane, Wm. Jones, Long Creek, Wm. Jones, W. T., John Ancrum, James Moore, Robt. Hogg, Alexander Lillington.

Wm. Robeson, Sam. Swann, Fred. Jones, sr., Jno. Colvin, Jno. Hollingsworth, Sam. Ashe, Geo. Merrick, And'w. Ronaldson, Arch'd Maclaine, James Wright, Jno. Marshall, Sampson Moseley, Thos. Devane.

For the county of Brunswick. Rich'd Quince, Sen., Rob't Howe, Thos. Davis, Rob't Ellis, Rich'd Quince, Jr., Parker Quince, Wm. Lord, Wm. Cain, Thos. Allen, Step. Daniel, Wm. Davis, James Bell.

For Bladen County. Nath'l Richardson, Thos. Owen, Walter Gibson, Thos. Brown, Faithful Graham.

For Duplin. Charles Ward.

The committee having met agreeable to summons, they proceeded to choose a chairman; accordingly Richard Quince, Sr. was unanimously chosen.

A letter from the committee of Cross Creek was read, and an answer was ordered to be wrote by the chairman to the said letter.

The Governor's proclamation, dated at Fort Johnston, the 16th inst. was ordered to be read.

On motion. Ordered that a committee be appointed to answer the said Proclamation; and that Rob't. Howe, Arch McLaine, and Samuel Ashe be a committee for that purpose.

On motion, for leave to ─────── Elletson to import his house servants from Jamaica, not exceeding six in number. It was carried against the motion, by a great majority.

The committee then adjourned to 10 o'clock to-morrow.

Wednesday, 10 o'clock.

The committee met according to adjournment.

On motion, ordered, That Cornelius Harnett be appointed to write to the committee of Cumberland County, to secure the gunpowder that may be in that county, for the use of the public.

On motion, For the more effectually disarming and keeping the negroes in order, within the county of New Hanover. It was unanimously agreed, by the members of the committee, for said county, to appoint Patrols to search for, and take from negroes, all kinds of arms whatsoever, and such guns or other arms found with negroes, shall be delivered to the Captain of the company of the District in which they are found, to be distributed by the said officers, to those of his company who may be in want of arms, and who are not able to purchase: and that the following persons be patrols, as follows:

From Beauford's Ferry, to the end of Geo. Moore's district: Sam'l Swann, Thos. Moseley, Geo. Palmer, Henry Beauford, Wm. Robeson, Luke Woodward.

Burgaw: Sampson Moseley, William Moseley, Jno. Ashe, Jr.

Black River: Geo. Robeson, Thos. Devane, Jno. Colvin, Thos. Corbit, Jr., Benj. Robeson, James Bloodworth.

Welch Tract: Barnaby Fuller, Geo. McGowan, Wm. Wright, Martin Wells, Morgan Swinney, David Jones.

Beatty's Swamp, to Perry's Creek; Elisha Atkinson, Bishop Swann, Aaron Erskins, Peter McClammy, Jno. Watkins, Edmond Moore, John Lucas.

Perry's Creek to Baldhead: James Middleton, Chas. Morris, Jno. Nichols, Samuel Marshall, Joseph Nichols, Jas. Ewing, George Stundere, Jas. Jones.

Long Creek: Wm. Jones, James Ratcliff, John Kenner, Thos. Bloodworth, Wm. Hennepy, Jno. Marshall.

Holly Shelter: Thos. Jones, Edward Doty, Henry Williams, Thos. Simmons, John Simmons, Joshua Sutton.

Resolved, That the following Association formerly agreed by the Committee of New Hanover county, stand as the Association of this Committee, and that it be recommended to the inhabitants of this district to sign the same as speedily as possible, and that the same, with this Resolution, be printed in the public newspaper.

ASSOCIATION.

Unanimously agreed to, by the inhabitants of New Hanover county in North Carolina, 19th June, 1775.

The actual commencement of hostilities against this Continent by the British troops, in the bloody scene, on the 19th April last, near Boston, the increase of arbitrary impositions from a wicked and despotic ministry; and the dread of instigated insurrections in the colonies, are causes sufficient to drive an oppressed people to the use of arms. We, therefore, the subscribers, inhabitants of New Hanover county, having ourselves bound by that most sacred of all obligations, the duty of good citizens toward an injured country; and, thoroughly convinced that, under our present distressed circumstances, we shall be justified before God and Man, in resisting force by force, do unite ourselves under every tie of religion and honor and associate as a band in her defence against every foe; hereby solemnly engaging that whenever our Continental or Provincial Councils shall decree it necessary we will go forth and be ready to sacrifice our lives and fortunes to secure her freedom and safety. This obligation to continue in full force until a reconciliation shall take place between Great Britain and America, upon constitutional principles, an event we most ardently desire and we will hold all those persons inimical to the liberties of the Colonies, who shall refuse to subscribe this Association. And we will in all things, follow the advice of our committee, respecting the purposes aforesaid, the preservation of peace and good order, and the safety of individual and private property.

The committee to answer the Governor's Proclamation of the 16th inst. returned the following answer, which was read and ordered to be printed in the public papers and in hand bills.

At a general meeting of the several committees of the District of Wilmington, held at the Court House in Wilmington, Tuesday 20th June, 1775.

Whereas, His Excellency, Josiah Martin, Esq., hath by Proclamation dated at Fort Johnston, the 16th day of June, 1775, and read this day in the committee, endeavored to persuade, seduce, and intimidate the good people of the province, from taking measures to preserve those rights, and that liberty, to which, as the subjects of a British King they have the most undoubted claim, without which, life would be but a futile consideration, and which, therefore, it is a duty they owe to themselves, their country, and posterity, by every effort, and at every risk, to maintain, support, and defend against any invasion or encroachment whatsoever.

And whereas, many unconstitutional and oppressive acts of Parliament, invasive of every right and privilege, and dangerous to the freedom of America, have laid the people of this colony under the fatal necessity of appointing committees for the several districts, towns, and counties of this province, who were instructed carefully to guard against every encroachment upon their invaluable rights, and steadily oppose the operation of those unconstitutional acts, framed by a wicked administration entirely to destroy the freedom of America: and as among other measures, those committees found it absolutely necessary either by themselves, or by persons appointed under them, to visit the people, and fully explain to them the nature and dangerous tendencies of those acts, which the tools of administration, were by every base art, endeavoring to prevail upon them to submit to; and his Excellency has endeavored by his Proclamation, to weaken the influence, and prejudice the characters of those committees, and the persons appointed under them, by wantonly, cruelly, and unjustly, representing them as illdisposed people, propagating false and scandalous reports, derogatory to the honor and justice of the King; and also, by other illiberal and scandalous imputations expressed in the said proclamation: We, then, the committees of the counties of New Hanover, Brunswick, Bladen, Duplin and Onslow, in order to permit the pernicious influence of the said proclamation, do, unanimously, resolve, that in our opinion, his excellency Josiah Martin, Esq.; hath by the said proclamation, and by the whole tenor of his conduct, since the unhappy disputes between Great Britain and the colonies, discovered himself to be an enemy to the happiness of this colony in particular, and to the freedom, rights and privileges of America in general.

Resolved, nem. con. That the said proclamation contains many things asserted to be facts, which are entirely without foundation; particularly the methods said to have been made use of, in order to compel the people to sign an association against any invasion, intestine insurrection, or unjust encroachments upon their rights and privileges; no person having signed such association but from the fullest conviction that it was essentially necessary to their freedom and safety; and that if his excellency founded such assertions upon information, it must have been derived from persons too weak or wicked to have any claim to his credit or attention.

Resolved, nem. con. That it is the opinion of this committee, that America owes much of its present sufferings to the information given by Governors and men in office, to administration, who having themselves adopted belief from improper informants, or, in order to sacrifice to the pleasure of the ministry, have falsely represented that His Majesty's American subjects were not generally averse from the arbitrary proceedings of a wicked administration, but that the opposition, made to such unconstitutional measures, arose from the influence of a few individuals upon the minds of the people, whom they have not failed to represent as "false, seditious and abandoned men"; by these means, induing the ministry to believe, that the Americans would be easily brought to submit to the cruel impositions so wickedly intended for them; that his excellency's proclamation is evidently calculated for this purpose, and is also replete with the most liberal abuse and scandalous imputations, tending to defame the characters of many respectable persons who zealously attached to the liberty of their country, were pursuing every laudable method to support it.

Resolved, nem. con. That the resolution respecting America, introduced by Lord North, into the British House of Parliament, which his Excellency, in his proclamation, alludes to, is such a glaring affront to the common sense of the Americans, that it added insult to the injury it intended them: That Lord North, himself, when he introduced it, declared to the House, that he did not believe America would accept of it, but that it might possibly tend to divide them, and if it broke one link in their chain of union, it would render the enforcing his truly detestable acts the more easy; therefore.

Resolved, That this was a low, base, flagitious, wicked attempt to entrap America into Slavery, and which they ought to reject with the contempt it deserves; that the uncandid and insidious manner in which his Excellency has mentioned the said resolution, is a poor artifice to seduce, mislead, and betray the ignorant and incautious into ruin and destruction, by inducing them to forfeit the inestimable blessings of freedom, with which nature and the British Constitution have so happily invested them; and also, indisputably proves, that his Excellency is ready to become an instrument in the hands of administration to rivet those chains so wickedly forged for America.

Resolved, nem. con. That at this alarming crisis, when the dearest rights and privileges of America are at stake, no confidence ought to be reposed in those, whose interest is to carry into execution every measure of administration, however profligate and abandoned; and who though they are conscious those measures will not bear the test of enquiry and examination, will endeavor to gloss over the most palpable violation of truth with plausibility, hoping, thereby, to blind, mislead, and delude the people; that this committee therefore, earnestly recommend it to the other committees of this province, and likewise to all our Brethren and suffering fellow subjects thereof, cautiously to guard against all those endeavors, which have been or shall be made to deceive them, and to treat such attempts as wicked efforts of the tools of Government calculated to throw this country into confusion, and by dividing to enslave it.

The committee adjourned till a meeting occasionally. Account of money received at this committee.

From Bladen county by the hands of Mr. Richardson, in good bills....................	£36 11s 2d
One Bill counterfeit of......................	2 0 0
From Cornelius Harnett, for sundry subscriptions to purchase gunpowder	49 15 6
From Wm. Jones, L. C., by the hand of R. Hogg for same purpose	10 0 0
From John Slingsby for same purpose..........	5 0 0
From Doct. Cobham for same purpose..........	2 10 0
From R'd. Bradley for same purpose...........	1 0 0
	£106 16 8

Money paid for sundries.

Paid for 350 lbs. Gunpowder in the hands of Burgwin, Humphrey & Co. pr. rec't............	£52 10s 0d
Paid John Slingsby for 50 pounds Gunpowder in his hands	7 10 0
Paid Wm. Grant to pay for cleaning out the court house	0 2 6
	£60 2 6

At an occasional meeting of the committee, June 1775.

Present: Cornelius Harnett, chairman; Rob't Hogg, Arch'd Maclaine, James Walker, Wm. Ewins, James Blythe, Sam'l Marshall.

Mr. James Ellotson Bowen applied to this committee for leave to land sundry household furniture, &c., imported in the ship Success, Edmund Cheeseman, commander, the property of ———— Ellotson, who is coming to reside in this province. The said Bowen being sworn upon the holy Evangelists of Almighty God; declared the list of furniture, &c., delivered to this committee, by him, is solely for the use of Ellotson, and that no part of it is, or was intended for sale, and that, if on opening the packages, any merchandise should be found, he will immediately acquaint the committee therewith, to be disposed of as they shall direct.

Rob't Hogg, a member of this committee, desired to withdraw himself from further attendance, as he is going to the back country.

The committee then adjourned to the next occasional meeting.

Monday, July 3, 1775.

At an occasional meeting of the committee.

Present: Cornelius Harnett, chairman, Francis Clayton, deputy chairman, Arch'd Maclaine, Jno. Robeson, Jno. Ancrum, Wm. Ewins, James Walker, Sam'l Marshall, Tim. Bloodworth.

Whereas, it was Resolved, at a session of the Honorable Continental Congress, now assembled at Philadelphia, that Thursday the 20th July next should be held as a day of fasting and prayer.

It was unanimously agreed to in committee met at Wilmington, that the humble observance of that day should be warmly inculcated on every inhabitant of this province and that the following resolve of the Honorable Continental Congress should be made public.

Ordered, That two hundred copies of the said resolve be printed in hand bills and distributed through this colony.

On motion, ordered, That the chairman of the committee write to Allen McDonald, of Cumberland county, to know from himself respecting the reports that circulate of his having an intention to raise troops to support the arbitrary measures of the ministry against the Americans, in this colony; and whether he had not made an offer of his services to Governor Martin for that purpose.

Ordered, That the following agreement be put up at the court house.

Whereas, several members of the Wilmington committee seem to find it inconvenient to give their attendance with that punctuality that the present exigence of affairs now demands, and as it has been the practice of all the Northern colonies since American politics have been drawing towards their present crisis, to re-elect their committee; for these reasons, and that the people may have an opportunity of confirming or annulling their former choice, it has been unanimously agreed to in committee held this day at Wilmington, to make the above public, and request the attendance of all the inhabitants qualified to vote, for members of assembly, to meet at the Court house on Thursday next, and elect a committee to represent said town and as it has been thought that the present committee is not sufficiently numerous, it is recommended to the electors to take the augmentation of the future one into consideration.

The committee then adjourned till the next occasional meeting.

Wednesday, July 5, 1775.

At an occasional meeting of the committee.

Present: Cornelius Harnett, chairman, Francis Clayton, deputy chairman, Arch'd Maclaine, James Walker, Jno. Ancrum, Sam'l Ashe, Jno. Ashe, James Blythe, Jno. Quince, Wm.

Ewins, Tim. Bloodworth, Wm. Purviance, Wm. Jones, Sam'l Swann, Joel Parish, An. Ronaldson.

A letter of the 27th June last, was received from the committee of intelligence, in Charlestown, S. C., by Captain Charles Cotesworth Pinkney, and read this day, requesting that this committee may give proper countenance to Captain Pinkney and such officers as accompany him, being sent with an intention to raise men for the defense of American liberty.

Resolved, therefore, That the chairman of this committee be empowered to write to the committees of the several counties and towns in this province, earnestly recommending aid and assistance to the officers from South Carolina, in raising such numbers of men as may be necessary to complete their levies now raising for the common defence and support of the liberties of America, and to express the sense this committee has of the noble and patriotic conduct of our sister colony in the common cause.

On motion, Resolved, That the exportation of all kinds of provision to the island of Nantucket, should be stopped until further orders by the Continental Congress, and it is recommended to the merchants of this port to observe the same.

John Thally was sent for and appeared before this committee, when he solemnly declared that he never had by any means whatsoever endeavored to alienate any person or persons from their duty in support of the general cause; and desired an advertisement which he signed to be put in the *Mercury*.

The committee then adjourned till next occasional meeting.

Thursday, July 6, 1775.

At an election for committee men, for the town of Wilmington, agreeable to a resolve of the late committee on Monday the 3d inst., the following persons were duly elected to represent the said town:

Cornelius Harnett, Francis Clayton, Archibald Maclaine,

Wm. Hooper, James Walker, Jno. Ancrum, Jno. Quince, Jno. Robeson, Wm. Purviance, Wm. Ewins, A. Ronaldson, James Blythe, Peter Mallett, Wm. Wilkinson, Adam Boyd, Hy Toomer, James Tate,* Jno. DuBois, John Forster, Doc't Jas. Geekie, Frans. Brice, Caleb Grainger, Wm. Campbell.

Friday, July 7, 1775.

At an occasional meeting of the committee.

Present, Cornelius Harnett, Francis Clayton, Archibald Maclaine, James Walker, Jno. Ancrum, Jno. Quince, Jno. Robeson, Wm. Ewins, A. Ronaldson, Peter Malett, Wm. Wilkinson, Adam Boyd,† Hy. Toomer, Jas. Tate, Jno. DuBois, Jno. Forster, Jas. Geekie, Francis Brice, Caleb Grainger, Wm. Campbell, Wm. Miller.

The new committee having met agreeable to a summons, proceeded to choose a chairman and deputy chairman.

Accordingly Cornelius Harnett, Esq, was unanimously chosen chairman, and Mr. Francis Clayton, deputy chairman.

On motion, Resolved, unanimously, as the opinion of this committee, that the immediate calling of a provincial convention is a measure absolutely necessary, and that the chairman do recommend the same to Samuel Johnston, Esq.

On motion, Resolved, unanimously, that every white man, capable of bearing arms, resident in Wilmington, shall, on or before Monday, the 10th instant, enroll himself in one of the two companies there, and that every man of the above description, who has not signed the association, apply to the subscriber, in whose possession for that purpose it is, and subscribe the same. A neglect of the above will be considered by the committee as a declaration of intentions inimical to the common cause of America; and the committee further direct that no master shall prevent his apprenticed servants from complying with the resolution—to be signed by the secretary.

---

* Preacher and teacher of classical school in 1760.

† Editor of the *Cape Fear Mercury*, and later Lieutenant and Chaplain in the Continental Line, and Brigade Chaplain Society of the Cincinnati after the Revolution.

On motion, Ordered, that Cornelius Harnett, Arch'd Maclaine, Francis Clayton, Adam Boyd, and John Ancrum, be a committee of correspondence till the next monthly meeting of the committee for the town and county.

On motion, Ordered, that the committee of Intelligence draw up a resolution to hold James Hepburn up to the public, as inimical to the liberties of his country and the common cause of America, which is as follows:

Whereas, this committee hath received information from undoubted authority, that James Hepburn of Cumberland county, attorney at law, did lately apply to the committee of that county, for orders to raise a company "under the Militia law, to preserve the independence of the subjects, and the dignity of the Government," and afterwards declared that, had the application met with success, the company was intended to act against the American cause. And, whereas, oath hath this day been made by James Clardy, of Bladen county, that the said James Hepburn, in a conversation with the said Clardy, after inquiring what officers had been chosen for the county of Bladen, and asking if the said Clardy was not a committee-man, said, in derision, that these were fine times when the country was to be governed by committees; and in order to intimidate the said James Clardy, and other the good people of this province, falsely and maliciously asserted that there were 50.000 Russians in his Majesty's pay, and that they had embarked, or were to embark immediately, in order to subdue the Americans; and whereas, it is notorious that the said James Hepburn, hath very lately been with Governor Martin at Fort Johnston, in company with some gentlemen lately settled in this province, as it is said, and universally believed, to offer their services to the said Governor, and to obtain his orders for raising mercenaries to suppress the noblest struggles of insulted liberty. It is, therefore,

Resolved, unanimously, That the said James Hepburn, is a false, scandalous, and seditious incendiary, who, destitute of property and influence, as he is of principle, basely and traitorously endeavors to make himself conspicuous in favor of tyranny and oppression, in hopes by violating the primary and fundamental laws of nature and the British constitution to raise a fortune to his family upon the subversion of liberty, and the destruction of his country.

Ordered, that this Resolve, and this preamble upon which it is founded, be published; in order that the friends to American Liberty may avoid all dealings and intercourse with such a wicked and detestable character.

The committee then adjourned till the next occasional meeting.

Wednesday, July 12, 1775.

At an occasional meeting of the committee; Francis Clayton, deputy chairman, Archibald Maclaine, James Walker, Caleb Grainger, William Campbell, William Ewins, Adam Boyd, Dr. Geekie, Jno. Ancrum, Peter Mallett, Andrew Ronaldson, William Purviance, Henry Toomer, James Blythe, Timothy Bloodworth, John Dubois, John Robeson.

On motion, ordered, that it is the opinion of this committee, a list of all the white male inhabitants of this town, from 15 to 60 years of age, should be taken, and that John Dubois, Jas. Blythe, Henry Toomer and Andrew Ronaldson, take such a list, and make return to this committee, or to the Secretary, as soon as possible. Also, a list of all the free mulattos and negroes in the said town.

The committee then adjourned till the next meeting.

Saturday, July 15, 1775.

At an occasional meeting of the committee; Cornelius Harnett, chairman, John Robeson, Wm. Wilkinson, John Forster, Wm. Campbell, Arch'd Maclaine, Wm. Purviance, Wm. Ewins, Timothy Bloodworth, James Blythe, Peter Mallett, Henry Toomer, James Geekie.

Resolved, unanimously, That a reinforcement of as many men as will voluntarily turn out, be immediately dispatched to join Colonel Howe who is now on his way to Fort Johnston and that it be recommended to the Captains of the Independent and Artillery companies in Wilmington, and the officers of several companies in this county, to muster their men, and immediately equip those who are willing to go on that service.

The committee then adjourned to the next meeting.

Thursday, July 20, 1775.

At a monthly meeting of the committee for the town of Wilmington, and county of New Hanover.

Cornelius Harnett, chairman, Francis Clayton, deputy chairman, Fred'k Jones, Sr., Alexander Lillington, Wm. Wilkinson, John Forster, Jno. Colvin, Jno. Hollingsworth, Thos. Devane, Jno. Devane, Henry Toomer, Jno. Ashe, Sam'l Ashe, James Geekie, Jno. Ancrum, James Moore, Wm. Purviance, Francis Brice, Adam Boyd, Archibald Maclaine, James Tate, Wm. Campbell, Andrew Ronaldson, Peter Mallette, Jno. Robeson, James Blythe, Sam. Swann, Wm. Jones, W. T., Wm. Jones, L. C., Joel Parish, Jas. Walker, Wm. Ewins, Thos. Bloodworth.

Visiting Members.

From Cumberland county.—Farquier Campbell, Rob. Cochran.

From Duplin county.—James Moore, Jno. James, Alex. Outlaw.

From Onslow county.—Jno. Ashe and Jno. Gibbs.

From Bladen county.—Thos. Robeson, Thos. Owen, Walter Gibson, Wm. Salter, James Council, Evan Ellis, Peter Robeson, Rob. Stuart, James Richardson, Jno. King, James White, Rob. Wells, Thomas Brown, Wm. Stuart.

Joseph Preston, being brought before the committee and examined, declared on oath, that it was a common report that John Collett, commander at Fort Johnson, had given encouragement to negroes to elope from their masters and promised to protect them.

The committee then adjourned to 7 o'clock to-morrow.

Friday, July 21st, 1775.

The committee met according to adjournment.

Present as before.

On motion ordered, That the Committee of Intelligence of this town, write to the committee of Cumberland and congratulate them on the favorable disposition of their committee and county, to support the common cause of America.

On motion, Resolved, That application be made to Mr. Samuel Campbell for the muskets he has in his possession, the property of the public, in order that they may be lodged with the secretary of this committee, to be distributed to those who may be in want of arms.

This committee having taken in consideration an act of the British Parliament for restraining the trade of the Colonies of New Jersey, Pennsylvania, the counties of Newcastle, Kent and Sussex on the Delaware, Maryland, Virginia and South Carolina, to Great Britain, Ireland and the British West Indies, which is to take place this day; it is

Resolved, unanimously, that the exception of this colony, and some others out of the said act, is a base and mean artifice, to seduce them into a desertion of the common cause of America.

Resolved, that we will not accept of the advantages insidiously thrown out by the said act, but will adhere strictly to such plans as have been, and shall be, entered into by the honorable Continental Congress; so as to keep up a perfect unanimity with our sister colonies.

The inhabitants of Poole (a seaport in the British Channel) having manifested themselves, not only inimical to America; but lost to every sense of honor and humanity, by petitioning Parliament to restrain the New England fisheries; by which iniquitous act, the virtuous inhabitants of those colonies, are cruelly deprived of the means of procuring a subsistence; and rendered almost dependent on the bounty of the neighbors; in testimony of our resentment of a conduct so injurious to our fellow citizens, and so disgraceful to human nature; we unanimously resolve, not to freight, or in any manner employ any shipping belonging to that town; and that we will not carry on any commercial intercourse with the selfish people of Poole.

Whereas, it appeared, upon incontestible evidence, that John Collett, commander of Fort Johnston, was preparing the said fort (under the auspices of Governor Martin) for the reception of a promised reinforcement, which was to be employed in reducing the good people in this province to a slavish submission to the will of a wicked and tyrannic minister, and for this diabolical purpose, had collected several abandoned profligates, whose crimes had rendered them unworthy of civil society; and that the said commander, had wantonly detained vessels, applying for bills of health, thereby defeating the salutary purposes for which the Fort had been established and continued, had threatened vengeance against magistrates, whose official opinion he chose to disapprove, had set at defiance the high sheriff of the county in the execution of his office, and treated the King's writs, when served on him for just debts, (which both as a soldier and a subject, it was his duty to obey) with the shameful contempt of wiping his b—k s—de with them, had with the most unparalled injustice, detained and embezzled a large quantity of goods, which having been wrecked near the fort, had the highest claim to his attention and care, for the benefit of the sufferers; in whose behalf, many and repeated applications had been legally made, in vain, to the said commander, had contrary to every principle of honor and honesty, most unwarrantably seized, by force, a quantity of corn, the private property of an individual; an act of robbery, the more inexcusable, as provisions were never withheld from him, whenever he would pay for them, had basely encouraged slaves from their masters, paid and employed them, and declared openly, that he would excite them to an insurrection; it also appeared that the said John Collett, had further declared, that, as soon as the expected reinforcements should arrive, the King's standard would be erected, and that, to it should be invited all those (as well slaves as others) who were base enough to take up arms against their country.

The Committee of New Hanover and Wilmington, having taken these things into consideration, judged it might be of the most pernicious consequences to the people at large, if the said John Collett should be suffered to remain in the fort, as he might thereby have opportunity of carrying his iniquitous schemes into execution. This opinion, having been communicated to the officers, and the committees of some neighboring counties, a great many volunteers were immediately collected; a party of whom reached Brunswick, when accounts were received, that the said commander had carried off all the small arms, ammunition and part of the artillery, (the property of this Province) together with his furniture, on board a transport, hired for that purpose, there to remain until the reinforcement should arrive, and then again take possession of the fort; the original design being thus frustrated, but the different detachments having met at Brunswick, about 500 men marched to the fort, and burnt and destroyed all the houses, &c., in and about the same; demolished, as far as they could, the back part of the fortification, and effectually dislodged that atrocious freebooter.

Resolved, therefore, that the thanks of the committee be given to the officers and soldiers who, with such ready alacrity, gave their attendance to effect a matter of so much real importance to the public.

The committee then adjourned to the next meeting.

Monday, July 31, 1775.

At an occasional meeting of the committee.

Present: Cornelius Harnett, chairman, Francis Clayton, deputy chairman, Henry Toomer, Wm. Purviance, James

Blythe, Wm. Ewins, Wm. Wilkinson, Jno. Forster, Tim. Bloodworth, Wm. Campbell, Jno. Ancrum, Peter Mallett, Andw. Ronaldson, Jno. DuBois, Adam Boyd.

The chairman presented to the committee, a letter from Mr. Rowan, inclosing one of the Governor's to a certain Lieu't Col. James Cotton; it was.

Resolved, unanimously, That the committee approve of Mr. Rowan's conduct; and that the committee of intelligence be requested to write to him on the subject.

Mr. Boyd read a letter from the Governor, requesting him to print an account of a late engagement at Bunker's Hill, between the King's troops and provincials; craved their opinion respecting the above application; it was

Resolved, unanimously, That he should acquaint the Governor, that the committee would not admit the separate publication in hand bills; but that if it was agreeable to him, it might be printed in the *Mercury*.

Whereas, we have learned from undoubted authority, that Governor Martin intends going into the back country, to collect a number of men for the purpose of disturbing the internal peace of this province.

Resolved, that the Governor's going into the back country may be of great prejudice to this province, as it is in all probability he intends kindling the flames of a civil war, and that the committees of the different counties should be advised of his intentions and requested to keep a strict lookout, and, if possible, arrest him in his progress.

The committee then adjourned to the next meeting.

Tuesday, August 8, 1775.

At an occasional meeting of the committee.

Present: Cornelius Harnett, chairman, Francis Clayton, deputy chairman, Arch'd McLaine, James Geekie, John Robeson, John DuBois, Francis Brice, Wm. Ewins, Samuel Collier, Timothy Bloodworth, John Hollingsworth, Sampson Moseley,

Thos. Nixon, John Campbell, Caleb Grainger, Andrew Ronaldson, Adam Boyd, William Purviance, A. Lillington, P. Mallett, James Tate, Samuel Ashe, John Forster, William Wilkinson, Wm. Campbell.

A letter from James Hepburn was received, with some others, and read to this committee, wherein he begs to be restored again to the favor of the public.

Ordered, that James Hepburn transmit to this committee, a deposition certified by a magistrate, respecting the matters with which he stands charged, a recantation of his conversation with James Clardy, and sign the Continental Association.

At an election held this day for additional delegates for this town and county, to represent them in general convention to be held at Hillsborough, on the 20th inst. Arch'd. Maclaine, esq., for the town, and Wm. Hooper, Alex. Lillington and James Moore, esq., for the county, were duly elected by the freeholders, as additional delegates, with Cornelius Harnett, esq. for the town, George Moore, John Ashe and Samuel Ashe, esqrs. for the county, chosen on a former election, to represent them in the aforesaid convention.

The committee then adjourned to the next meeting.

Wednesday, Aug. 9, 1775.

At an occasional meeting of the committee.

Present: Cornelius Harnett, chairman, Archibald Maclaine, John Robeson, James Geekie, John Forster, Adam Boyd, Peter Mallett, Francis Brice, Jno. DuBois, Tim. Bloodworth, Thos. Bloodworth, Henry Toomer, Jas. Blythe, Wm. Purviance, Jno. Ancrum, Jas. Tate.

Whereas, the late Continental Congress, in the fourth article of their association, for themselves and their constituents, agree that the earnest desire they had, not to injure their fellow subjects in Great Britain, Ireland and the West Indies, induced them to suspend a non-exportation, until the 10th day of September, 1775; at which time, if the said acts, and parts of acts of the British Parliament thereinafter mentioned, should not be repealed; they would not directly or indirectly export any commodity whatsoever, to Great Britain, Ireland or the West Indies, except rice, to Europe. And, whereas, information hath been made to the committee, that several merchants and traders, in the town of Wilmington, understand the said article, in this sense, that is to say, that if any ship or vessel should before the said 10th day of Sep., begin to load, time and liberty would be allowed to complete the loading, at any time, however, extended, after the said 10th day of September, which would be a flagrant infraction of the said Association.

Resolved, therefore, That no ship or vessel, on any pretence whatever, shall take on board any merchandise or commodities from and after the 10th day of September next; nor shall any person or persons presume to ship any goods, wares, or merchandise, on board of any ship or vessel, from and after the said 10th day of September, on pain of the displeasure of the public.

Friday, August 11th, 1775.

At an occasional meeting of the committee. Present: Cornelius Harnett, chairman, Arch'd Maclaine, Peter Mallet, Henry Toomer, Wm. Purviance, Adam Boyd, Thos. Devane, Timothy Bloodworth, Wm. Campbell, John Forster, James Geekie, Jno. DuBois, Wm. Wilkinson, Francis Brice, James Blythe, John Ancrum.

On application made by John Gifford, from the committee of Wake, for a supply of gunpowder.

Ordered, that the committee of intelligence write to the committee of Wake, and acquaint them of our inability to supply them with gunpowder at this time: that whenever we have any to spare they may depend on our assistance.

Whereas, this committee has transmitted to the committee of Cumberland, sundry papers that were thought necessary to be kept secret, and at the same time enclosed with them the opinion of this committee and the oath of secrecy, which this committee have reason to believe they have neglected, by which means the contents of the said papers have transpired:

Resolved therefore, that this committee can not for the future transmit to the committee of Cumberland, any papers of a secret nature, until we are satisfied that the oath of secrecy has been taken by that committee, and that the committee of intelligence write to them accordingly.

Resolved, That Messrs. John Robeson, Wm. Campbell, and Wm. Wilkinson, be appointed to collect and take into their possession, all carriage guns and swivels, whether the property of the public or of private persons, for which they are to give such sufficient receipts as are necessary.

Thursday, August 17, 1775.

At an occasional meeting of the committee, Present Francis Clayton Deputy Chairman, Wm. Campbell, John DuBois, Henry Toomer, Caleb Grainger, John Forster, Wm. Wilkinson, Wm. Ewans, James Blythe, Saml. Marshall, James Tate, William Purviance, John Ancrum, Peter Mallett, Francis Brice, Andrew Ronaldson.

On intelligence from Richard Quince, esq., concerning a quantity of gunpowder being sold by a negro in this town; on examination of the parties it appears that one Peter Brown must have been privy to this affair; and that a negro called Nicholas, was the negro who sold the powder.

Resolved, That the said Peter Brown shall give security for his appearance, when called on by this committee, when he produced William Miller, and Thomas Brown as his securities; and the said Peter Brown became bound for his appearance in the penal sum of £50, and each of his securities in the sum of £25, proc. money to be forfeited on failure of the said Brown's appearance when called upon by this committee.

Resolved, That the said negro (Nicholas) be sent to gaol till the examination of Sparrow.

Thursday afternoon, August 17, 1775.

At an occasional meeting of the committee. Present Francis Clayton Dep. Chairman, Wm. Campbell, John DuBois, Henry Toomer, Caleb Grainger, John Forster, Will. Wilkinson, Wm. Ewins, James Blythe, Samuel Marshall, James Tate, Peter Mallett, John Ancrum, Wm. Purviance, Francis Brice, Andrew Ronaldson.

A letter was produced from Richard Quince intimating some alarming information made in Brunswick, relative to the Governors wicked intentions. Resolved, that Mr. J. Ancrum and Mr. J. DuBois, wait on the committee at Brunswick to procure a certain account of that information that proves satisfactory to this committee—that a letter be wrote to the Brunswick Committee, informing them that Mr. Ancrum and Mr. DuBois were sent to get the account or information on oath, till which was done, this committee could not comply with the request of sending down men for the protection and safety of the inhabitants of Brunswick, as the intelligence from thence was so imperfect that it was impossible to act with propriety. The committee then adjourned.

Friday morning, August 18, 1775.

At an occasional meeting of the committee: Present Francis Clayton Dep. Chairman, Wm. Purviance, James Tate, Thos. Bloodworth, James Blythe, Timothy Bloodworth, Jno. Robeson, Andrew Ronaldson, Wm. Ewins, Wm. Wilkinson, John Forster, Wm. Campbell, James Walker, Peter Mallett, Francis Brice, Caleb Grainger, Henry Toomer.

Several letters were received that had been taken from an express, sent by his Excellency to the back country with dispatches: those of any importance were taken to the Congress by Col. James Moore.

A letter was read from the Governor to Dr. Cobham, desiring he would send down some particular medicines. Resolved,

That Dr. Cobham be desired not to send the medicines, which he readily agreed to on being called into committee. Mr. Samuel Campbell waited on this committee and produced an instrument of Writing, styled by the Governor a Proclamation: the said piece was read by Fran's Clayton after which it was ordered to be kept in the possession of the committee. The committee then adjourned.

Friday afternoon, 3 o'clock.

At an occasional meeting of the committee: present Francis Clayton, Dep. Chairman, Will. Purviance, James Tate, Thomas Bloodworth, James Blythe, And'r Rolandson, Timothy Bloodworth, John Robeson, Wm. Ewins, John DuBois, Will Wilkinson, John Forster, Wm. Campbell, James Walker, Peter Mallett, Francis Brice, Caleb Grainger, Henry Toomer, John Ancrum. On motion, Ordered, that Lt. Col. Cotton be sent for, and escorted here by a guard (for that purpose) who attended accordingly.

After his examination he was remanded to confinement. Mr. Williams, Sen'r—was then ordered in and attended—passed examination, and remanded back to confinement.

On motion, Ordered, that Mr. Clayton write to Bladen a letter of thanks to that committee for apprehending the above men.

The committee adjourned till 9 o'clock to-morrow morning.

Saturday Morning, 9 o'clock.

The committee met according to adjournment. Present Francis Clayton Deputy Chairman, John Forster, Peter Mallett, A. Ronaldson, James Blythe, Timothy Bloodworth, John Ancrum, Thomas Bloodworth, Wm. Campbell, John DuBois, Wm. Ewins, John Robeson, Francis Brice, James Walker, Wm. Wilkinson, Henry Toomer.

Mr. Cotton, Mr. Samuel Williams, and his son Jacob Williams, being ordered before the committee they all, and voluntarily of their own accord, signed the association entered into by the inhabitants of this country, and readily took an oath drawn up by the deputy chairman.

The said James Cotton, Sam'l and Jacob Williams, very cheerfully consented to go to the Congress, to be held at Hillsboro on the 21 inst., there to pass whatever examination may be thought proper by the said Congress.

Ordered, That they be attended by a few gentlemen who are going to Hillsborough: and that the Deputy Chairman write to the Congress, giving an account of these men since they were taken in Bladen county.

Captain Thomas Fitch appeared before the committee and swore on the Holy Evangelists of Almighty God, that the cargo he had on board the Schooner Swallow, was not intended, nor should not be landed, at any port except in some of the West India islands; and that he is to proceed to Hispaniola, and from thence to Jamaica.

Ordered that the certificate produced by Captain Fitch from Humphrey and Jewkes be filed among the committee papers.

Saturday evening, 8 o'clock.

At an occasional meeting of the committee; Present Francis Clayton Dep. Chairman, Wm. Wilkinson, James Blythe, Wm. Ewins, Henry Toomer, John DuBois, Jno. Forster, Francis Brice, Wm. Campbell, John Ancrum, Peter Mallett.

Ordered, That Mr. Cotton and the two Williams be allowed to go up to the convention by way of X Creek.

The committee then adjourned.

Monday, August 21, 1775.

At a meeting of the Committee; Present Francis Clayton Dep. Chairman, Wm. Purviance, Fred'k Jones, Sampson Moseley, Wm. Campbell, J. Hollingsworth, Sam'l Marshall, And'w Rolandson, Timothy Bloodworth, Thomas Nixon, W. Wilkinson, Henry Toomer, Jno. Forster, John DuBois, John Robeson, Francis Brice, Sam'l Swann, Peter Mallett, James Tate.

On motion made whether Captain Maclean, (who has shown himself inimical to the liberties of America,) should not in a limited time depart this provnce.

Resolved, That if Captain Maclean does not come into this committee and make a recantation of his sentiments in regard to America within 30 days from this date that he be ordered to depart this province.

October 6, 1775.

At an occasional meeting of the committee. Present Cornelius Harnett Chairman, Timothy Bloodworth, A. Lillington, John Devane, John Hollingsworth, James Moore, A. Rolandson, Wm. Wilkinson, Wm. Ewins, Wm. Campbell, Jno. Ancrum, Wm. Purviance, Adam Boyd, Caleb Grainger.

Whereas it appears to this committee that several vessels, landed and cleared out by the officers of His Majesty's customs, are still remaining in this river.

Resolved, That every vessel now in the river of Cape Fear loaded and cleared out as above (before the 10th day of Sept. last), do proceed on their respective voyages within ten days from this date.

It appears to this committee that Moses Buchanan is confined in the county gaol, by virtue of the writ served on him (since the 10th day of September last,) at the suit of Robert Bannerman contrary to a resolve of the Congress of this colony, lately held at Hillsborough, prohibiting the commencement of any civil suite without the consent of a committee.

Ordered, That in pursuance of such resolve the said Moses Buchanan be discharged from his confinement.

October 11, 1775.

At an occasional meeting of the Committee. Present, John Ancrum in the chair, A. Maclaine, James Geekie, John Forster, Wm. Ewins, P. Mallett, A. Rolandson, Andw. Boyd.

Col. James Moore having applied to this committee for 150 lbs. of gunpowder and 6 cwt. of lead or ball for the use of the troops under his command, ordered that the above quantity of ammunition be delivered to Col. Moore, on his order as he may have occasion for the same.

Mr. Daniel Southerland applied for leave to import a cargo of salt from the West Indies, whereupon the question being put this committee declined giving any opinion, and referred it to the committee of safety.

Monday, October 16, 1775.

At an occasional meeting of the committee: Present John Ancrum in the chair, A. Maclaine, P. Mallett, Wm. Ewans, F. Brice, J. Forster, Wm. Williamson, A. Rolandson, James Tate.

On application from Capt. McGill, of the sloop Ranger, for permission to clear out his sloop in ballast. Ordered, that Capt. McGill have leave to clear out for the port of New York only, and that he be allowed to take on board any quantity of deer skins he may choose. Grant paid 8s.

On application from Alex. Hostler, Ordered, that the paper imported in Capt. Weir's vessel, and now in the hands of Adam Boyd, be sold at vendue for the use of the Press only, or be immediately delivered to A. Hostler to be re-shipped.

Ordered, that Francis Brice be appointed secretary to this committee, during the absence of Thomas Craike.

Wilmington, Tuesday, October 17, 1775.

Present Jno. Ashe, Jno. Devane, Wm. Jones, Sr., Wm. Jones, Jr., Charles Hollingsworth, Timothy Bloodworth.

142   HISTORY OF NEW HANOVER COUNTY.

Ordered, That Francis Brice be appointed to keep the Poll for the election of delegates, and appointment of committeemen for the county.

At an election this day, agreeable to a Resolve of the late Congress of this Colony, for the appointment of Delegates to represent this town and county in Congress the ensuing year; Cornelius Harnett, Esqr., was duly elected as a delegate to represent this town; and Sam'l Ashe, John Ashe, Sampson Moseley, John Hollingsworth and John Devane, Esqr., were also duly elected to represent the county. The committee for the town and county were also nominated agreeable to a resolve of the said Congress.

Those for the town were, John Ancrum, Jas. Walker, Jno. Quince, Peter Mallett, Wm. Campbell, Sam. Campbell, Wm. Ewins, Henry Toomer, Jno. Slingsby, Wm. Wilkinson, John Forster, Jas. Geekie, John Robeson, Chas. Jewkes, Andrew Ronaldson.

Wednesday, October 25, 1775.

At an occasional meeting of the new committee. Present John Ancrum, Charles Jewkes, John Slingsby, Peter Mallett, Henry Toomer, Wm. Campbell, James Geekie, John Forster, Wm. Ewins.

The committee proceeded to choose a chairman and deputy chairman; the question being put, John Ancrum was chosen as chairman, and Jas. Walker, deputy chairman.

Samuel Campbell appeared, and declined serving as a committeeman, as it would be very inconvenient for him to attend. Andrew Ronaldson also declined serving, as he was not allowed to be a freeholder at the election, therefore, had no right to be a committeeman. The committee nominated, in their room, John DuBois and John Kirkwood, who being sent for readily agreed to serve in committee.

This committee then proceeded to appoint a Committee on Secrecy and Correspondence. John Ancrum, Jas. Walker, Wm.

Campbell, Charles Jewkes, John Slingsby, John DuBois, and Peter Mallett, were accordingly nominated.

On motion, Ordered, that the paper now in the hands of Adam Boyd, be sold to-morrow morning at 11 o'clock; that J. Slingsby, Wm. Campbell and Peter Mallett see that the same is sold. Also, Ordered, that one ream of paper be purchased for the use of this committee only.

Monday, October 30, 1775.

At an occasional meeting of the committee. Present John Ancrum, chairman, John Slingsby, John Forster, John Kirkwood, James Geekie, Wm. Wilkinson, John DuBois, Wm. Ewins, and Henry Toomer.

On motion ordered, that John Ancrum, John DuBois, John Kirkwood, and James Geekie, Wm. Wilkinson and William Campbell take a list of the inhabitants of Wilmington, agreeable to a resolve of the Congress of this Colony, lately held at Hillsborough; and that they make a return of the same at the next meeting of this committee.

Friday, November 3, 1775.

On application from Mr. John Hunt, the committee met. Present John Ancrum, chairman, Peter Mallett, John Slingsby, Wm. Wilkinson, John Forster, John DuBois, Wm. Ewins, Henry Toomer.

Mr. John Hunt came in, and produced two letters to his Excellency, recommending said Hunt as Register for Granville county; and the Rev. Mr. Wm. McKenzie as a clergyman for said county. On examination of John Hunt, on oath; found he had no other papers for the Governor; therefore,

Ordered, That Mr. John Hunt be allowed to go down to His Excellency on board the Crusier, to obtain such papers from the Governor that he may have occasion for, relative to the Register's Office; and that on his return he shall produce what papers he may receive from the Governor to this committee. Grant was paid.

On application from Mr. Peter Mallett, Ordered, That if Adam Boyd does not pay P. Mallett (on Monday next or before) for the paper sold some days ago, (as well as what paper A. Boyd has in his hands,) that P. Mallett have leave to dispose of the same on Tuesday next; or any time after, to such persons who may choose to purchase it.

Monday, November 13, 1775.

At an occasional meeting of the committee. Present: John Ancrum, chairman, Charles Jewkes, John Forster, James Geekie, Wm. Wilkinson, Henry Toomer, John Kirkwood.

Mr. Chairman produced a letter from Rich'd Quince, Esq., of Brunswick, purporting that a man of war and a ship with transports, (or troops) were arrived at Fort Johnston.

On reading the above letter, it was ordered, that Messrs. Forster, Mallett, Wilkinson and Jewkes, go round the town, and examine the arms that may be in each family; after reserving one gun for each white man that may be in the house, the remainder shall be valued by the above gentlemen, and a receipt given for them, mentioning their value. Those who have new guns to dispose of, shall be allowed three for one; (in order to obtain an immediate supply of arms on this immergent occasion) a receipt shall also be given for such guns on account of the public, and for the use of the first regiment under the command of Col. James Moore.

On application from Capt. John Walker, Ordered, that 56 pounds of gunpowder and 221 pounds of lead, be immediately delivered to Capt. Walker, to be sent to the Camps at Bernard's Creek, and that Captain Walker's receipt be taken for the same.

Wednesday, November 15th, 1775.

At an occasional meeting of the committee. Present: John Ancrum, chairman, Wm. Wilkinson, John DuBois, Henry Toomer, John Forster, Wm. Ewins, James Geekie, John Kirkwood, Charles Jewkes.

Mr. Timothy Bloodworth came in with a message from the county committee, desiring that both the committees should be united; and that this committee send a member to the next meeting of the county committee to acquaint them with the opinion of this committee relative to their uniting.

Resolved, That it is the opinion of this committee, that for the good order and safety of the county and town, a union should be effected between the two committees; Ordered, That all the members of this committee, attend at the next meeting of the county committee, to acquaint them with the opinion of this committee.

Ordered, That notice be given to the white male inhabitants to meet on Monday next, at 10 o'clock, in the forenoon, at the Court House, to form themselves into companies of militia, agreeable to a resolve of the Congress lately held at Hillsborough; and that it be recommended to the inhabitants to have the officers chosen to each respective company on the same day.

Thursday, 16, 1775.

Whereas, the committee inadvertently nominated John DuBois and John Kirkwood as members of this committee, in the room of Samuel Campbell and Andrew Ronaldson, who declined serving in committee, instead of giving notice to the Freeholders to choose other persons in their place; Resolved, that the said nomination be void, and that the order relative thereto be rescinded; and as many members have since declined serving.

Ordered, That the secretary issue notice thereof to the Freeholders, summoning them to meet at the Court House, to-morrow morning, at 10 o'clock, to appoint others in the place of those who declined.

Friday, November 17, 1775.

Agreeable to the notice of yesterday the Freeholders met at the Court House, and elected Cornelius Harnett, Arch'd Maclaine, John DuBois, John Dunbibin, John Kirkwood, and Herald Blackmore to serve in committee in place of James Walker, William Campbell, Samuel Campbell, Andrew Ronaldson, John Quince and John Robeson, who declined serving.

Saturday, November 18th, 1775.

Present: John Ancrum, Chairman, Cornelius Harnett, A. Maclaine, John Forster, Wm. Wilkinson, Henry Toomer, Charles Jewkes, Wm. Ewans, James Geekie, Peter Mallett.

Resolved, That no vessel whatever shall load any cargo, to any part of the world from this port, until further orders from this committee or some superior power.

Monday, November 20, 1775.

At an occasional meeting.

Present: John Ancrum, chairman, Cornelius Harnett, Wm. Wilkinson, Henry Toomer, Wm. Ewins, John DuBois, John Forster, James Geekie, John Kirkwood, Jona. Dunbibbin, Arch. Maclaine.

On motion William Wilkinson was chosen deputy chairman, in place of James Walker, who declined serving in committee.

A letter was produced from Rich'd Quince, Sr., of Brunswick, informing that the committee of that town were of opinion that a battery might be raised to defend the town; and requested that the cannon be sent from hence for that purpose.

Resolved, That the carriage guns be sent down, and delivered to Col. James Moore.

On application from Mr. Sam. Campbell, for leave to send down provisions for the cruiser man-of-war, Resolved, That (as the Commander of the Sloop hath fired a number of times on the troops under the command of Col. Moore, without their giving any provocation for such conduct) no provisions of any kind be sent down to the cruiser, or any other ship belonging to the navy, till further orders.

This Committee taking into consideration the danger with which the inhabitants on Cape Fear River are threatened by the King's Ships now in the harbor; and the avowed contempt and violation of justice, in the conduct of Governor Martin, who with the assistance of the said ships is endeavoring to carry off the artillery, the property of this Province, and the gift of his late Majesty of blessed memory, for our protection from foreign invasions; have

Resolved, That Messrs. John Forster, William Wilkinson and John Slingsby, or any one of them be impowered to procure necessary vessels, boats and chains to such part of the channel as they or any of them may think proper, to agree for the purchase of such boats and other materials as may be wanted; and to have them valued, that the owners may be reimbursed by the public. And it is further ordered that the said John Forster, &c., do consult the committee of Brunswick on this measure, and request their concurrence.

Ordered, That the Committee of Intelligence write to Col. Howe and the committee of Newbern, and inform them of the dangerous situation of the inhabitants of Cape Fear, and request an immediate supply of gunpowder to be sent by wagons or carts over land.

Friday, November 24, 1775.

At an occasional meeting of the committee.

Present: John Ancrum, chairman, Cornelius Harnett, H. Toomer, John Kirkwood, James Geekie, Arch'd Maclaine, Charles Jewkes, Wm. Ewins, John DuBois.

Ordered, That the Committee of Intelligence write to the Chairman of the county committee, requesting him to procure all the fire-arms he possibly can for the use of Provincial Regulars; as by information from Col. Moore, it is imagined that the men of war now at Fort Johnson, have an intention to attempt burning Brunswick, and afterwards proceed to this town.

Ordered, That the Committee of Intelligence, write to the committee of Safety for the district of Salisbury, informing them of the danger the inhabitants of the Cape Fear are in, from the ships of war, now in the harbor; and requesting them if they can do it with safety to themselves, to order down the troops stationed in that part of the Colony, armed as completely as possible.

Ordered, That the resolve of the committee, forbidding vessels to load in this Port, be delivered to Captain Batchelor, and that he be informed if he perseveres in loading his vessel, he will be treated as an enemy of American liberty.

Ordered, that Messrs. Samuel Ashe, Frederick Jones, Robert Shawe, Benjamin Stone, William Lord, William Hill, Richard Quince, junior, Richard Bradley, William Purviance and John Smith, be requested to attend in this town on the 29th day of November, instant, in order to value the houses, buildings and other improvements therein, that may be liable to be destroyed, and that they or any three of them, do value the same upon oath, and make a return thereof to this committee under their hands.

Ordered, that this committee purchase up what lead may be found in this town, that the same be run into balls of different sizes, as soon as possible, and that Samuel Hewitt be employed in making the same, as also cartridges; and that this committee also purchase what Salt Petre and Brimstone may be had.

This committee being informed that the above Samuel Hewitt has in his possession two 2 pound pieces: Ordered, that he produce the same to this committee, as soon as possible.

Thursday, December 7, 1775.

At an occasional meeting of the committee.

Present: John Ancrum, chairman, William Wilkinson, deputy chairman, Charles Jewkes, John DuBois, Will Ewins, John Slingsby, James Geekie, John Kirkwood, Jona. Dunbibbin, Archibald Maclaine.

On application from William Gibbs, for leave to charter a vessel in this River, to load with naval stores, that he has at Cape Lookout and Bogue, and intends to bring round here, if allowed by this committee, he having already obtained permission from the committee of Safety for the District of Newbern, to ship a quantity he had cast away on the 2d of September last. It is the opinion of this committee that should Mr. Gibbs charter Capt. Batchelder's vessel (or any other vessel) to load with naval stores, that the vessel shall not take said cargo on board in this river.

Ordered, that Messrs. Henry Young, Geo. Hooper, William Whitfield, Phillip Jones, David Girdwood, and Richard Rundle, be requested to join the gentlemen formerly chosen to value the houses, &c., in town, and that they be desired to meet for that purpose on Tuesday the 12th inst.

Tuesday, December 19th, 1775.

Present: John Ancrum, chairman, Will Wilkinson, deputy chairman, Archibald Maclaine, John Forster, James Geekie, John Kirkwood, William Ewans, Jona. Dunbibin.

Ordered, that Ralph Millar be immediately supplied with 25 lbs. of Salt Petre, 7 lbs. Brimstone, and a large mortar and pestle, to enable him to make Gunpowder, which he is to produce to this committee, and that he be also supplied with 20 yards of Osnaburgs and two small weights; that F. Brice shall procure the above articles, and have them sent up to John Nichols' Landing, in Bladen for said Millar.

Wednesday, Dec. 20, 1775.

Present: William Wilkinson, deputy chairman, Arch'd Maclaine, John Forster, Henry Toomer, Charles Jewkes, John Kirkwood, Wm. Ewins, Herold Blackmore, Jona. Dunbibin.

On application made by Jona. Dix and David Thompson, of the Massachusetts and Rhode Island government, for a pass to travel to their respective families; as the said Dix and Thompson have not given a satisfactory account to this Committee; and as there are some circumstances that make them appear inimical to the American cause:

Ordered, That the said J. Dix and David Thompson be put under guard of Captain Dixon's Company, till inquiry shall be made about them; and an order of this committee shall be their releasement.

Friday, December 22d, 1775.

Present: Wm. Wilkinson, deputy chairman, Arch'd Maclaine, John Forster, Henry Toomer, Charles Jewkes, John Kirkwood, Wm. Ewins, John DuBois, James Geekie.

On examination of Jona. Dix and David Thompson (who were put under a guard on the 20th inst:—also, the papers they had in their possession (by which nothing could be found to prove them our enemies,) and their readiness to take and sign an oath administered by the chairman, declaring themselves friends to America; therefore,

Ordered, That the said Jonathan Dix and David Thompson be immediately released, and that a copy of the oath taken by them be delivered by the Secretary to enable them to pursue their journey without any further hindrence.

Tuesday, January 2, 1776.

Present: John Ancrum, chairman, Wm. Wilkinson, deputy chairman, John Forster, H. Blackmore, Will Ewins, James Geekie, John DuBois, Henry Toomer, Jona. Dunbibin.

This committee having received a letter from the county committee, requesting the attendance of this committee at the Bridge this day; Ordered, that the chairman of this committee and Herold Blackmore attend the county committee. Captain Batchelder applied for leave to clear out his Brig in ballast, for New York.

Resolved, that no vessel, whatever, in this port, clear out for any other port, until further orders from this committee or a superior power, and that Captain Batchelder be served with a copy of this order.

Friday, January 5, 1776.

At a meeting of the committee.

Present: John Ancrum, chairman, Wm. Wilkinson, deputy chairman, A. Maclaine, John Forster, Wm. Ewins, Jona. Dunbibin, Henry Toomer, John DuBois, James Geekie, John Kirkwood, H. Blackmore.

The trade of this port depending so much upon good pilots, and the ships of war in the harbor having already one or more of the branch pilots in their custody; and the captain of the Scorpion exacted from Thomas Bridges (another of the said pilots), his parole of honor to return on board the said ship, with an intention, as it is conjectured, not only to deprive the good people of this colony, of all benefits of trade, but to pilot our enemies up the river when it shall be thought expedient to destroy the property of the inhabitants. It is the opinion of this committee, that all the pilots of this river, be immediately secured, and that Col. Moore be requested to take them into his custody; and it is

Resolved, That as soon as the said pilots shall be safely secured that notice be given to the captain of the Scorpion, that the said Thomas Bridges is detained by order of the committee.

Ordered, That the two companies of Militia of this town, appear on the usual place of parading, properly armed and accoutred on next Monday week, as well as every other inhabitant that has not drawn in either of the said companies, and that they do draw before the above day, and that the test prescribed by the Provincial Council be signed.

Ordered, That Messrs. Wilkinson and Toomer provide a house in this town as an additional barrack for the Regulars under the command of Col. Moore, to be appropriated to the use of an hospital, and that a nurse be provided to take care of the sick.

Saturday, January 6, 1776.

At a meeting of the Committee. Present: John Ancrum chairman, W. Wilkinson, Deputy Chairman, A. Maclains, John Forster, Will. Ewans, John Kirkwood, John DuBois, James Geekie, Herold Blackmore.

Mr. W. Campbell came into committee and presented a letter from the Governor, requesting Mr. Campbell to send down two or three barrels of flour, a tub of butter, and some vegetables

Ordered, That Mr. Campbell have leave to send down two or three barrels of flour, a tub of butter, and some vegetables for His Excellency.

A. Maclaine produced a letter from the Governor to Capt. Maclean ordering him as a half pay officer, to embark for England, and Capt. Maclean was of opinion, that should he wait on his Excellency, he might obtain leave to continue in this Province some time longer.

Resolved, that Capt. Maclean shall not have leave to wait on the Governor, but he may write to the Governor, and that he shall show the letter to this committee, pursuant to a resolve of the Provincial Council.

Ordered, that the custom house officers do not clear out any vessels from this port hereafter, without leave from this committee, or some superior power and that the officers be served with this order.

Pursuant to an order of this committee, empowering certain

persons therein named, or any three of them, to value the houses, buildings, and enclosure in the town of Wilmington; a paper has been returned by seven of the said, purporting to be a valuation of the buildings, &c., in the said town; but as it appears that several of the said houses and buildings have been omitted; that many of the fixtures, particularly those in the still house of Harnett and Washington, have been totally overlooked; and the said valuers declared that they did not include the fences and inclosures in their valuation; this committee have

Resolved, That the said valuation is incomplete, inasmuch that this order has not been complied with; and it is further

Resolved, That John Cheeseborough, Andrew Ronaldson, James Blythe, George Jacobs, Malatia Hamilton, Wm. Purviance and Henry Button, (or any three of them), be empowered to value all of the said houses, buildings and enclosures in the said town, on oath: and that they be sworn before they enter upon the said business; and that they value the houses of C. Harnett, Esq., above the town, and those of Wm. Hooper, Esq., and the late Dr. Green below.

Tuesday, January 9, 1776.

At a meeting of this Committee.

Present: Wm. Wilkinson, deputy chairman, Cornelius Harnett, A. Maclaine, Jno. Forster, John Kirkwood, Will Ewans, H. Blackmore, Jona. Dunbibbin.

Resolved, that Jacob Phelps, one of the pilots in this river, be employed with his boat, to carry freight and passengers between Wilmington and Brunswick, and no further, without permission; and that the said J. Phelps do not presume to take any passengers or freight, without leave of one of the two committee of the said towns, or the commanding officers of the forces at Brunswick or Wilmington; and it is recommended to the people in general, that they employ the said Jacob Phelps' boat only, as a passage boat; and it is further Resolved, that no other persons, but such as the said Phelps may employ, shall have liberty to carry any freight or passengers to Brunswick, without the leave of this committee, or the commanding officer at Wilmington, to the end that such persons as may have inimical designs against the country, may be prevented from carrying intelligence to the Governor or Ships of War.

Resolved, that Jonathan Swann, another of the pilots, have liberty to remove with his family from his usual place of residence, about two or three miles back; that Benjamin Bill may be employed, if he thinks proper, on Board the Provincial Ship, but that he shall not have liberty to go to his usual place of residence, and that Thomas Galloway continue at some convenient place near the New Inlet, in order to be ready to pilot in any vessels which may be allowed to trade in this province, and that it be recommended to the Provincial Council and Committee of Safety for Wilmington district, to make an adequate allowance to the said Thomas Galloway toward the maintenance of his family.

Ordered, That Mr. John Forster, receive all the Salt Petre, Lead and Brimstone, in Wilmington, that he give receipts for the same. And that 4s. per lb. be allowed for all salt petre.

Saturday, January 12th, 1776.

Present: John Ancrum, chairman, A. Maclaine, John Forster, Jno. Kirkwood, Wm. Ewins, John Slingsby, J. Dunbibbin, John DuBois, James Geekie, Henry Toomer.

Ordered, That Dr. Geekie supply the following articles for the use of the Hospital, that he be repaid by this committee; a middle size pot, a small ditto, 2 skillets, a water jug, 2 pint mugs, 4 pint bowls, 2 large tea pots, 2 jardens, one half dozen pewter spoons.

Ordered, That the chairman write to Ralph Millar, requesting his attendance on this committee, and informing him, that they are willing to allow him 10s. per day for himself (he finding charcoal and making 20 lbs. powder per day; that he attend as soon as possible to enter into an agreement for that purpose and take the negroes into his possession.

Monday, January 15, 1776.

At a meeting of the committee:
Present: John Ancrum, chairman, Wm. Wilkinson, deputy chairman, A. Maclaine, Jno. Forster, H. Blackmore, Henry Toomer, Jas. Geekie, Jno. Slingsby, Jno. Kirkwood, Wm. Ewans.

A paper writing, containing two sheets signed, a Lawyer, and addressed *"To those who have a true sense of distributive justice and untrammeled liberty, residents of the borough of Wilmington,"* having been produced by the chairman, who found it put up to public view under the Court House, and it having been acknowledged by a certain William Green to be his hand writing, and the said Will. Green having made oath that he received the writing from which it was copied from Dr. Fallon, returned the original as well as the copy, and the said Dr. Fallon, in person, having justified the said papers: It is therefore, Resolved, that the said Dr. Fallon appears to this committee to be the author and publisher of the said paper.

Resolved, That the said paper contains many false and scandalous reflections on this committee, tending to inflame the minds of the people: to create divisions and dissentions amongst us by destroying that unanimity so essentially necessary to our mutual defence; and also containing an illiberal and groundless charge against a respectable gentleman deservedly high in office in this colony:

Resolved, also, that the said Dr. Fallon be kept in close custody, until he give security for his good behavior for and during the space of six months, in the sum of £500, proclamation money. And the said Dr. Fallon having refused to give such security, was ordered into custody.

Tuesday, January 16, 1776.

Present: John Ancrum, chairman, Wm. Wilkinson, deputy chairman, Arch'd Maclaine, John Forster, Herald Blackmore, Henry Toomer, John Slingsby, James Geekie, Wm. Ewans, John Kirkwood.

At a meeting of the committee:

Whereas, the Continental Congress, on the 1st day of November last, "Resolved, that New York, the lower counties on Delaware, North Carolina, and Georgia, ought not to avail themselves of the benefit allowed to them by the late restraining act, and therefore, that no person should apply at the custom house in those Colonies for clearances of other documents, which other Colonies are deprived of by said restraining act, for securing the navigation of vessels with cargoes from their Ports." It is, therefore,

Resolved, That no person, whatever, do presume to apply to the Custom house for clearances, without first obtaining leave from this or some other Committee for that purpose; and that this Resolve be made public, and a copy delivered to the officers of the Customs.

Resolved, that the resolution of this committee, passed the 6th inst., ordering the Custom-house officers not to clear out vessels without leave be rescinded.

Captain Alexander Maclean having gone down to the ship Cruiser, and been with the Governor, contrary to a resolve of the Provincial council, and also, an order of this committee.

Resolved, therefore, that he, the said Alexander Maclean be sent for, to come before this committee, to answer such breach aforesaid, and give security for his good behavior; which he has accordingly done, himself, James Walker and Arch'd Maclaine, in the sum of five hundred pounds proclamation money, for six months, if he continues in the Province so long.

Ordered, that permission be granted to Captain Butterfield to clear out his schooner in ballast only. Also, to Captain Batchelder to clear his brig out, he having nothing on board but ballast and necessary sea stores. Captain Batchelder also had leave to send a letter to the Governor, desiring to know if his vessel would be prevented from going out of this river.

Ordered, that William Wilkinson be appointed to receive all the Salt Petre, brimstone and lead, in the room of John Forster, who was appointed on the 9th inst., for that purpose, and that Mr. Wilkinson give receipts for the same.

Messrs. Forster and Geekie having called on Dr. Fallon to know if he intended to give security required by the committee, they reported to this committee that Dr. Fallon refused to give any security.

The committee adjourned to 5 o'clock this evening.

Tuesday evening, 5 o'clock.

The committee met according to adjournment.

Present: John Ancrum, chairman, Wm. Wilkinson, deputy chairman, Henry Toomer, H. Blackmore, Jno. Forster, Jona. Dunbibbin, James Geekie, Arch'd Maclaine, Jno. Slingsby, Wm. Ewins, John Kirkwood.

Resolved, that Dr. Fallon be continued under guard for the present time, and that Colonel Moore be requested to refuse admittance to any person, but such as he or the officer on guard may think proper; and that Dr. Fallon be not precluded from the use of pen, ink, and paper, but that when the officer on guard may think he has any letters to send out, and requests admittance for any particular person, such person may be admitted for so long a time as the officer may think proper, but that such person be carefully searched on his departure, and any letters that may be found upon him, to be carried to the commanding officer.

The committee adjourned.

Wednesday, January 17, 1776.

At a meeting of the committee:

Present: John Ancrum, chairman, Wm. Wilkinson, deputy

chairman, Arch'd Maclaine, Cornelius Harnett, Herold Blackmore, Jona Dunbibbin, John Kirkwood, Henry Toomer, John Slingsby, John DuBois.

Col. Moore having requested of this committee to furnish him with 50 stand of arms.

On motion, ordered that John Ancrum chairman, Wm. Wilkinson, John DuBois, and Jona. Dunbibin be requested to call respectively on the inhabitants of this town to-morrow, and borrow from them such guns as they can spare, to supply Col. Moore, as soon as possible with the number of guns he wants—they having such guns valued, and giving proper receipts for them to the owners.

Col. Moore having informed this committee that he looks upon Dr. Fallon to be an insinuating and dangerous person among the soldiers, and that he can not, without injuring the common cause, and running the risk of the public safety, any longer keep the said Fallon in the Guard House.

Resolved, That he, the said Dr. Fallon be committed to the common jail to-morrow morning, at eleven o'clock, there to remain until he makes a full concession for his offences to the public, and asks pardon of this committee for the repeated insults which he has in person offered.

Resolved, That Col. Moore be requested to order a Guard to attend near the jail and to give strict orders that the soldiers shall not converse with Dr. Fallon, that no person be admitted to speak to him but by leave of the officer on Guard, and that no letter or writing be suffered to be sent out by the Doctor without the inspection of such officer.

The committee then adjourned.

Thursday, January 18, 1776.

At a meeting of the committee.

Present: Wm. Wilkinson, deputy chairman, Henry Toomer, John Slingsby, John Forster, Arch'd Maclaine, James Geekie, Wm. Ewins, Jona. Dunbibin.

A letter from John Ashe, Esq., to Dr. Fallon, requesting the Doctor to attend his family, being laid before this committee, in answer thereto, Resolved, that a copy of the Resolves of this Committee relative to Dr. Fallon, be inclosed by the Secretary to Col. Ashe.

The committee adjourned.

Saturday, January 20, 1776.

At a meeting of the committee: Present John Ancrum, Chairman, Wm. Wilkinson, Dep. Chairman, Henry Toomer, John Forster, Arch'd Maclaine, John DuBois, James Geekie, John Kirkwood, Herold Blackmore:

On the application of William Gause, and others, in behalf of themselves and the inhabitants of Challotte (Shalotte) and Lockwoods Folly, setting forth their apprehensions of danger from the people of Waggamaw, and requesting of this committee a small supply of powder, to enable them to act in their own defence in case they should be attacked.

Ordered, that 20 lbs. of Gunpowder be supplied to William Gause from the stock of this Committee, for the use of the inhabitants of Lockwoods Folly and Shallotte, when the said Gause applies for the same.

Whereas, this committee on the 17th inst., issued a Mittimus to the Sheriff of New Hanover Co., requiring the said Sheriff and the keeper of the jail, safely to keep the body of James Fallon, until he should give sufficient security for his good behavior to the public, for the space of six months, in the sum of £500 proc. money; and until he should make a full concession for his offences to the public, and ask pardon of this Committee for the repeated insults which he has in person offered, and whereas it appears to this committee that the prison door has been kept open and all such persons as applied for admission to Dr. Fallon have had liberty to enter and the said Dr. Fallon has been permitted to write letters and send them out without any inspection, altho in one of these letters to the Sheriff he continues to repeat and justify his offences and as the intention of imprisoning the said Dr. Fallon was to prevent him from the future from disturbing the peace of society, this committee have Resolved, That the Sheriff and Jailor give strict orders that no person be admitted to Dr. Fallon (except in case of sickness) but a servant to carry his necessaries and keep his department clean, and that the said Fallon shall not be suffered to send out any letters or writings but such as may be approved by this committee or the commanding officer of the forces, and that the prison door be kept locked. Ordered that a copy of the above be sent to the Sheriff.

Resolved that a resolve on the 18th inst to send copies of the proceedings of this committee to John Ashe, Esq., be rescinded.

Saturday night, 9 o'clock.

At a meeting of the committee: Present John Ancrum, Chairman, Wm. Wilkinson, Dep. Chairman, John Forster, Herald Blackmore, John Kirkwood, Dr. Geekie, Arch'd Maclaine, John DuBois, Wm. Ewins, Henry Toomer:

Resolved, That it be recommended to the Commanding officers of the militia in Wilmington to warn their companies to be ready at the Court House to-night completely accoutered at the beat of the drum.

Monday, January 22, 1776.

At a meeting of the committee; Present Wm. Wilkinson Deputy Chairman, John Forster, James Geekie, Wm. Ewins, John Kirkwood, Henry Toomer, Jona Dunbibbin.

Dr. Fallon having applied by letter to the Chairman of this committee for a copy of a paper writing signed "A Lawyer," and the proceedings of the committee against him, Ordered that the Secretary supply Dr. Fallon with a copy of the proceedings of this committee against him as author of a certain paper signed "A Lawyer," but not with a copy of the said paper. The committee adjourned.

Saturday, January 27, 1776.

At a meeting of the committee: Present John Ancrum Chairman, William Wilkinson, Dep. Chairman, John Forster, Arch'd Maclaine, John Kirkwood, Wm. Ewins, James Geekie, Herold Blackmore, Jona. Dunbibbin, John DuBois.

The Governor having summoned his Majesty's Council to attend him on board the Scorpion, Sloop of War, and several of his Majesty's Council being in this town on their way to attend on the Governor agreeable to said summons: Resolved that this committee are bound by a resolve of the Provincial Congress to prevent any person from waiting on Governor Martin, and particularly at this present time this committee can not consistent with the safety of the country permit his Majesty's Council to attend the Governor, and the Chairman is ordered to respectfully..........to each of the Council who may be in town and acquaint them with this resolve.

A letter from Capt Parry, commander of the cruiser, to Captain Bachelder informing him he would give him leave to pass with his vessel provided he brought down the provisions demanded from Mr. Campbell; Thereupon, Resolved, that the requisition of Captain Parry is an insult to this Committee, and for the future, if any provisions are suffered to go down to the man of war they shall be sent down in small boats as usual.

The Committee adjourned.

Saturday, Jan'y 28, 1776.

At a meeting of the Committee:

Capt. Walker informed this Committee that he had in custody, under a Guard, Mr. William Mactier, who was, about 10 o'clock last night, with three other persons going to Brunswick in a boat, that Mr. Mactier refused to comply with his requisition in giving his word of honor that he would not go further than Brunswick, without applying to Col. Moore; and Mr. Mactier being brought before the committee, and alleging that he had leave from some of the members thereof, and it appearing that no leave had been granted:

Resolved, That Captain Walker has done his duty in taking Mr. Mactier into custody, and keeping him under a Guard.

Resolved, Also (Mactier having declined for the present to sign the test recommended by the Provincial Congress) that he shall not leave to go down the river on any pretence whatever, until he satisfies this Committee that he is a friend to the American cause, and enter into such obligation as may be thought necessary.

Resolved, That Captain Walker discharge Mr. Mactier from the Guard.

Wednesday, January 31, 1776.

At a meeting of the Committee.

Present: John Ancrum Chairman, Wm. Wilkinson Deputy Chairman, John Forster, Dr. Geekie, Arch'd Maclaine, Henry Toomer, Jona. Dunbibbin, Wm. Ewans, John Kirkwood, John DuBois.

Major Clark having applied to this committee for 2 dozen spades, to finish the entrenchments begun below the town of Wilmington:

Ordered, that Cap Clark may purchase 2 dozen spades and give receipts for the same, to be paid by a warrant from the Provincial Council on the Treasury.

Whereas a former order passed in this committee for Mr. Hewitt to be employed to make cartridges.

Ordered, that Mr. Hewitt be immediately set to work to make cartridges, and be allowed one dollar per day, when employed in that service, till a further agreement with him, and that he be supplied with paper, &c., for that purpose, and that

Mr. Dunbibin purchase and give receipts for the same in the name of the committee.

The committee adjourned.

Friday, February 2, 1776.

At a meeting of the committee. Present: John Ancrum chairman, John Forster, Wm. Ewins, John Kirkwood, Henry Toomer, John DuBois, James Geekie, Jona. Dunbibbin, Herold Blackmore, John Slingsby.

Information having been made to this committee, that a certain —— Mixon, who lives on the Sound near to Hasell's, goes frequently on board the Man of War, and that John Porter, a miller to Mr. J. Robeson, can inform this committee particularly of Mr. Mixon's conduct.

Ordered that the chairman, Capt. Forster, and John Slingsby be appointed to examine John Porter and if any proof should appear against the said Mixon, acting inimical to the American cause, or going on board the Man of War, they are to apply to the Commanding officer in town to take him in custody.

Whereas, a former Resolve of this Committee passed requesting all persons who had not signed the test, recommended by the Provincial Council, to sign the same, and as many persons have neglected to comply with such request, it is, therefore

Resolved, That James Grant call on all those who have not signed and tender them the test, and such persons as refuse to sign, he is to make a return of their names to this Committee.

The Committee adjourned.

Monday, February 5, 1776.

At a meeting of the committee. Present: John Ancrum Chairman, Wm. Wilkinson, Deputy Chairman, John Forster, Jno. Slingsby, Jno. DuBois, John Kirkwood, Jona. Dunbibbin,

Henry Toomer, Wm. Ewins, Arch'd Maclaine, Herold Blackmore.

Mr. Nash presented to the chairman, a letter from Governor Martin to Maurice Moore, Esq., in answer to one the committee permitted him to send to the Governor—which was read in Committee, and returned to Mr. Nash.

A letter from the Governor to the Council was also read in answer to theirs read in Committee 28th January.

Col. Moore having informed this Committee that the Men of War, lying at Fort Johnston, had committed hostilities on the Continental Troops under his command, by firing on them at the said Fort; and as the Committee of Safety passed a Resolve that the "Cruizer," sloop of war, might be supplied with provision from time to time, so long as she did not commit hostilities on the persons or properties of the good people of this Province.

Resolved, That the ships of war now lying in this river, have actually committed hostilities against the inhabitants of this Province, and therefore, this Committee in obedience to the said resolve of the Committee of safety, can not suffer any more provision to go down to the Men of War, for the future.

Ordered, that a copy of the above resolve be delivered to the agent for supplying the stationed ship in this Port.

Dr. Fallon, by letter, to the chairman, having signified an intention to come under recognizance to the public for his good behavior:

Ordered, that Arch'd Maclaine, Captain Blackmore, Dr. Geekie and John Slingsby, be appointed to make out a form of recognizance for Dr. Fallon to sign, and that he be served with a copy.

The Committee adjourned.

February 9, 1776.

At a meeting of the committee: Present John Ancrum chairman, Wm. Wilkinson, Deputy chairman, Wm. Ewins, John DuBois, Cornelius Harnett, Herold Blackmore, John Kirkwood, Jona. Dunbibbin, Henry Toomer.

I, A. B. do free and voluntarily swear, that in my opinion and sincere belief, neither the Parliament of Great Britain, nor any member or constituent branch thereof, have a right to impose taxes upon the American colonies, to regulate the internal policies thereof, and that all attempts by fraud or force to establish and exercise such claims and powers are violations of the peace and security of the people, and ought to be resisted to the utmost; and that the people of this Colony singly and collectively are bound by the acts of the Continental and Provincial Congress, because in both they are freely represented by persons chosen by themselves; and I do solemnly swear to support, maintain and defend all and every the acts, resolutions and regulations of the said Continental and Provincial Congresses, to the utmost of my power and abilities—So help me God.

The Committee took the above oath, and Resolved that the Captains of the two Companies shall muster their men immediately, and tender the same to every man in Wilmington, without exception, and whoever shall refuse or decline voluntarily to take the s'd Oath, shall by the Militia Officers aforesaid, be disarmed as inimical to the liberties of America.

CHAPTER V

BURNING OF FORT JOHNSTON AND EXPULSION OF GOVERNOR MARTIN—VIGILANCE OF THE WILMINGTON COMMITTEE—MOVEMENT OF SCOTCH HIGHLANDERS—BATTLE OF MOORE'S CREEK—COLONEL MOORE'S REPORT—LETTER OF COLONEL PURVIANCE.

Prior to the beginning of 1775, the excitement throughout the Province had increased to a great height, and when the Mecklenburg proceedings in May took place it burst into a blaze of enthusiasm, although the still lingering desire to be reconciled to Great Britain, if possible, and the fear of too great haste in precipitating a conflict, restrained and embarrassed the more conservative and timid spirits.

But among the people of the lower Cape Fear, the determination to "begin business" was soon manifested,* and the Committee at Wilmington early in July sent word to those in other counties, that they proposed to take the fort at the mouth of the river, whereupon volunteers began to assemble, and on the 15th of July, Col. Robert Howe, of Brunswick County, and on the 16th Col. John Ashe, of New Hanover, started with detachments for the fort, the two numbering about five hundred men, and meeting at the town of Brunswick; but before they reached the fort, the commanding officer, Captain Collet, after removing his arms, ammunition and other supplies to a transport lying in the river, joined Governor Martin, (who had fled from New Bern) on the sloop of war "Cruizer," then in the harbor, from the deck of which, on the night of the 18th they witnessed the burning of the fort to which the troops had set fire. This was the opening scene of actual war in North Carolina.

The people of Bladen County, on hearing of this movement,

---
* See proceedings of Safety Committee, June 20 and July 21.

Moore's Creek Battle Ground — the Brave Scotch Highlanders

Erected in 1907 to the Heroic Women of Cape Fear Section, 1775-1781

Moore's Creek Bridge Original Monument, Erected 1

assembled immediately, and about three hundred of them met Ashe and Howe when returning from the fort.*

Being nearer to the Governor's place of refuge than their compatriots, the Wilmington Committee could keep a more vigilant watch upon his movements and learn more of his designs. They soon discovered that he strongly desired, and intended, if possible, to get into the interior and take personal command of the army of Loyalists, particularly the Scotch Highlanders, of whom he asked the King to appoint him commander. His request was not granted, and it was fortunate for him that it was not, for, although a lieutenant-colonel in the British service and said to be a very competent officer, he would have met the fate which General McDonald met at Moore's Creek and landed in jail as he did, or been killed like poor McLeod if he had undertaken to lead the assault as he did. It is more than probable, however, that if he had received the appointment he would never have reached his friends, for the ever vigilant Wilmington Committee kept the other committees informed of his aims, and they were ready to arrest and imprison him on sight. The only army experience the Governor ever got during the Revolution was as a guest of Lord Cornwallis in South Carolina, and later of Major Craig in one of his raids out of Wilmington in 1781.†

Governor Martin remained on the "Cruizer," as he dared not make his appearance ashore, and from this, his new and only home in America, issued pamphlets to the Loyalists which were circulated by secret agents. He had been expecting for some time to receive help, and at last, in November, he was notified that seven British regiments were on the way to him, but disappointment again awaited him, for the expected aid did

---

* Colonial Records, X, 114-115. Governor Martin so hated Howe that, in a letter dated two days before the burning of the fort and addressed to the Earl of Dartmouth, he thus spoke of him: "Robert Howes is commonly called Howe, he having impudently assumed that name for some years past in affectation of the noble family that bears it, whose least eminent virtues have ever been far beyond his imitation."—*Colonial Records*, X, 98.

† President Swain, in his "lecture on the Invasion of North Carolina in 1776," says that Governor Martin not only suggested that campaign "but that the entire system of operations for the reduction of North Carolina until the retirement of Cornwallis in May, 1781, was prosecuted to some extent under his immediate supervision."

not arrive until too late for the movements he was contemplating, and indeed not until after the glorious victory of Moore's Creek Bridge had entirely destroyed all hope of overrunning and subduing North Carolina.

The Revolution had now actually begun in earnest, Howe's expedition to Virginia in November and an expedition to South Carolina in December under Rutherford, Polk, Martin and others, having been successful, and the spirit of the patriots was exultant.

On the 5th of February, 1776, the movement of the Tories, for which the Governor had impatiently waited, began, and they marched to Cross Creek (Fayetteville) under command of General McDonald. On the 9th the news of this movement reached Wilmington, and about the same time was received elsewhere. Its effect was electrical. At Wilmington Col. James Moore, who, at the session of the Provincial Congress at Hillsborough in the previous August, had been appointed Colonel of the first regiment, Continental Line, Howe being appointed Colonel of the second, immediately ordered his regiment to get ready to move against McDonald, and, after three or four days of continuous hard labor in preparation, began his march with his regiment and a field battery consisting of five guns. He was joined as he passed through Bladen by a part of the militia of that county and reached, took possession of, and fortified Rockfish Bridge, seven miles east of Cross Creek, on the 15th. On the 19th he was joined by Colonel Alexander Lillington, with one hundred and fifty of the Wilmington Minute Men, and Colonel Kenan, with about one hundred of the volunteer independent rangers, making his command number about one thousand. McDonald's army numbered about fifteen hundred, and with these he marched on the 20th to within four miles of Moore's position, and sent a letter with Governor Martin's proclamation offering pardon to Moore and his command if they would surrender and take the oath of allegiance. Moore, knowing that Col. Alex. Martin and Colonel Thackston were approaching the rear of McDonald with troops from the up-country, and that Colonel

Caswell was coming from the east with eight hundred men,
sent a reply that he would answer definitely the next day, his
purpose being to give Martin and Thackston time to get into
position to cut off his retreat, when he intended to move out
and attack McDonald in front and rear. McDonald's men had
already begun to desert, two companies having left in a body
on the night of the 20th, just at the time that McDonald,
learning of Caswell's coming, had commenced to escape, which
he did that night and next morning by crossing the river at
Campbellton with his whole force, and after sinking and destroying all the boats, taking the shortest road to Negro Head
Point, opposite to Wilmington.

On discovering the movement as soon as it was made, Moore
had the first opportunity of his brief but brilliant career to
exhibit his qualities as a military commander—qualities which
caused his immediate promotion to the rank of Brigadier General (March 13th) and within a year secured for him the command of the whole Southern department. His report to the
President of the Provincial Council, Cornelius Harnett—the
Council being then in session at New Bern—recites the facts as
we have given them up to this movement of McDonald, and
then continues in the following words:

"I then dispatched an express to Colonel Caswell, who was on his
march to join us with about eight hundred men, and directed him to
return and take possession of Corbett's Ferry over Black River, and
by every means to obstruct, harass and distress them in their march.
At the same time I directed Colonel Martin and Colonel Thackston to
take possession of Cross Creek in order to prevent their return that
way. Colonel Lillington and Colonel Ashe I ordered by a forced march
to endeavor, if possible, to reinforce Colonel Caswell; but if that could
not be effected to take possession of Moore's Creek Bridge while I proceeded back with the remainder of our army to cross the Northwest
at Elizabethtown so as either to meet them on their way to Corbett's
Ferry, or fall in their rear and surrender them there. On the 23rd I
crossed the river at Elizabethtown, where I was compelled to wait for a
supply of provisions until the 24th at night, having learned that
Colonel Caswell was almost entirely without. Just when I was prepared to march I received an express from Colonel Caswell, informing

me that the Tories had raised a flat which had been sunk in Black River about five miles above him, and by erecting a bridge had passed it with the whole army. I then determined as a last expedient to proceed immediately in boats down the NorthWest River to Dollerson's Landing, about sixty miles, and to take possession of Moore's Creek Bridge, about ten miles from there; at the same time acquainting Colonel Caswell of my intentions, and recommending to him to retreat to Moore's Creek Bridge if possible, but if not, to follow on in their rear. The next day by four o'clock we arrived at Dollerson's Landing, but as we could not possibly march that night, for the want of horses for the artillery, I dispatched an express to Moore's Creek Bridge to learn the situation of affairs there, and was informed that Colonel Lillington, who had the day before taken his stand at the bridge was, that afternoon, reinforced by Colonel Caswell, and that they had raised a small breastwork and destroyed a part of the bridge.

"The next morning, the 27th at break of day, an alarm gun was fired, immediately after which, scarce allowing our people a moment to prepare, the Tory army, with Captain McLeod at the head, made their attack on Colonel Caswell and Colonel Lillington, and finding a small intrenchment next the bridge on our side empty, concluded that our people had abandoned their post, and in the most furious manner advanced within thirty paces of our breastwork and artillery, where they met a very proper reception. Captain McLeod and Captain Campbell fell within a few paces of the breastwork, the former of whom received upward of twenty balls in his body; and in a very few minutes their whole army was put to flight, and most shamefully abandoned their General, who was next day taken prisoner. The loss of the enemy in this action, from the best accounts we have been able to learn, is about thirty killed and wounded, but as numbers of them must have fallen into the creek, besides many more that were carried off, I suppose their loss may be estimated at about fifty.

"We had only two wounded, one of them died this day." [This dead hero was John Grady, of Duplin.]

Colonel Moore, owing to the circumstances recited in his letter, did not reach the battlefield in time to take command, but, as also appears, he directed all the movements of the different detachments, immediately upon a sudden change of operations by his wily and able opponent. This fact was for a long time lost sight of in the subsequent controversy between the friends of Caswell and Lillington as to which of the two commanded in the fight.*

---

* See vote of thanks to Colonel Moore. Preface to Col. Rec., X, 12.

It was the first clear and overwhelming triumph of the Americans in the Revolution, and its results not only in the capture of eight hundred and fifty prisoners and in the value of captured material, including seventy five thousand dollars in gold, fifteen hundred rifles, three hundred and fifty shotguns, one hundred and fifty swords and dirks, two medicine chests worth more than fifteen hundred dollars, and thirteen wagons and teams—but in its moral effects upon both patriots and Tories, were almost incalculable.* Governor Martin, of course, tried to minimize these results by writing to the Government that what he called the "little check to the Loyalists" was a small matter that would not have any very serious effects, but the victory produced a wave of joyous exultation throughout North Carolina among the patriots, and for a time utterly crushed the spirit of the Tories.

The British fleet, with seven regiments under Clinton and Lord Cornwallis, which Governor Martin had been so long expecting, and to form a junction with which was the purpose of McDonald's Tory army, did not arrive in the Cape Fear River until about the first of May, just two months after the battle of Moore's Creek. Its arrival was at once made known by General Moore to the Provincial Congress, then sitting at Halifax, which immediately ordered all the regiments of regulars to report to him at Wilmington, but these regulars constituted only a part of the force that turned out to meet the invaders, for the volunteers and militia flocked in to the number of several thousand, making the total force on the Cape Fear more than six thousand men.†

There is an interesting letter from Col. Wm. Purviance, of New Hanover, dated February 23,‡ and addressed to the Council, giving an account of the preparations under his directions

---

* And yet a distinguished Senator from Massachusetts, a few years ago, when a small appropriation was asked from Congress to erect a monument on the battlefield, declared he had never before heard of the battle of Moore's Creek Bridge.

† Saunders (Preface to Col. Rec., Y, 13) regarded the first estimate of 9400 men as somewhat exaggerated.

‡ Col. Rec., X, 464-8.

for the defence of Wilmington after Colonel Moore had gone to Cross Creek, before the arrival of the fleet and while the "Cruizer" and "Scorpion" were committing depredations along the river. The letter shows that Colonel Purviance, though disclaiming any military skill, was exceedingly vigilant and efficient in the performance of this duty, as the following extracts from it prove:

After telling of his orders from Colonel Moore to prepare for marching, and of his work "during upwards of eighty hours of severe service night and day, with the assistance of the regulars and minute men whilst they were here," he says he had "happily effected everything necessary." "The two companies of minute men in this county and somewhat above eighty others, under the command of John Ashe, Esq., and stiling themselves Volunteers, together with a considerable number of disaffected persons, reduced the number of fighting men in my county so much that it was thought necessary with so small a number that remained that I should stay behind to protect the Town and adjacent Country from any insults that might be offered in the Absence of the Troops, by the Ships of War; Unequal as I know myself, and as indeed I must necessarily be, to any military command, I chearfully exerted myself to fill a department which of course fell upon me and which there was not any other to undertake."

He says that Lieutenant-Colonel Devane had nobly relinquished his rank to take command of a Minute Company which otherwise could not have been raised, and that he had assigned Major Ward to act as lieutenant-colonel and Captain Young to be first major and adjutant, Dubois to be second major, "they being two of the most active officers I have and the best acquainted with military discipline." Reports having been received from Brunswick on the 14th February, that the sloop of war "Cruizer", with a tender, had passed that town on her way up the river, great excitement ensued and the noncombatants began to move their families and effects out of danger.

"Since that time," he says, "I have been reinforced by Captain

Clinton's company of minute men from Duplin, a minute company from Onslow and part of the militia of this last county under the command of Colonel Cray. I have also had between fifty and sixty men under Major Quince from Brunswick County, and with all those forces I have been almost constantly employed in throwing up breastworks on the principal Streets and Wharfs and the hills above and below the Town; these I shall soon have compleated so as to prevent the landing of any men from the Ships. I am making the necessary preparations for fire rafts and shall be able to make use of what swivels are mounted and of a number of blunderbusses.

"But I am now assured the ships never will venture to Wilmington. They too much dread the rifle-men to approach us. The Cruizer and her tender attempted to go up the North West River on the West side of the Great Island opposite to Town,* but found there was not sufficient water all the way, and they returned. It is thought the intention was to favor the Regulators and the highland banditti, whom they expected to Triumph and protect the Provision Boats which would consequently come from Cross Creek for their Army and Ships. After the Cruizer had fallen down below the Island her people went several times on Shore at Mr. Ancrum's Plantation,† carried off his live stock and vegetables, and attempted to seize his Negroes who fled to the woods.

"They have even taken away a parcel of printed Books, Old Clothes, &c., and threatened to burn the house. I therefore thought it necessary to dispatch Major Quince with his detachment to protect the inhabitants on the West Side of the River as I found that the more necessary as Col. Davis of Brunswick County, informed me yesterday that there were fifty men from the Ships at the fort pillaging the Inhabitants. Capt. Dupree with only fifteen men arrived at Mr. Ancrum's plantation just as the Cruizer's boat was coming ashore the third time, fired upon them, which was returned and kept up

---

* Now called Brunswick River.
† The "Old Town" plantation.

about a minute, when the Sailors pushed off with precipitation. We certainly did some execution tho' they carried off their Men. The Cruizer fired three Guns without effect; since this the ship is gone down below the flats.

* * * * * * *

"The Ships of War which threatened us for some time are all fallen down to Brunswick. Their people have been so much harassed on both sides of the River by the Riflemen that I imagine their station became uneasy."*

---
* It is to be regretted that it has been impossible to secure a record of Colonel Purviance and his descendants, although he was a prominent man in the history of the county at that period. As elsewhore stated, the creek leading into Masonborough Sound through his lands was long known as Purviance Creek.

SPENCER COMPTON, EARL OF WILMINGTON
(From portrait painted for James Sprunt, Esq.)

CHAPTER VI

MARTIN'S AND PARRY'S CORRESPONDENCE WITH THE COMMITTEE—CLINTON'S PROCLAMATION—HOWE'S PLANTATION PLUNDERED—BRITISH ABANDON THE CAPE FEAR UNTIL 1781—CRAIG COMES IN 1781—HIS OPERATIONS.

It was a remarkable fact that what happened just ten years before, when Governor Tryon and Captain Lobb, of the sloop of war "Viper" tried to scare the people of Wilmington for refusing to supply the men of war with provisions, should have happened again exactly on the same day of the same month ten years later, when Governor Martin and Captain Parry, of the sloop of war "Cruizer," tried the same experiment. Mayor DeRosset received Tryon's letter February 27, 1766, and Harnett received Martin's and Parry's letters February 27, 1776.* The insolent threat of the latter assumes a comic aspect in view of the fact that at the very hour of the correspondence, McDonald's army, on whose immediate arrival the Governor was confidently relying, had been beaten and captured; and the change of tone in Captain Parry's last note, when news of the victory had doubtless been received—namely, "must beg you will send a few quarters of good beef"—is pitiful. The following is the correspondence, as contained in the Colonial Records, Vol. 10, 477-481 :

To the Magistrates and Inhabitants of the Town of Wilmington:

It is expected and hereby required that the Inhabitants of the Town of Wilmington do furnish for his Majestie's service one thousand barrels of good flour on or before Saturday next, being the second day of March, which will be paid for at Market price.   JO. MARTIN.

Cruizer Sloop of War,
Off Wilmington, Feb. 27th, 1776.

CRUIZER, WILMINGTON RIVER,
Feb. 27th, 1776.

His Majestie's ships not having received provisions agreeable to their regular Demands, I shall as soon as possible, be off Wilmington with

---

* The reply to these demands is not signed, but Martin plainly refers to Harnett as the author by attributing it to "the Chairman of a Combination," and so forth.

his Majestie's sloop Cruizer and other armed vessels under my command to know the reason of their not being supplied.

I expect to be supplied by six this evening with the provisions I have now demanded of the contractor.

If his Majestie's ships or Boats are in the least annoyed it will be my duty to oppose it.
FRAN. PARRY.

To the Magistrates and Inhabitants of Wilmington.

The Inhabitants of Wilmington, by their representatives in Committee, in answer to your Excellencie's Demand of One Thousand Barrels of flour for his Majestie's service, beg leave to assure your Excellency that they have been always most cordially disposed to promote his Majestie's real service which they think consistent only with the good of the whole British empire. But the inhabitants are astonished at the quantum of your Excellencie's requisition as they cannot conceive what service his Majesty has in this part of the world for so much flour. In the most quiet and peaceable Times when the Ports were open and Trade flourished it would have been impossible to procure such a quantity in the Town in so short a time as your Excellency mentions. How then can your Excellency expect a compliance from the Inhabitants of Wilmington during the present stagnation of Commerce? At a time, too, when you well know that an army raised and commissioned by your Excellency hath been for some time possessed of Cross Creek and the adjacent country, from whence only we can expect the Article you have thought to Demand.

We can with Truth assure your Excellency that it is not in our power to comply with your requisition, either in whole or in part, many of the inhabitants having for some time passed wanted flour for private use and the dread of Military Execution by the ships of War hath induced most of the Inhabitants to remove their effects.

The Inhabitants, Sir, sincerely wish they had not reason to expect that your Excellency's Demand is only a prelude to the intended destruction of the devoted Town of Wilmington.

If this should be the case it will not, however, make any alteration in their determination. It will be their duty to defend their property to the utmost, and if they do not succeed altogether to their wish they have one consolation left, that their friends will in a few days have it in their power to make ample retribution upon those whom your Excellency thinks proper to dignify with the epithets of friends of Government. These faithless and selfish people are now surrounded by three armies above four times their number, and the Town of Cross Creek, now in our hands will make some, tho, a very inadequate compensation for the destruction of Wilmington.

This, Sir, is no boast and we would not treat your Excellency with so much disrespect as to make use of Threats.

The Account we have given you is sacredly true, and we have the most convincing proof of it in our possession.

I have the honor to be, by order of the Committee,
Sir, Your Excellency's most Obt. Serv't.

WILMINGTON, 27th Feb., 1776.
Sir:

The reasons why his Majestie's ships have not been supplied with the usual quantity of provisions is so obvious that it cannot possibly have escaped the sagacity of Cap't. Parry.

The trade of this colony hath been distressed by the King's Ships even contrary to the Acts of the British Parliament. The Military stores, the property of the People, have been seized with an avowed intention to subjugate them to slavery. The fort, which the People had built at a great Expense for the protection of their Trade made use of for a purpose the very reverse, and when they attempted to demolish it they have been fired upon by the ships of war.

The slaves of the American Inhabitants have been pursued, and many of them seized and inveigled from their duty, and their live stock and other property killed and plundered long before the Committee thought it necessary to deny the ships a supply of provisions; and to Crown all you, Sir, for the Second Time, have brought up the Cruizer and several Armed Vessels to cover the landing of an army Composed of highland banditti, most of whom are as destitute of Property as they are of Principle, and none of whom you will ever see unless as fugitives imploring protection.

Tho' you should come up before the Town you can not expect any other answer than what we now give you.

We have not the least intention of opposing either your ships or Boats, unless you should attempt to injure us, and whenever you may think proper to treat the Inhabitants as his Majestie's officers did heretofore, we shall be happy to receive you in the manner which we always wish to receive those who have the honor to bear His Majestie's commissions.

I am, by order of the Committee,
Sir, Your Obt. Serv't.
To CAP'T. PARRY.

To the Magistrates and Inhabitants of the Town of Wilmington:

I have been much surprised to receive an answer to my requisition directed to The Magistrates and Inhabitants of Wilmington, from a member of the lawfull Magistracy in the name and under the Traitorous Guise of a Combination unknown to the laws and Constitution of this Country, as if the Magistrates and Inhabitants of Wilmington chose rather to appear in the Garb of Rebellion than in the character of his Majestie's loyal and faithful subjects.

The quantity of flour that I required for his Majestie's service I concluded, from the information I had received, that the Town of Wilmington might have well supplied within the Time I appointed by my note and I should have been contented with the quantity that was obtainable. The requisition was not made, as the answer to it imports, for a prelude to the destruction of that Town, which has not been in contemplation, but was intended as a Test of the disposition of the Inhabitants, whose sense, I am willing to believe, is known to the little arbitrary Junto (stiling itself a Committee) which has presumed to answer for the People in this and other Instances.

The Revilings of Rebellion, and the Gasconadings of Rebels are below the contempt of the loyal and faithful People whom I have most justly stiled Friends of Government and the forbearance of menaces I have little reason to consider as a mark of Respect from the Chairman of a Committee founded in usurpation and Rebellion.

Jo. MARTIN.

SIR:—The Committee of Wilmington have not only been chosen by the people but on the present occasion these very people (consisting of the freeholders) have been consulted on the propriety of their answer. That Committees are unknown to the Constitution, let those who have driven the people to that dreadful necessity account for.

I may venture to assure your Excellency that the greater part of the People in arms against the Inhabitants of this country are, in the opinion of every gentleman and man of understanding, unworthy to be considered as respectable members of Society. That there may be some of them of a better sort embarked in a cause which, right or wrong, does them little honor, is a circumstance for which it is easy to account.

The Inhabitants of this Town are extremely pleased to find that his Majestie's service is not in any immediate want of the flour which your Excellency thought proper to require, as it is impossible for them to comply, even in part. Whoever was your Excellencie's informant that the Town of Wilmington could now, or at any other period, procure so large a quantity in so short a time has grossly deceived you.

The conduct of the inhabitants of this Town is well known to your Excellency, and you might have been long since assured that there did not want any new proof of their zeal for his Majestie's service on the one hand, or a firm attachment to their Liberties on the other. And whilst they are conscious of no Acts but those which tended to assert the rights of God and nature, they have reason to believe that they do not deserve the epithets of rebels and traitors with which your Excellency hath so liberally loaded them.

Time alone must convince your Excellency that the Committee can not, for any interested purposes, condescend to convey an untruth which candor would be ashamed of.

To the Magistrates and Inhabitants of Wilmington:

As I am informed it is inconvenient to supply his Majestie's sloop Cruizer with salt provisions, must beg you will send a few quarters of good beef. FRAN'S. PARRY.
Cruizer, Wilmington River, Feb. 28, 1776.

It was on the 5th of May and while the great fleet was lying off Fort Johnston, that Clinton, the British commander-in-chief, under whom was Lord Cornwallis, issued the celebrated proclamation to the people of North Carolina, offering pardon to all who would return to their allegiance to the Crown, but specifically excepting from the offer Robert Howe and Cornelius Harnett, who were particularly obnoxious because of their active and continuous opposition to the measures of the government from the very beginning of the Revolution, the one now being a Brigadier General of troops in the field, and the other the chief civil officer of the State.

This was the first appearance of Cornwallis in the South, and seven days after the issue of the proclamation, on Sunday May 12th, he began his career by landing nine hundred men at Orton with the intention of capturing an outpost of one hundred and fifty men under Maj. Wm. Davis of the first Regiment, Continental Line, who were stationed at the mill on that plantation; but Davis's pickets gave the alarm in time, and he retired, taking his supplies with him, after killing one, wounding several, and capturing a sergeant of Cornwallis's celebrated 33rd Regiment. After burning the mill, Cornwallis went two or three miles down to General Howe's plantation at Howe's Point, which he plundered, carrying away as the spoils of his warfare about twenty steers for his beef-eaters.

After this exploit five of the seven regiments occupied Fort Johnston, one was stationed on Baldhead, and the other remained aboard ship.* There was a camp of Americans not

---
* Martin I, 534.

very far from Fort Johnston which the British might have attacked, the main force of the former being in and near Wilmington, and it may be that they did attack it, as that would account for the tradition that a sharp fight occurred, in which much blood was spilled, on the margin of "Liberty Pond," a half mile or so in rear of the town of Brunswick, although it is more probable that the skirmish with Major Davis's pickets is what the tradition refers to.

Clinton concluded to abandon a campaign in North Carolina and to proceed to attack Charleston. He left some vessels, however, in the Cape Fear, and taking Governor Martin with him he set sail for that city in the latter part of the month which he had so fruitlessly spent in this State.

About the same time the Provincial Congress, having by resolutions nominated a number of persons from the different districts to be a Council of Safety, these persons concluded to hold their first session at Wilmington, and accordingly assembled there on the 5th of June, when Cornelius Harnett was unanimously elected President of the Council, and they at once proceeded to business. Evidently when this meeting was appointed to be held it was supposed that Clinton would still be in the river, and it was a bold act of defiance to him, but although, as just stated, there were some of his ships still in the river, he had just sailed for Charleston, where he arrived on the 7th.

The Council of Safety continued in session from the 5th to the 15th inclusive, and then adjourned to meet at the residence of Mr. William Whitfield, on Neuse River in Dobbs County, on the 19th. Their proceedings during their stay in Wilmington were interesting, and almost exclusively directed to the appointment and transfer of officers to and from different regiments, and similar military preparations, but they also took time to look after certain disaffected ones of the gentler sex who, with their families, were ordered to remove from Wilmington at least twenty miles up the river within eight days, and directed General Moore to see to the execution of the order.

During Clinton's stay, General Moore, who was vigilantly preparing for any movement of the enemy, vigorously drilled his command twice a day. He did not go in person to participate in the defense of Charleston, but about June 1st, sent two of his regiments, Nash's and Martin's, which distinguished themselves and gained great reputation by their gallant conduct, winning high praise from Gen. Charles Lee, commander-in-chief, who, in his report, pronounced them "admirable soldiers." General Moore remained in Wilmington all the summer, keeping a watch on the enemy, several of whose ships were still in the river and a detachment of whose troops were still on Bald Head. In the latter part of September, however, the British, after burning two of the tenders and the sloop of war "Cruizer," took their departure from the Cape Fear, to return no more for several years, as the war had been transferred to the north.

Thus the strictly Revolutionary history of the county of New Hanover ceased to be especially interesting until the beginning of the year 1781. But in the meantime the utmost vigilance was practiced to suppress threatened insurrection by the Tories, who were constantly instigated by British emissaries to give trouble. Among the emissaries in 1779 was George Carey, British naval officer, who "came in a vessel to the Cape Fear under a flag of truce, to distribute manifestoes offering terms of settlement to the people without regard to continental or State authorities. He was promptly seized and thrown into jail by Francis Clayton and John Walker."*

In May, 1780, Charleston having been surrendered and the movements of the British toward our southern border being imminent, there was a general exodus of the people from that region. Mr. Iredell, writing to his wife from New Bern on the 21st of May, says: "The people in this State are very much distressed and everywhere flying from home. Wilmington is

---

* State Records, XIII, 296.

crowded with some of the first families. Fourteen ladies are said to have arrived there last Friday, and several were there before," and on the 28th, writing from Mr. Hooper's residence on Masonboro Sound, he says: "Col. Washington's Light Horse have fled to Wilmington, and are now there and will be, I suppose, joined to-day by a legion of about 200, part horse and part foot, commanded by one Col. Armand, who is on his way from the northward."*

Mich. Gorman, writing from New Bern, September 5th, to Governor Nash, says:

"Stanley's ship" (the General Nash) "has arrived at Wilmington and brought in two armed Brigs, one from Greenock in Scotland, with the most valuable cargo ever imported into this State, the other from St. Kitts with dry goods, rum, sugar and fruit." This cargo of the prize from Scotland was estimated by him to be worth fifteen thousand pounds sterling.†

On the 29th of January, 1781, Major Craig, of the British army, an officer on the staff of General Burgoyne, arrived in Wilmington with about five hundred men and escorted by three men of war and some galleys. The men of war were the Blonde, 36 guns, the Delight, 16 guns, and the Otter, 16 guns. He came expecting to cooperate with the Tory forces of the upper Cape Fear in weakening the opposition to Cornwallis by drawing away some of the American troops, but his expectations were not realized. Cornwallis, retreating after the battle of Guilford Court House, arrived in Wilmington, April 7th, despondent and with a badly crippled force, and at the same time General Green returned to recover South Carolina. Cornwallis remained in Wilmington until the 24th April, when he set out for Virginia, where he afterwards surrendered at Yorktown. During his stay in Wilmington he occupied the residence (still standing) on the southwest corner of Third and Market street, opposite St. James's church, and his cavalry occupied the church for their headquarters.

The best contemporary account of the treatment of the

---

*McRee, I, 453.   † State Records, XV, 71-72.

people along the route of Cornwallis's march to Virginia is contained in the letters of William Dickson, of Duplin County, which were published in 1901 by J. O. Carr, Esq., a member of the Wilmington Bar, and a descendant of Mr. Dickson's brother.

After describing Craig's attack on Lillington at the great bridge hereafter mentioned and the result of the battle of Guilford Court House and Cornwallis's retreat to Wilmington, Mr. Dickson says:

"Cornwallis arrived at Wilmington, and General Greene, being gone to South Carolina, seemed to strike terror on our militia then at their post. General Lillington, who then commanded the post at the great bridge, ordered our retreat from that to Kinston on the Neuse River, about thirty miles above New Bern, where on the 28th of April he discharged all the militia except one company to guard the artillery and stores. The militia, thus discharged (we had not the name of any army in North Carolina) every man was now to look to himself. The next day after being discharged we returned home. Cornwallis's army was then in the middle of our county, encamped at my brother, Robert Dickson's, plantation. The whole country was struck with terror; almost every man quit his habitation and fled, leaving his family and property to the merciless enemies. Horses, cattle and sheep, and every kind of stock were driven off from every plantation, corn and forage taken for the supply of the army, and no compensation given, houses plundered and robbed, chests, trunks, etc., broke, women and children's clothes, etc., as well as men's wearing apparel, and every kind of household furniture, taken away. The outrages were committed mostly by a train of loyal refugees, as they termed themselves, whose business it was to follow the camps, and under the protection of the army enrich themselves on the plunder they took from the distressed inhabitants, who were not able to defend it. We were also distressed by another swarm of beings (not better than harpies). These were women who followed the army in the character of officers' and soldiers' wives. They were generally considered by the inhabitants to be more insolent than the soldiers. They were generally mounted on the best horses and side-saddles, dressed in the finest and best clothes that could be taken from the inhabitants as the army marched through the country."

He then tells how his brothers and their families were treated, and says that, not content with the ordinary plundering, at his brother-in-law's house they "took away all the bedding, all the apparel, even the baby's clothes, stripped the rings off my sister's fingers, and the shoes and buckles off her feet, choked the children to make them confess if their father had not hid his money, and to tell where it was, etc., and many of the neighbors were treated in the same brutish manner."

Then for a short while after Cornwallis left, the Tories, thinking they had everything their own way, were, Mr. Dickson says, "more cruel to the distressed inhabitants than Cornwallis's army had been before," but as soon as both Cornwallis and Craig were out of the way the men of Duplin gathered a small force of about eighty men, attacked them and wreaked so fearful a vengeance upon them that they never attempted to embody again.*

Craig's arrival with the ships in the river, produced a panic, and there was, among the Whigs, a general exodus, but some considered it safe to leave their families, believing that they would not be subjected to indignities, or plundered.† Others, living out of town, fearing to trust their families to the danger

---

* The writer has before him an original letter from Col. Wm. Caswell to Col. John Walker, dated May 2, 1781, and referring to the movement of Cornwallis's column on its march, of which the following is a copy. Colonel Walker (generally called "Major Jack") had organized the militia of New Hanover county not included in Lillington's brigade:

KINGSTON, 2nd May, 1781.

DEAR SIR :—I am happy to have it in my power to acknowledge the receipt of your favor of yesterday's date, tho' nothing new in any of the movements of the enemy. I have an express just come into Camp Kingston who was in the rear of the enemy yesterday and saw them encamped at Capt. John Taylor's mill on Goshen, and they moved this morning. The remainder of General Lillington's brigade left yesterday for Pitt.

By an express from General Greene of the 21st April, he says that he lays before the [illegible] Camden ; that he has not sufficient force to storm the place, nor has he battering cannon to beat down their works, and the only way he can take the place will be by starving them.   I am in haste, yours, &c.,   W. CASWELL.

† Thomas Bloodworth, Commissioner of specific taxes for New Hanover county, put on board a vessel all the stores, with vouchers and papers belonging to them, and sent them up the Northeast River, but Craig overtook and burned them. Bloodworth was, by act of the legislature in 1788, exempted from responsibility.—*Colonial Reecords, XXI, 648.*

of marauding parties, removed them into the town, and among the latter was Mr. Hooper, who, in a letter to Mr. Iredell, said: "In an enemy's country, at all events, I thought it best to trust them to the mercy of the principal officers who would be at Wilmington and preserve some order there." He credited Craig with a virtue he did not possess, for that officer expelled Mrs. Hooper and other ladies from the town, forbidding them to use their carriages or other means of conveyance or to take with them anything but their wearing apparel; but finally, after keeping them standing for hours under a hot sun, upon the solicitation of others allowed them to use a boat and an escort of a ten year-old boy to go up the river a few miles, where they got into communication with General Rutherford's outpost and were taken care of.

There were many, and much worse, instances of cruelty and barbarism perpetrated by Craig and his command in and around Wilmington, one of the most notable of which was the treatment of Cornelius Harnett. Mr. Harnett was ill and suffering great pain at the house of Colonel Spicer, about thirty miles from Wilmington, at which place he was compelled by his condition, to stop on his way to the interior of the State. Craig, having learned through a spy, (of whom there were many) where he was, sent a detachment to arrest him, for, although a citizen and not a soldier, he was the most obnoxious individual to the British in the country. Harnett, sick and suffering, was at first, according to tradition, compelled to walk beside the mounted men who captured him until he fell exhausted, and was then, according to the testimony of an eyewitness,* brought into Wilmington "thrown across a horse like a sack of meal." From this treatment and his imprisonment, from which he was released upon the intercession of loyalist friends, he soon died.

With such examples set them by their commanding officer, it is no wonder that subordinates and common soldiers were

---

* Dr. A. J. DeRosset, Sr., who frequently made this statement to his grandson, Colonel W. L. DeRosset, and other members of his family, by whom this is authorized.

merciless in their conduct, one illustration of which was what has always been referred to as "the massacre of the eight-mile house." This eight-mile house was on the lower or sound road from Wilmington to New Bern, and was a tavern kept by a man named Rouse. Some of the militia officers who were stationed in that neighborhood to keep a watch on the movements of the British, foolishly gathered there to have a frolic, and with strange disregard of consequences neglected to post sentinels. "They were betrayed," McRee says, "by a merchant of Wilmington,"* a party of dragoons swooped down on them, and in their defenceless condition, instead of capturing, literally butchered all except Lieutenant Love, who, according to one version of the affair, escaped, but according to another was killed and was buried under a mulberry tree by Timothy Bloodworth, who tried to rescue them on hearing the firing, but was too late.†

These sudden expeditions of the cavalry were repeated in different directions from the town, and the town itself was protected by intrenchments, but although General Lillington, who commanded the militia, had not sufficient force to assault the works, the detachments under command of Colonel Kenan, of Duplin, Captain Alfred Moore, of Brunswick, and others were active in skirmishing and patrolling the surrounding country. Lillington, with the main body of his command, took post on the west side of the Northeast River at Heron's bridge, about ten miles above the town, and about the end of February Craig moved out at night with a strong force to attack him, and after driving away the outpost opened with artillery on his intrenchments across the river, but the militia stood the fire gallantly and made the woods ring with their rifles and shotguns, and after staying there two days without

---

* He was disguised in British uniform, but was recognized, and was an object of scorn ever afterwards.
† *Our Living and Our Dead*, for October, 1875.

crossing the river, Craig withdrew.* He built a field work at
Rutherford's Mills, about seven or eight miles to the northeast
of where this engagement occurred, and used the mills to
grind the grain gathered from the adjoining plantations.†

The conditions on the upper Northwest River, in Bladen,
and the adjoining counties, were at this time terrible for the
patriots, as the Tories who dominated that region were harry-
ing them, destroying all their property, burning their houses,
and murdering them. They were not only outnumbered but
were unsupplied with arms and ammunition, while Craig abun-
dantly supplied their enemies with both, and kept them encouraged by assurances of success. It was almost as bad in
Duplin, where, as Mr. Dickson wrote, they took numbers of
citizens and carried them to Wilmington, where they died on
prison ships.‡ The smallpox raged there, and one of the
victims of that disease was Gen. John Ashe, who had been
wounded, captured and imprisoned, and a few days after his release in October died from the effects of his treatment. His
son, who had also been captured, was put in irons on a prison
ship by Craig, who threatened to hang him and others.§

All through the summer and fall of 1781, while Craig occupied Wilmington, engagements of a minor kind occurred, some
of them being bloody, between the Tories and militia in Bladen,
Duplin and New Hanover.||

As a specimen of the British reports of these engagements,
we give the following, taken from the *Royal Gazette,* published at Charleston, S. C., September 8th, 1781, from which it
will be evident that there were "war correspondents" at that
time with largely developed powers of imagination:

---

* Upon his withdrawal some of Lillington's officers crossed the river and burned the house he had occupied as headquarters, called Mount Blake, belonging to John McKenzie. At the December, 1790, session of the Legislature McKenzie memorialized that body ask- ing compensation, but was refused on the ground that Lillington did not authorize the burning.—*State Records, XXI, 829.*

† McRee, I, 526. Also "Dickson Letters," the first of which gives a full account of the outrages perpetrated on the people of Duplin by the British.

‡ Dickson Letters.

§ Craig's letter to Governor Nash, State Records, XXII, 1024.

|| In November Maj. Joseph Graham attacked and defeated 100 Tories at Buchoi, Alfred Moore's plantation, within three miles of Wilmington, killing and wounding twelve, and next day attacked "the brick house," still nearer town, unsuccessfully.

188   HISTORY OF NEW HANOVER COUNTY.

CHARLESTON, September 8.

On Thursday an armed schooner arrived with dispatches from Wilmington, after a passage of 23 hours.

We have the pleasure to inform the Public, from very good authority, that Major Craig, after his gallant attack on the Rebels at Rockfish (when between 60 and 70 of the enemy were cut to pieces, and 31 made prisoners) directed his march towards Newbern in such an able manner as to prevent the junction of the several Rebel parties that were collected in the different counties to oppose him. Being informed on his arrival at William's Bridge, that a considerable body of General Lillington's men were posted 6 miles below, he left the cannon and baggage under a guard, and notwithstanding his long march, proceeded to attack them, but the enemy having learnt his intentions, went off with some precipitation. The detachment halted and had just taken up their ground, when a few Rebel light horse were reported to be in the adjacent woods. Major Craig immediately pushed forward with the cavalry, consisting of forty-three men, officers included, and at about 500 yards beyond his picquets, found a line of 250 chosen light horse, headed by their General Caswell, with every officer of rank or influence among them. Maj. Craig was within 30 yards of the enemy before he perceived their great number; he formed directly, sending for the Yagers and North Carolina Regiment to his support; but being justly apprehensive of their encircling his little party, and relying on the bravery and good conduct of the 82d. and Cap't. Gordon's Troops, without waiting for the Infantry, he ordered them to charge, which was immediately obeyed with the most distinguished alacrity. The Rebels gave their fire at 12 yards distance, which did not in the smallest degree check the ardour of the Troops, who rushed among and dispersed them, notwithstanding their great superiority, killing ten and taking the same number prisoners. Lieut. Dunlop, with the 82nd. Troop, pursued them above four miles with little effect, the whole of the Rebel Party being mounted on selected horses; a few being entangled in the swamps, fell into the hands of the Loyal Militia. It has since been understood that a very considerable number were wounded. Gen. Caswell escaped with difficulty.

We have to lament the loss of that most deserving officer, Captain Gordon, of the Independent Troops, who was the only person killed on this occasion. His fall sensibly damps the satisfaction we feel at the inconsiderable loss on our side, in so very disproportionate a contest. One Quartermaster of the Legion, a sergeant and one private of the 82d were wounded, and 15 horses killed and wounded.

The march of the Troops from thence to Newbern, which they reached on the 20th ultimo, was uninterrupted. A disposition for the defence of the Town had been made by Gallies and some Inhabitants, which had no other effect than causing the exchange of a few shot. The Town was taken possession of, and the Stores, consisting of above 3000 bushels of salt, and a large quantity of rum, with all the shipping and merchandise at the wharfs, were immediately destroyed. Major Craig intended remaining only two days, but getting information of Mr. Caswell's being posted with about 500 men at Coore's Creek, (18 miles from Town) intrenching himself, he moved with an intention to attack him. Mr. Caswell escaped about twenty minutes before his arrival. Finding it difficult to procure subsistence in that exhausted country, Major Craig returned to Rutherford's Mills to the Sound, on which he is now encamped.

By the accounts from Wilmington we are happy to find, that the Inhabitants in general of North Carolina, are daily manifesting their attachment to His Majesty's Government, by joining in large bodies, even to the amount of 1200 men, and otherwise assisting in the suppression of this wicked and unnatural Rebellion.

The most notable of these engagements was the splendid performance at Elizabethtown on the night of the 29th of August, when about one hundred men under the lead of Colonels Brown, Owen, Morehead, Robeson,* Irvine, Gillespie, Dickinson and Wright, who had been driven from the county by the Tories, returned, and fording the river below the town, made a furious attack just before dawn on the garrison, which consisted of about four hundred men commanded by Colonels Slingsby† and Godden, both of whom were killed, and about twenty of their men, while the loss of the attacking force was only one man wounded. The particulars of this desperate undertaking as given by Caruthers and others constitute one of the most thrilling episodes of the war. A number of

---

* Col. Thomas Robeson was a grandson of Andrew Robeson, of Scotland, who was a graduate of Oxford University, and emigrated to Pennsylvania, where he became a Councilor of that Province and Chief Justice. His son Thomas, father of Colonel Robeson, came at a very early period to North Carolina, and settled in Bladen county, where he married Sarah Singletary, and settled on a plantation which he named Walnut Grove, and which is still in possession of his descendants. Colonel Robeson was born at Walnut Grove January 11, 1740. He and his brother Peter were at the battle of Moore's Creek Bridge. They were hated by the Tories, and in 1781 Fanning burned their houses, for which and other similar acts Peter wreaked such vengeance as gave him the sobriquet of "bloody Peter."

The command of the patriot force at the battle of Elizabethtown, according to tradition, was held by Colonel Brown, but it is alleged that Colonel Brown was at that time suffering from a wound, and that Colonel Robeson (who was his brother-in-law) actually commanded. Brown was the senior officer in rank and in age in his county. Colonel Robeson died May 21, 1785, and was buried at Council's Bluff in Bladen county.

† Colonel Slingsby was an ancestor of that distinguished family of educators in North Carolina, the Binghams, and was as highly esteemed by the Whigs as by the Tories for his magnanimous and kindly spirit.

patriots who had been captured by the Tories, and were held by them at the time of the assault, were released, and valuable supplies, including a large amount of arms, ammunition, and other greatly needed supplies, were taken. The victory was a death blow to the Tories in that part of the country, and greatly revived the spirits of the patriots.

A perpetual memento of this brilliant action is still preserved in a deep ravine in which the panic-stricken garrison took refuge, and which has ever since been called "the Tory Hole."

General Rutherford, who had for some time been a prisoner in Florida, returned and resumed command of the forces on the upper Cape Fear, and determined to invest Wilmington, which he did, establishing his camp near the same bridge on the Northeast River where Lillington had the skirmish with Craig in February. While waiting there to complete his arrangements for driving Craig out of the town, General "Light Horse Harry" Lee arrived on the 18th November at the camp on his way to General Greene in South Carolina, and brought the news of Cornwallis's surrender on the 19th of October, and on the same day Craig evacuated Wilmington, and Rutherford marched in before the vessels carrying Craig's force had got out of sight down the river. And thus ended the actual military operations on the lower Cape Fear.

CHAPTER VII

WILMINGTON.

About the year 1730 a little settlement was begun on the east side of the Cape Fear River opposite the junction of its two main branches, which was dignified by the name of New Liverpool.

In 1732 the name was changed to Newtown or Newton. In 1733 John Watson obtained a grant for 640 acres adjoining the settlement on the north, and James Wimble, Joshua Granger, Michael Dyer and others obtained other grants, and these persons laid out the town. In 1734 the English traveler, mentioned in the first chapter, spent the night "in a hut" there.

On November 2, 1734, Governor Gabriel Johnston began his administration of the Province, and in the following March began to carry into execution his purpose to destroy the town of Brunswick and the influence of its founders by establishing Newton as its successful rival, just as Burrington had previously attempted. Johnston completely succeeded, and experience proved the wisdom of the change, although the motive for it was selfish and the method of effecting it—by packing the Council to make a tie and allowing the President, after voting to make the tie, to cast another vote to break it and give a majority for Newton—was an arbitrary and unjust proceeding which reflected no honor on those engaged in it, and afforded the first sample of "machine" politics in our history.

Having ordered a meeting of the Council, a term of the Court of Oyer and Terminer, a Court of Exchequer, and the opening of a land office there, all on the 13th of April, 1735, he proceeded to buy property there, and some of his Council and other friends did the same, which gave a great impetus to the movement in favor of Newton. He supplemented this local action by active correspondence with persons in England, Scotland and Ireland, in which he held out strong inducements to immigration to the Cape Fear, and in the course of the year these immigrants began to arrive, but only a few settled in Newton, most of them being desirous of becoming landholders, and planters.

Like other Governors (and notably among them his successor, Governor Dobbs), Johnston brought over with him some friends, the most deserving of whom, perhaps, was James Innes, a soldier and man of high character, who afterwards became the most prominent military officer of the Province, and of whom we have already spoken in a previous chapter. Innes bought land in Newton, as Johnston and some of his other friends did, and got one or more grants for large tracts in the country on the Black River and the Northeast branch of the Cape Fear.

At the session of the Assembly held at New Bern February 25, 1739, among the private acts passed was one entitled "An Act for erecting the village called Newton, in New Hanover County, into a town and township by the name of Wilmington, and regulating and ascertaining the bounds thereof"—the new name having been suggested by the Governor in honor of the Earl of Wilmington—and at the next session of the Assembly, held August 21, 1740, "An Act for the further and better regulation of the town called Wilmington, in New Hanover County; and to establish the Church of the parish of St. James, to be built in the said town" was passed. In 1741 the Assembly met in Wilmington, but no acts of any importance were passed, and none affecting the interests of the town.

As an evidence of the progress made in trade and business on the Cape Fear at the time Wilmington was established, Governor Johnston reported that during the year ending December 12, 1734, forty two ships had gone out of the river loaded. This, of course, indicated returns either of cash or imported goods, but the domestic business, because of the scarcity of money, was conducted chiefly by barter and exchange of commodities.

Between 1740 and 1748 four different invasions of the

Province by Spanish vessels occurred, but only the last one affected the people of Wilmington especially. This, which happened in September, 1748, has been described in a former chapter, and the only memorial of it is the painting that still hangs in the vestry room of St. James's church.

When Governor Dobbs took charge of the Government, in 1754, he reported the population of Wilmington to consist of seventy families, while the population of Brunswick had been reduced to twenty families. In regard to the commerce on the Cape Fear, he said: "Above one hundred vessels annually enter this river and their number is increasing; there were sixteen in the river when I went down."

In 1760 Wilmington was erected into a borough and the municipal government was entitled "The Mayor, Recorder, and Aldermen of the Borough of Wilmington." In 1764 an act was passed "for regulating the proceedings in the court held for the borough of Wilmington." Two years later, in 1766, the name of the municipality was changed to "Commissioners of the Town of Wilmington." (It is worthy of remark that just one hundred years afterwards, in 1866, the name was finally changed by the incorporation of "The City of Wilmington.")

The first meeting of a public kind of which we have any record was held April 5, 1743, at which the freeholders met to elect commissioners for the ensuing year, as prescribed by the Act of Assembly, on which occasion they elected five gentlemen; but on the 27th of April there was a call for a general meeting of the inhabitants and freeholders to concert measures for laying out the streets of the town in a more exact manner, in which meeting the elected commissioners seem to have been ignored (with one exception) and three commissioners were selected, who were empowered to agree with a proper surveyor and necessary assistants to re-survey the streets, and fix proper stakes, etc. To meet the cost of the re-survey a subscription was made, but the commissioners were forbidden to complete the negotiations until they gave three days notice at the court-house of the time and place appointed for making such agreement, when the consent of the subscribers should be necessary to complete it—a very conservative start toward municipal improvement, it must be admitted. Before even doing this much, however, the freeholders got Michael Higgines, one of the original proprietors, to make a sworn statement in regard to the original survey, which he did in the following deposition, which, as an interesting bit of authentic contemporary evidence, should be perpetuated:

NORTH CAROLINA, NEW HANOVER COUNTY.

Michael Higgines, late of the town of Wilmington, Ordinary Keeper, at the request of many of the inhabitants and freeholders of the said town, maketh oath that in the year of our Lord 1733, John Watson, planter, was possessed of a tract of land containing 640 acres by virtue of a warrant from Governor Burrington, beginning at John Maultsby's line to Col. Halton's line, then along his line south to the corner thereof and thence several courses down the northeast branch of the Cape Fear River; that in March or April, 1733, he, this deponent, and Joshua Granger, Sr., bought of the said John Watson fifty acres, part of the said tract of land, beginning at a tree which then grew in a hollow where Wm. Faris' tar house now stands, fronting down the river near a quarter of a mile, and running back for the complement; that on or about the said month of April, James Wimble, Mariner, bought of the said John Watson the remaining part of the said tract that was below the land purchased by this deponent and Mr. Granger; and this said tract was divided between John Watson, (who still continued to possess the other upper part of it,) this deponent, Joshua Granger and James Wimble. And the said John Watson, this deponent, Joshua Granger and James Wimble, in the month of April or thereabouts, entered into an agreement to lay out part of the said tract of land into lots and streets for a town, and to fix a centre in the Market St. where the town house now stands, and the same was accordingly laid out, on or about the said month of April, by William Gray, Surveyor, in the following manner, viz: "Beginning at a place where now lies the threshold of the north door next to the .... house, now possessed by Hugh Blanning, thence running northwest three poles, which station was agreed and fixed upon by us, said place to be the middle of Market Street aforesaid, and as the course of the said street was a half point north and this deponent having now reviewed the front street of the said town, saith: "That he verily believes that the post standing in the northeast corner of the yard possessed by Hugh Blanning, is exactly in the western line of Front Street, which street was run at right angle with Market St. of the width of four poles and all the other streets in the bounds of the then intended town were laid out four poles wide, and were exactly parallel either to Front Street or Market Street before ascertained, and that all the lots aforesaid were of the length of 20 poles with a breadth of four poles except the water lots, which were likewise four poles wide down to the low water mark." And this deponent further saith: "That when the said Surveyor, running along Front Street, went down steep or declining places, he ordered the chief chain-bearer to hold up the chain and the other one to hold down the chain and to the contrary in going up; in order and with the intention that all the lots might be of equal breadth," further saith not.

Sworn and subscribed by Michael Higgines, on the 9th of May, 1743, before me.   JA. MURRAY, J. P.

In pursuance of the agreement the freeholders employed Jeremiah Vail to make the re-survey "agreeable to the oath of Michael Higgines, and that the said surveyor be upon oath to do the same justly and truly without fraud," for the sum of one hundred and fifty pounds; and on the 12th of July they petitioned the Assembly to establish the town in accordance with Vail's survey, which was done by the Act of 1745, "for the better regulating the town of Wilmington and for confirming and establishing the late survey of the same, with the plan annexed."

On November 30, 1745, Richard Hellier was appointed town clerk, the market was ordered to be kept under the town house temporarily, and excellent regulations for it and against forestalling were made. The method of improving the streets was to call out all the "taxables" at stated periods, who had to appear at the court-house at six o'clock in the morning with the necessary tools and work from three to six days according to the necessities of the case, and, strange to say, they were required to work not only on the streets and bridges of the town (of which latter there were a good many) but also on the opposite side of the river on the road from Point Peter up to Mount Misery.

The taxes were not levied by the commissioners of the town, but apparently by a vote of the inhabitants, as such entries as the following are found, viz: "A majority of the inhabitants having agreed to a tax of," etc.; and again, "Wm. Robinson and a majority of the inhabitants having agreed to a tax," etc. (Why Wm. Robinson *and* a majority were required is beyond us, although we cheerfully acknowledge the great antiquity and title to precedence of that name.)

In the years 1755 and 1756 the people seemed to be much exercised on the subject of fires, several having occurred, and they laid a special tax on every house in the town to buy an engine, and appointed night watches to prevent further damage. The fire engine, which was ordered through Capt. Benjamin Heron, cost (with freight and insurance) one hundred and thirty one pounds and fourteen shillings. The fires do not seem to have been incendiary, but from foul chimneys, and a penalty of forty shillings was imposed upon every person whose chimney caught afire. Mr. Alexander Duncan contracted to keep the fire engine and hose "in order and oyld, and to play it once a month," for which care two of his family were exempt from working on the streets.

It was on the 15th of January, 1760, that Governor Dobbs issued the letters patent erecting the town into a borough, the government to consist of a Mayor, Recorder and eleven Aldermen, out of the latter of whom the Mayor was to be elected by the freeholders on the first Monday of each January. The first Mayor elected was John Sampson; the first Recorder, Marmaduke Jones, and the first Aldermen, William Dry, Cornelius Harnett, John Lyon, Frederick Gregg, Caleb Granger, Daniel Dunbibin, Arthur Mabson and Moses John DeRosset.

On the 3d of January, 1763, Frederick Gregg was elected Mayor.

On the 3d January, 1764, for some inexplicable cause, the freeholders are recorded as having chosen commissioners instead of a Mayor, Recorder and Alderman, but on the 29th of the next January the record says "the Mayor, Aldermen and Freeholders of Wilmington convened in common council at the court-house," Gregg being still Mayor, but a different lot of Aldermen attending. It was at this meeting that the following refreshing resolution was adopted: "Resolved, That the following rule be observed by the Mayor, Recorder, Aldermen and Freeholders in all debates: That the party speaking should not leave the subject in debate to fall upon the person of any member of the Common Council, or other person; *and whereas great abuses are daily committed by mixing milk with water and other such mixtures and afterwards exposing such milk for sale in the said borough, be it therefore ordained,*" etc.!

On the 6th of January, 1766, Caleb Mason, one of the Aldermen, was elected Mayor, but refused to qualify and resigned on the 14th at a meeting called for that purpose, and on the 20th Moses John DeRosset was chosen to that office. This occurred at the culmination of the excitement about the Stamp Act—the two vessels, the Dobbs and the Patience, having been seized on the 14th—and justifies the suspicion that Mason preferred "the calm sequestered vale of life" to the cares of office at so critical a period, while it reflects great honor on DeRosset, in that it showed the confidence of the people in his courage and capacity, a confidence fully justified by his conduct as Mayor, and his manly letter to Governor Tryon.

On the 11th of February the Mayor, Recorder and Aldermen, having been directed to elect a Representative from the borough to the General Assembly, the Mayor certified that Cornelius Harnett had been unanimously chosen, and on the 23d of June, William Hooper was elected Recorder in place of Marmaduke Jones, resigned.

Mayor DeRosset died in 1767, and in 1768 (for some reason unknown, as there is a gap in the record from June, 1766, to January, 1768,) the authorities of the town again resumed the name of Commissioners, and continued under that name, one of the notable performances of the Commissioners being at their meeting on the 14th day of June, 1774, when it was

"Ordered, that a Ducking Stool be provided for the use of the town, and that same be paid for out of the town tax."

So that, regardless of their pending Revolution, the fathers of the town would have a little fun, even in an official way.

The first press and the first newspaper were established in Wilmington in 1764, when Andrew Stewart, who had come from Philadelphia, where he had a press and book shop, issued in September of that year, the first number of the *North Carolina Gazette and Weekly Post Boy*. He started well, but in a year or two fell into disgrace because of some serious charge against him, and for want of support the paper failed and was discontinued in 1767. Stewart was drowned while bathing in the river in 1769.*

The first political pamphlet known to have been issued from a North Carolina press, was one written by Judge Maurice Moore, and published by Stewart in 1766, entitled:

"Justice and policy of taxing the American Colonies in Great Britain considered; wherein is showed that the Colonists are not a conquered people; that they are constitutionally entitled to be taxed only by their own consent; and that the imposing a stamp duty on the Colonists is as impossible as it is inconsistent with their rights—*Non sibi sed patriæ*.

"By Maurice Moore, Esquire, Wilmington, N. C. Printed by Andrew Stewart, and sold at his office near the Exchange 1766."

This pamphlet is in the archives of the University of North Carolina.

The second newspaper was started in the following October by Adam Boyd, who had bought Stewart's press and material, and his paper was called the *Cape Fear Mercury*. Exactly how long he continued to publish it is not known, but it appears, from the proceedings of the Safety Committee of Wilmington on the 30th of January, 1775, that he applied to them for encouragement to his newspaper "some time ago laid aside," and received their support on certain terms. Governor Martin, on the 8th of August, issued a proclamation in which he said, referring to the action of the people of Mecklenburg in May preceding, "I have also seen a most infamous publi-

---
* Weeks, The Press in North Carolina.

cation in the *Cape Fear Mercury,"* etc., which shows that the *Mercury* still existed in the summer of 1775.

Adam Boyd deserves more than a passing notice. He was the son of Adam Boyd and his wife, Jane Craighead, and came to Wilmington from Pennsylvania prior to January, 1764, as appears from one of his letters, in which he says he was initiated in the Masonic lodge there in January, 1764; that Peter Mallett and Colonel DeKeyser were in the lodge with him, and that on St. John's Day, 1770, "at the dinner at Emmet's house, a little back from the street," he and Mr. London acted as stewards. He had been a Presbyterian licentiate, but not an ordained minister. He early joined the Continental army, first as ensign, then became lieutenant, and finally, chaplain. At the close of the war he helped to organize the North Carolina Society of the Cincinnati at their first meeting at Hillsborough in October, 1783, was appointed secretary of the society and its first brigade chaplain.* In 1788 he was ordained a minister of the Episcopal church by Bishop Seabury and officiated for a short time at St. James's church in Wilmington, although not the actual rector. Dr. Boyd was a great sufferer from asthma, which was aggravated by the climate of Wilmington, and removed to Augusta, Ga., where he served as minister from 1790 to 1799, and died at Natchez, Miss., in 1803. He married the widow of Moses John DeRosset, the Mayor of Wilmington during the Stamp Act troubles, and was esteemed a very good man and true patriot, but in his old age became the victim of money-sharks and was robbed of his last resource, the land granted to him for his Revolutionary services.†

Dr. Boyd's letter, from Natchez, Dec. 30, 1802, to Dr. DeRosset, asking him to send Boyd's certificate of membership in the Masonic lodge in Wilmington, into which he was initiated in January, 1764, suggests a notice of that venerable institution. It is said that the first charter for a Masonic lodge

---

* "The N. C. Society of the Cincinnati." Gen. Charles L. Davis.
† Annals of the DeRosset Family, Mrs. C. DeR. Meares.

in the Province was for a lodge at Brunswick, in 1733, called King Solomon Lodge, of which Benjamin Smith, who was afterwards Grand Master and Governor of the State, was a member, but that the records of that lodge were destroyed. On the records of the Grand Lodge of England, under date of March, 1755, there is an entry of the grant of a charter to a lodge "213 at Wilmington on the Cape Fear River in the Province of North Carolina," but whether that was for the lodge that later met at Hooper's residence on Masonboro Sound, or the original Wilmington Lodge, which was re-chartered in 1794, and has ever since borne the name of St. John's Lodge, No. 1, (the oldest one in the State) or whether the two were one and the same, is not known, as the earliest records were lost, as were the records of the Grand Lodge of the State, in 1787. The most distinguished men of the Cape Fear region belonged to this lodge. Hooper, Harnett, Maclaine, Lillington, Edward Jones, Joshua G. Wright and many others were members.

The lodge had erected a building in Wilmington as early as 1758, which was valued for taxation that year at one hundred and forty pounds, and which, tradition says, was located on Red Cross street. They built, in 1803, the house on the south side of Orange street, between Front and Second streets, afterwards owned by Thomas W. Brown (and which is still standing and owned by one of his family), and held their meetings in it from that date until 1843, when St. John's Lodge building was erected on the north side of Market street, between Front and Second streets.

CHURCHES.

The church buildings in Wilmington and in Brunswick were both authorized to be constructed by the Act of 1751, although the establishment of the two parishes had been provided for some years earlier. In giving the history of St. Philip's at Brunswick, as we have done in the first chapter, the history of St. James's at Wilmington was necessarily given, the same ministers as a rule during that period having served both parishes. There was no other church building in either town prior to the Revolution nor until some years after it.

The original church of St. James was not to be compared to the edifice at Brunswick, which was the most imposing one in the Province. It was a plain, barn-like brick building, destitute of the least pretension to architectural beauty, which, perhaps, the more readily reconciled the consciences of the British cavalry officers in using it for barracks during their occupation of the town in 1781. The lot on which it was built was at the southwest corner of Market and Fourth streets, and had been used for a public burying ground. It was sold by Michael Higgines to James Smallwood, June 28, 1745, for two hundred pounds, and on the 12th July, 1749, Smallwood conveyed it, with the adjoining lot, to John Rutherford and Lewis DeRosset, wardens of St. James's parish, for the construction of the church. By the Act of 1752 thirty feet of Market street was allowed to be used for the site of it, and it stood there until 1839.*

The graveyard lying south of the old church was used as the common burying ground of the people of the town of all denominations for many years, and until Oakdale cemetery was established in 1853, the first burial in the latter being on the 5th of February, 1854.

Some of the great men of the Cape Fear were buried in the old St. James graveyard, and among them Cornelius Harnett, in 1781, but, as heretofore stated, the planters generally were buried in their family graveyards, nearly all of which have gone to ruin, while many have wholly disappeared. This old graveyard has been the theme of numerous writers, as most of the ancient burying places in the country have been, and many traditions have been preserved in regard to it. One of these traditions was so well authenticated by the testimony of unimpeachable witnesses living at the time—which testimony was put in writing—and presents so remarkable a case of the fulfill-

---

* William Farris, merchant, died in 1757, after leaving part of his estate to Cornelius Harnett and Marmaduke Jones, trustees, to be used in finishing the church.

ment of a "vision" as to be worthy of record. The facts were recited by the late Col. James G. Burr, in a lecture delivered in the opera house in Wilmington February 3, 1890, and, stated in condensed form, were as follows:

In March, 1810, Samuel R. Jocelyn, son of a distinguished lawyer of the same name in Wilmington, and himself a promising man—not long after conversing with his friend Alexander Hostler and others about the possibility of a man's returning to earth after death and making his presence known, and after making an agreement with Hostler that the first of the two who died should, if possible, reveal himself to the survivor—was killed by accident, and buried in St. James's churchyard. Hostler was greatly afflicted by the death of his friend, and, while sitting alone in his room a day or two after the funeral, was overwhelmed by the sudden appearance of Jocelyn, who said to him: "How could you let me be buried when I was not dead?" "Not dead?" exclaimed the horror-stricken survivor. "No, I was not," replied his visitor; "open the coffin and you will see I am not lying in the position in which you placed me," and vanished immediately. Hostler, though greatly affected, believed he was the victim of delusion and tried to rid himself of it, but at the same hour on the next evening, and again at the same hour on the third evening, the apparition confronted him with the same mournful query. He then determined to exhume the body and see whether the fact was true or not. He told the story to Mr. Lewis Toomer, and asked his assistance in the disinterment, which he agreed to give. They went together at night and opened the grave, and upon removing the lid of the coffin and turning the light of a dark lantern on the body, discovered it lying face downward. Hostler communicated the facts to Colonel Burr's mother, who was his near relative, and between whom and himself there was an affectionate intimacy, and Mr. Toomer told the facts of the disinterment in the presence of another venerable lady, Mrs. C. G. Kennedy, who put the statement in writing for Colonel Burr, who read it during the course of his lecture.

Thomas Godfrey, author of the first American drama, "A Prince of Parthia," and whose history is an interesting one, is buried in St. James's churchyard.

EDUCATION.

While the facts in regard to the educational interests of the people of the Province of North Carolina, like those of other provinces outside of New England, were lamentable, there was not such an absolute destitution of educational facilities as has sometimes been represented. The contrast has generally been drawn between the lack of schools here and the ample supply of them in New England, without considering the very marked differences in the circumstances that surrounded the settlement of these respective colonies.

New England was settled by clusters of families, who from the beginning organized communities; North Carolina was settled by individuals, with or without families, in very small groups, or separate from each other. New England was settled by people of the same religious faith and the same social ideas; North Carolina was settled by people of every kind of faith, and different social customs.

From the start, towns were established in New England; no town was established in North Carolina until 1704 when Bath was settled, and there were only twelve houses in it. A little later Beaufort was laid out, and still later New Bern. The population of North Carolina was composed of English Churchmen, Roman Catholics, Baptists, Scotch and Scotch-Irish Presbyterians, French Protestants, German Lutherans, and Quakers. They were distributed over a large territory, and their differences of faith as well as their separation from each other was an insuperable barrier to the concentration of efforts to organize schools, such as existed in New England. Besides all this it was against the declared policy of the British authorities to encourage education among the people of North Carolina, except under restrictions that amounted to a practical prohibition of it. Among Governor Burrington's instructions from the home government in 1731 was one forbidding any schoolmaster to teach unless licensed by the Bishop of London, as well as by the Governor.

There was no legislation in favor of schools until 1745, and nothing came of that. The first school actually put in operation *by law* was the school at New Bern, which was incorporated in 1766, only ten years before the Revolution, and the master of this school was required to be a communicant of the Church of England, and the school itself to be subject to the control of that church, as also was the school later established at Edenton, in 1770.

On the Cape Fear some of the earlier ministers taught schools. With the immigration of the Scotch, which began as early as the administration of Governor Johnston and continued up to 1775, school-teachers came, but they settled in the upper Cape Fear region and taught the children of their countrymen.

Of course this brief discussion has been in reference to public schools authorized by law, or private schools established in communities and taught for pay, such as the classical school opened by Rev. James Tate in Wilmington in 1760. The first free school of which there is any record, and which was the first one founded by private benevolence, was the Innes Academy in Wilmington, named in honor of Col. James Innes, who left nearly all of his estate in 1759 to found it, and which was incorporated under that name.

But these schools, public and private, by no means represented all the educational facilities of the people, for there were private tutors in the families of the planters and wealthier citizens, and the sons of these families, when sufficiently advanced, were sent to Harvard or Princeton or to England for the completion of their education. A number of Wilmington and lower Cape Fear boys were thus educated, some of them being sent to England when quite young and remaining there for years* Their fathers were in many cases well

---

* General Waddell's three sons, after his death in 1773, were sent to England for their education, and the eldest one, returning in 1784, died and was buried at sea, the others remaining several years.

educated and cultured men, who owned good libraries and read much of the best literature. But the want of schools for popular education was deplorable, and was a source of sincere and profound regret among the more enlightened, and a subject of remonstrance, repeated by successive Governors and other officials.

EARLY INDUSTRIES.

One of the early industries of Wilmington was that of shipbuilding. Several of the first settlers of the town engaged in the business, and one of the sites on which it was conducted is still so used, this being the shipyard originally founded by Joshua Granger at the foot of Church street. There was another established a little lower down by Michael Dyer, and two others, the sites of which are unknown, by James Wimble and Archibald Corbett, the latter of whom is recorded as having built a vessel for the Glasgow firm of Beard & Walker. (Matthew Rowan, afterwards acting Governor of the Province, was a ship-builder and came to the Cape Fear for that purpose.) Wimble was master of a vessel, the brigantine "Penelope," and was also an excellent surveyor, whose map of the coast, made in 1738, is well known and was for a long time the most valuable and accurate one in use. These ship-builders were attracted by the forest timbers generally, and especially by the plentiful supply of live oak, which far surpassed any other for their purpose, particularly in its adaptability for "knees" and the like. A very considerable part of the vessels trading to and from the Cape Fear, as appears by the Custom House records of Brunswick, one large volume of which still exists in a mutilated condition,* were entered as "plantation-built" to distinguish them from foreign-built ones. They were not large, their tonnage ranging from forty to one hundred and fifty tons, but they were well adapted to the coast and West Indies trade of that time, although a modern seaman would regard employment on such craft as extra-hazardous. The exports were

---

* See Note, Chapter I.

naval stores, lumber, staves, rice, indigo, hides and tobacco, and after the year 1735 the commerce increased rapidly, especially in the exportation of rice, the cultivation of which annually grew larger, and finally became the chief agricultural industry of the lower Cape Fear region.

Indigo ceased to be cultivated after the Revolution, and later the cultivation of tobacco for commercial purposes was transferred to the more western and northern sections of the State.*

PUBLIC BUILDINGS.

The public buildings of the town of Wilmington in the early days consisted of a town hall, situated at the intersection of Market and Second streets, which was a brick building of greater length than breadth, surmounted by a cupola, and having a market place under it, afterwards called the "mud market" to distinguish it from the market later erected in the middle of Market street between Front street and the river; a court-house, which stood in the middle of the crossing at Front and Market streets, and which had three arches on each side and each end, on the ground floor, the middle ones open and the others closed by benches for the convenience of the public; a jail, which originally stood on the south side of Market street between Second and Third streets, but the locality of which was changed several times, and a custom-house on the river front at the foot of Nun street, south side.

Neither of the Colonial Governors had a permanent residence in Wilmington, although Johnston bought property in the town, and Tryon seems to have occasionally occupied temporary quarters in it. Tradition has not been uniform as to the locality of the latter, one story giving the south side of Market street near the river, and another the north side of Dock near Second street, as the place. Fifth street was the boundary street, and

---

* On 29th March, 1764, Governor Dobbs, in a long letter to the Board of Trade describing the condition of the Province, says: "At Cape Fear, instead of having had all our flour from the northward they have increased in sowing wheat and erecting bolting mills [so] that they have of late exported several hundred barrels of flour to the West Indies, and have increased in their export of naval stores to 36,647 barrels per annum, and in lumber and scantling above 30,000,000 feet, having erected about forty sawmills on the branches of the Cape Fear river."

on the earliest maps that part of Market street beyond Fifth
was marked: "Road to Newbern."

BOROUGH REPRESENTATION.

As above stated, Wilmington was, by letters patent issued by
Governor Dobbs, January 15, 1760, erected into a borough,
but there is no record of an election of a borough representative
to the Assembly until 11th of February, 1766, when Cornelius
Harnett was unanimously chosen.

This borough representation was not abolished in the State
until 1835, when the convention, called to amend the Constitution, restricted the election of representatives to the counties,
and did away with the old borough system. As long as it
lasted Wilmington was represented by very able men, particularly in the earlier period when such men as Harnett, Hooper,
Maclaine, Edward Jones, and Joshua G. Wright were elected;
the last named serving continuously for sixteen years, from
1792 to 1809, when he was elected judge. The borough representatives were additional to those of the counties.

When the Revolution ended, antagonisms almost as bitter as
those existing between Whigs and Tories during its continuance
arose in regard to various matters. A demagogical crusade
against all lawyers was inaugurated, which doubtless had its
origin in the time of the Regulators; there were disgraceful
squabbles between the judges and sometimes between them and
members of the bar; there were confiscations of the estates of
persons who had been openly, or secretly, British sympathizers;
there were prosecutions for treason, but no executions of those
accused; there was a strong feeling in favor of pardon and
oblivion of the past, and an equally strong feeling against such
clemency; there were the usual conflicts of personal ambition
among public men, and radical differences in regard to matters
of public administration.

These antagonisms were as fierce in the Cape Fear section as
in any part of the State. As the time approached when the
relations between the States and the general government had

to be finally considered and established by a constitutional convention, these differences were crystallized by the formation of two political parties, one of which strenuously objected to conceding more than a very limited power to the Federal government, and the other equally anxious to invest that government with powers adequate to its proper administration. The latter were called Federalists, and the former Anti-Federalists, and afterwards Republicans.

When the convention to consider the proposed Constitution of the United States was called to meet at Hillsborough in July, 1788, the first furious political campaign in our State was inaugurated. Mr. Hooper, one of the leaders of the Federalists, had removed his residence from Wilmington (which borough he had represented for some years in the legislature) to Hillsborough, and was succeeded by Archd. Maclaine, another leading Federalist, who was elected a delegate to the convention from the town. Timothy Bloodworth, the most active Anti-Federalist in New Hanover, was also elected from the county. He was a devoted follower of Willie Jones, the leader of that party and "the most influential politician in the State," and of General Thomas Person, another radical Republican who, according to the testimony of a respectable witness, denounced General Washington as "a damned rascal and traitor to his country for putting his hand to such an infamous paper as the new Constitution."* Thus New Hanover was represented in the convention by two men who were, and had been for some time, bitter political enemies. Maclaine was a leader of the bar, and much the more cultured of the two, but did not possess the poise and good nature of Bloodworth, who was a much better politician. Prior to the election Maclaine published an address, and gave free rein to his tongue; and in his private correspondence with his political allies his pen was dipped in gall and sparkled with satire and humor. As a specimen of the latter he thus refers to one of the best and most useful men of

---

* McRee, II, 225.

the period, the Rev. James Tate, who opened the first classical school in Wilmington.

"Parson Tate has picked up all the arguments, good or bad, that have been published against the new form of government. The only original objection he had was the want of a mint in each State; this, he alleges is a never-failing mark of sovereignty, and is to keep the money with us; he appears to be greatly distressed that we shall be obliged to send our *bullion* to the seat of government. It is indeed truly distressing."*

Maclaine and Bloodworth had some sharp encounters in the convention, but all the logic and eloquence of Iredell, and Johnston, and Maclaine and others was unavailing, and the convention, by a large majority, (184 to 84), refused to adopt the Constitution, although it was adopted the next year, when its opponents found that a continued refusal by North Carolina to become a member of the Union meant ruin to the State.

One of the questions considered by the convention of 1788, was the location of a site for the permanent capital of the State, and Bloodworth, although it was confidently expected by the Cape Fear people that he would vote in favor of Fayetteville (which was the choice of an overwhelming majority of them), grievously disappointed them by voting in favor of a place "in the vicinity of the farm of Isaac Hunter" in Wake County, which place was chosen and the City of Raleigh was built upon it.

The convention of 1789 and the Legislature both met in Fayetteville on the same day, November 2d, and among other things, the legislature ordered elections for members of the National Congress, and Bloodworth was one of those chosen. He was afterwards (1795) elected to the United States Senate by a majority of one over Alfred Moore and, upon his retirement after one term, was comfortably provided for by his appointment to the office of Collector of the Port Wilmington.

In the legislature of 1788 Edward Jones represented the

---
* Maclaine to Iredell.—McRee, II, 217.

borough of Wilmington, and Thomas Devane the county of New Hanover. Mr. Jones, who was a lovable man and a good lawyer, was elected by the next legislature to the newly established office of Solicitor General of the State. Mr. Devane was, as were several of his family in that and succeeding generations, a planter of high character, and sound judgment.

In the next year (1790) Mr. Hooper, who had so long served his State and country with great distinction, died at his home in Hillsborough, and very soon thereafter the able and fiery Maclaine also passed away, at his home near Wilmington. In 1792 Joshua G. Wright, of New Hanover, a lawyer of ability and high character, began his public career as a member of the Legislature, and continued to represent the county until 1809, when he was elected judge.

In 1795 Judge Samuel Ashe, of New Hanover, was elected Governor of the State, and brought to the performance of the duties of that station the experience of twenty years of public service as a legislator and judge. He was reelected for a second and a third term. He had been from the first organization of the two parties an extremely radical Anti-Federal leader, and died in that faith at the age of 88, in 1813.

On the 20th of April, 1791, General Washington arrived in Wilmington on his southern tour, coming from New Bern, and was met some miles from the town by the Light Horse Company and escorted into the town, where he was received with salvos from a four-gun light battery, and the acclamations of a large crowd. He occupied the residence of Mrs. John Quince, on the southeast corner of Dock and Front streets, which that lady put at his service, it being one of the best in the town. The next day he was entertained at a large dinner by the gentlemen of the town, during which there was more artillery firing, and at night there was a general illumination and a grand ball. The day after, he proceeded on his journey, again, escorted by the Light Horse Company for many miles*
There is a tradition that during his stay what afterwards be-

---
* Letter of Anna Jean Simpson, 25th April, 1791, to Mrs. Christian Fleming, published in the *Wilmington Messenger*, April 25, 1901.

came a threadbare joke, was perpetrated by Laurence (called Lal) Dorsey, as follows: Dorsey kept the inn where the dinner was given, and the General, remarking upon the very flat and sometimes swampy nature of the surrounding country, asked Dorsey what sort of drinking water was used and if it was good, to which Dorsey (who was an impudent jester) replied that he really didn't know—that he never drank it.

CHAPTER VIII

FORT JOHNSTON AND SMITHVILLE (NOW SOUTHPORT).

The beautifully located town near the mouth of the Cape Fear River, rejoicing, from 1792 up to 1887, in the name of Smithville—so called in honor of Gen. Benjamin Smith—was in the latter year incorporated under the name Southport, through the solicitation of some northern speculators, who proposed to build a railroad to it and make it a city, but who have utterly failed to accomplish their benevolent design, except on paper.

It was built on the level ground surrounding Fort Johnston, and the town was always called "The Fort" by the Wilmington people who owned summer residences there, but by those who found Smithville too hard a word to pronounce, was designated as "Smiffle." The fort was built under the Acts of 1745, ch. 6, and 1748, ch. 10, and the commissioners appointed to erect it were "His Excellency Gabriel Johnston, Esq., Governor; the Honorable Nathaniel Rice, Robert Halton, Eleazer Allen, Matthew Rowan, Edward Moseley, Roger Moore, William Forbes, Esqs., and Col. James Innes, Wm. Faris, Esq., Major John Swann and George Moore, Esq.," and the act says "it shall be called Johnston's fort, and shall be large enough to contain at least twenty-four cannon, with barracks and other conveniences for soldiers." It was completed in 1748 The officer or officers commanding it prior to 1755 are unknown to us, but in that year it was commanded by Capt. John Dalrymple, who was appointed by General Braddock. In 1758 it was commanded by Capt. James Moore, afterwards Brigadier General in the Revolution, who, although quite young, was very highly spoken of by Governor Dobbs, and from 1766 to 1774 by Capt. Robert Howe, afterwards a distinguished Major-General in the Revolution. In less than two years after he gave up the command, Howe and Ashe burned the fort, while Captain Col-

GOVERNOR BENJAMIN SMITH

let, its commander, and Governor Martin looked on in impotent rage from the deck of the "Cruizer," on which they had taken refuge. At that time, there were only the officers' quarters and small barracks, with one or two outhouses, on the premises, and no residents around it, except possibly a pilot or two. In the month of May, 1776, as heretofore stated, five British regiments occupied the fort.

About 1790 the first start toward a settlement there by citizens was made, and an account of it was written by a chief actor in the movement, Joshua Potts, a part of which has been preserved and was recently republished by the University under the title "James Sprunt, Historical Monograph No. 4," as follows:

Matters, even of consequence, have sometimes originated more by chance than design. A number of instances might be cited. It was the case relative to Smithville though a place not yet of great importance. The first movement happened as follows:

About the year 1786 Joshua Potts, the writer hereof, then living in Wilmington, was taken sick and by medical attendance had got better, but notwithstanding, still continued very weak and a loss of appetite, etc. So it happened that his old friend, Capt. John Brown, who had been master of a packet that plied between Wilmington and Charleston, meeting me one day asked me to take a sail with him in an open boat down the river, saying that the salt air might recruit me, etc.

Accordingly, debilitated as I was, I proceeded with him down the river Clarendon, or Cape Fear, in an open boat, being at the time only able to sit up. Captain Brown had put on board some eatable refreshments, but I had no thought of partaking any. We had not proceeded farther down than opposite the New Inlet when Capt. B. asked me to eat something. I listened to what he said, and discovered an inclination to partake of such cold collation as he had set forth. My appetite returned and in a day or two I felt myself braced up by the effects of the salubrious breeze from the sea, although I was exposed in camping out, etc., for at that time there were only two or three pilots' houses on the bank. I returned to Wilmington in a few days perfectly recovered.

I was at that time single, but in a year or two more became a married man, and in a summer season determined that my family should retire from Wilmington to Fort Johnston and there experience the cool and healthy sea breezes. Accordingly I carried my then small family down to the fort and rented the loft of a pilot house (Joe Swain's) where we were all stowed away, breathing health and rough pleasure.

While thus living a fisherman's life, I received a letter from John Huske, Esq., of Wilmington, then in low health, on the subject of having a town laid off on the level, near Fort Johnston. Mr. Huske wished to reside there for the sake of his health. This letter was dated Wilmington, October 18, 1790, and it is herewith enclosed, No. 1.

Mr. Huske would have called the proposed town Nashton had an act of the Assembly been passed, concerning which intelligence shall hereafter be given.

Mr. Huske was the first mover of a town near the fort, and I myself was to become the operator. I stepped off the ground from the old fort southward to the first small creek. The distance was shorter than what was wished. I accordingly wrote Mr. Huske; notwithstanding I was prevailed on to form a petition to be circulated through Brunswick County setting forth the prayer of the inhabitants that an act of the Assembly might be passed for the establishment of such a town.

The said petition accompanies the report, No. 2. J. Potts, having written said petition, was applied to for it by Charles Gause, Esq., a leading inhabitant of Brunswick County, who undertook the exhibition of it in order to obtain subscribers' names. This was performed and introduced in the General Assembly, which in that year sat in Fayetteville.

The whole intention was unexpectedly opposed by General Smith, who was then a member of and for Brunswick County. It was said he supported his negative role on account of two or three pilots who had built their houses by public permission promiscuously on said land. As it was, however, he had influence sufficient to stop the proceeding in the Assembly, and thus ended the prospects of a town at that time.

Some people in Wilmington and others in Brunswick County, being disappointed in their expectations of a town, were said to have imputed the opposition of General S. to the cause, not of pilots, but that he had not been previously consulted in and about the business.

Now, so it was that the old Fort Johnston as well as the surrounding lands was the property of the State of North Carolina, and that power alone the petitioners had relied on for the grant alluded to.

Capt. John Brown and Joshua Potts determined, however, not to abandon the place, and, fearless of any molestation, proceeded to occupy as a temporary residence for summer and autumn, each a few square feet near the shore, and accordingly proceeded to have each a cabin formed and framed in Wilmington, and procured a sufficiency of the boards and shingles to complete these; employed a pettiauger and put on board the frames and other materials of both houses, engaged carpenters with their tools, and both families of said John and Joshua, with plenty of provisions, etc., all together went on board the lighter at Wilmington, arrived at Fort Johnston and there landed the whole.

In a few days afterwards we had erected each a summer house, in a temporary manner, near the water, between where is now Mrs. Wade's and the beach. The said two houses, or camps, had not chimneys of any kind, and only rough shutters to the windows (no glass), the whole of the sawmill roughness, as a plane had not been used about them. Our two families were thus coarsely encamped; and instead of a kitchen our cooking fires were made among thick bushes near hand, which screened the inconvenience of the wind, but rain would sometimes moisten our cooking and depredating hogs would run off with our hot cakes in their mouths.

In this way our families enjoyed health, cool breezes and a coarse way of living several summers. In the meantime Captain B. and myself became expert fishermen.

During these rugged scenes there was no town laid off and only a few neighbors, pilots and their families.

The first twelve months had nearly expired after the failure of the bill at Fayetteville, and the General Assembly were next to sit at New Bern. Who should come in my cabin at the fort but the same old Mr. Charles Gause, whose business was to get me to write and renew the petition for the establishment of said town. I remember reminding Mr. Gause that any such attempt must be of no use, as no doubt General Smith would oppose it as before. Mr. Gause replied in a positive voice that if I would copy off the petition he would advocate it as before, and that General Smith should not be sent to the Assembly unless he would use his endeavors to have a suitable act passed for the intended purpose. (The election was then pending.)

Conformably to the request of Gause, I then wrote off a new petition much after the tenor of the first.

The venerable old man made good his word. General S. was elected, went to New Bern and assisted to get the act passed, and which is herewith enclosed. See No. 3, passed at New Bern, November session, 1792.

The writer hereof remembers hearing General S. say, when he returned from the Assembly, that on his making a motion and offering the bill for the act, Mr. Macon or some other respectable member made an observation that many applications had been acted upon for different towns in the State, but that few, if any of them, had succeeded; that the said worthy member said as General S. has applied in behalf of this petty town, it should be called Smithville, as if by way of derision to the applicant, should the town (like many others) not succeed.

The next desirable object was to secure my attention and services in laying off and beginning the necessary operations to form the town. See a letter from General Smith, dated Belvidere, January 29, 1792, No. 4.

By reading over the first Act of the Assembly, No. 3, it will be seen that the town was to consist of one hundred lots, with streets and squares; that each subscriber should pay forty shillings or four dollars, to the State, for each and every lot of half an acre he might determine, but no one person might subscribe to more than six lots, that many might have a chance. The plan of the town was at length sketched off by General Smith and J. Potts, and the lots numbered thereon from No. 1 to No. 100. Meanwhile all the lots were subscribed for.

The rest of the manuscript, and also the documents referred to, are lost. Mr. Potts was a leading citizen of Wilmington.

After the Revolution, the site of Fort Johnston reverted, as a matter of course, to the State of North Carolina, and it was in December, 1809, ceded to the United States by an Act of the Legislature of the State. The fort was a battery on the bluff above the river bank, and occupied a square in the center of what afterwards became the river front of the town. It was built of a material called "tapia," and the original construction of it was so good that Lieutenant Swift, afterwards General and Chief of Engineers of the United State Army, writing of it in 1804, said:

"In clearing away the sand I found much of the tapia walls then erected, finer in their whole length, on a front of the ordinary half bastion flanks and curtain of two hundred and forty feet extent, far superior to our contemplated plan for the battery of tapia."

This tapia was "a composition consisting of equal parts of lime, raw shells and sand, and water sufficient to form a species of paste, or batter as the negroes term it," which was poured into boxes six feet high by seven feet in thickness, and constituted the parapet, and when hardened was probably sufficient to resist a bombardment by such artillery as was then in use. The fort was garrisoned by United States soldiers for many years after its reconstruction, and indeed up to within a few years before the war between the States. It was the favorite resort of the people on summer evenings, and especially of the young gallants and their sweethearts, who found the sea breeze and the moonlight on the bay fit accompaniments to love-making.

CHAPTER IX

INTERESTING ITEMS FROM COURT MINUTES.

As an introduction to these interesting court minutes an incident, recently related to the writer by the venerable Mr. Richard J. Jones, now in his eighty-eighth year, is worthy of record.

Mr. Jones was coroner, and on the death of the sheriff became, by virtue of his office, Sheriff of New Hanover County at the close of the war of 1861-65, and he found the papers in the office of the sheriff and clerk scattered about the floor. Seeing one ancient looking bundle from which a part of the wrapper had been torn, he picked it up to restore it to a pigeonhole and found that it contained an execution which had been returned by the Sheriff of Onslow County *nearly a hundred years before,* marked "satisfied," and enclosed in it in Continental money (N. C. currency) was the amount called for by the execution. He preserved some of the bills and has them now. Probably the invasion by the British in 1776, or 1781 (which closed the courts) may account for the loss, or oversight, of the package for so many years.

COUNTY COURT.

The earliest court record (imperfect) is that of December Term, 1736, of the county court at Brunswick, and consisted chiefly of the probate of deeds, the one of earliest date being a deed from Porter to Moore, March 4, 1731. The first twenty-six pages of this record are missing, and therefore the names of the justices who held the court do not appear, but at the next term (March, 1737) Robt. Halton, Cornelius Harnett, James Innes, James Murray, and Nathaniel Rice were the presiding justices.

These gentlemen were certainly model officials in one respect, for it appears from the proceedings of Thursday of that term that the court opened at eight o'clock. At this session the bounds of the several districts of New Hanover precinct were prescribed, these districts being Lockwood's Folly, Brunswick, Town Creek, Newton (Wilmington), The Sound, Rocky Point, and Welsh Tract.* In the last two, Burgo Creek, (now spelled Burgaw) is named as a limit. At this term also we first find that the marks and brands of cattle were recorded, and that a list of defaulting jurors were fined thirty shillings each; also the probate of a power of attorney from Ex-Governor Burrington to his wife Mary (whom he left in this country.)

The court was held at Brunswick quarterly until the year 1740, when it began to be held at Wilmington, the first term there being held June 10, 1740, when "His Majesty's Commission of the Peace" was read and Matthew Rowan, Wm. Farris, James Murray, Sam. Woodward, Robt. Walker, Richard Eagles and Thos. Clark, Esqs., qualified as justices of said court, and Daniel Dunbibin produced the Governor's commission as "Notary Public and Tabellion" and qualified as such. This is the first appearance in our records of this ancient Roman and French official title, which continued in use for many years afterwards, and until 1802.

At this term an interesting question was presented to the court when Mr. Samuel Swann offered for probate a paper described as the "intended will" of a man who had neglected to sign it, but which had been signed by three witnesses, one of whom was examined, etc. Mr. Swann argued the motion for probate, and the court recommended to the Governor to grant letters testamentary.

At the June term, 1741, the first entry of the names of slaves authorized to carry guns as hunters on their masters' plantations was made by "Hon. Edwd. Moseley, Esq." for four men on his four plantations† and also the following: "Archd. Hamilton moved that Richd. Quince be excused from attending as a juror, it appearing he is a Freeman of one of the Cinque

---

* So called from an intended Welsh settlement there.

† At July Term, 1768, "Cornelius Harnett prayed leave for his man Jack to carry a gun at his two plantations, *Maynard* and *Poplar Grove*. Granted.

ports in Great Britain, of which he produced sufficient testimony. Granted."

At a later period "searchers" were appointed for Brunswick and Wilmington, and "patroles" for the districts, the latter being often prominent men, such as "Saml. Watters, Capt. George Gibbs, and Danl. McFarland for Northwest district in St. Philip's Parish." Many licenses to men and women to keep "ordinaries" in town and country were granted, (some being refused), and in one instance an application to keep a *coffee-house*, with license to sell liquors, was refused by the court on the ground that they had no authority under the law to grant such a license except to the keepers of ordinaries, although the court thought a *coffee-house* would be a public advantage.

In 1759 it was ordered that all travelers passing over Mount Misery ferry, "except inhabitants of New Hanover and Bladen," should pay four pence Proc. (proclamation money) for ferriage. Licenses were required to build mills, and sometimes land of adjacent owners was condemned for that purpose.

An entry at the November term, 1759, says: *"The Court and Jury* proceeded to choose grand and petit jurors for the next *Supreme Court,"* but how they proceeded is not stated, whether by a boy drawing from a prepared list out of a box or hat, as at present, or not, does not appear. Of course the "Supreme" Court for which the jurors were chosen was the next Superior Court.

At June term, 1760, Mr. Fred. Gregg brought into court an inventory of Governor Burrington's estate—a fair evidence of his recent death, the exact date of which has never been published.

About this period it was customary to fix tavern rates, chiefly for wines and liquors, of which there were many varieties.

There were no courts from January, 1773, to April, 1774, because of the everlasting quarrels between the Governor and Council, and the Assembly, about various matters of legislation, neither of them being willing to do what the other desired, but the sessions of the County Court in New Hanover were resumed in April 1774, at which term one of the first entries is the probate of the will of the distinguished lawyer and former Speaker of the Assembly, Samuel Swann.

At April term, 1775, Alfred Moore made his first appearance with a license from the Governor to practice law, and qualified; and at the same term Timothy Bloodworth (who twenty years afterwards beat him for the United States Senate) was appointed to keep the ferry between Wilmington and Negro Head Point. At October term, 1775, the clerk of the court, John London, was granted twelve months leave of absence to go to England on private business, and was authorized to appoint a proper person to officiate in his absence, and at the next (January, 1776) term he appointed Jonathan Dunbibin. The minutes from April term, 1776, to January term, 1777, are missing. This was attributable probably to the arrival of the British fleet under Sir Peter Parker, which entered the river April 18th and stayed until some time in June, as we see by the minutes of January term, 1777, that Jonathan Dunbibbin was allowed £10 Proc. "for the care of the records and for removing them from place to place to secure them from the enemy."

At January term, 1780, guardianship of Jane Quince and Ann Quince, daughters of Richard Quince, was granted to Richard and Parker Quince, they giving separate bonds for each ward in the sum of £300,000 each, showing that the estate was an unusually large one. At this term also, Henry Toomer, Wm. Hill and John Walker, Esqs., were appointed commissioners for taking into their possession the forfeited estates in the county, "agreeable to law," and at the next term each of them gave a separate bond in the sum of £200,000.

At the April term, 1780, the court chose three persons, viz, Francis Clayton, Francis Brice and John Walker, to "inspect money in this county."* At the January term, 1781, the fol-

---

* This was for the purpose of detecting counterfeits, which appear to have been largely issued, and against which the most severe legislation had been enacted. See Acts of 1748, and up to 1784.

lowing note is entered by the clerk at the end of the minutes: "Note—The British forces having landed at Wilmington under command of Maj. James Henry Craig on the 29th of January, 1781, prevented the court being held until January term, 1782."

At the January term, 1782, the will of Cornelius Harnett was proved and his widow, Mary, qualified as executrix, and administration on the estate of Gen. James Moore was granted to Alfred Moore during the absence of the executor, James Walker. At this term also a long list of absentees "supposed to be inimical to this State and to have forfeited their property," were required to appear and show cause why their several estates should not be confiscated.

At October term, 1785, it was "ordered that each of the constables in this county during the sittings of the court do appear in the court-house with a white staff not less than six feet long as a badge of their office." At the January term, 1786, a census of all free citizens was ordered to be taken by the captains of each company in the county.

At the April term, 1786, the will of Gen. Alex. Lillington was proved. At the July term, 1786, the court (which had been meeting at private houses), adjourned from Mr. Jenning's house *to the church,* where they met, and the only business transacted there was the probate of the will of Lewis H. DeRosset, upon whose motion years before, (1750) in the Colonial Assembly, the church had been constructed. If this proceeding was without reference to that fact (and no mention is made of it) it was a strange coincidence.

At the October term, 1786, the will of "the late Maj. Gen. John Ashe" was proved.

At the October term, 1787, the following curious entry is made:

"Thomas Lamb, having made it appear to the court that he could not bear the smell of hair-powder, flour, or wheat, it is ordered that he be exempted from attending as a juror this court."

January term, 1788, "ordered that fifteen shillings be allowed for the scalps of bears, panthers and wolves, and two shillings for scalps of wildcats," and the same day a boy fourteen years old came into court and asked that a record be made of the fact that some time previously he lost part of his ear by the bite of a horse. The fact was fully proved and ordered to be recorded. The reason, of course, was that he wished to be protected from the suspicion that his ear had been clipped for crime, which was one mode of punishment. At the June term, 1804, an entry was made that the Court was of the opinion that the scalp tax (on bears, wolves, panthers and wildcats), ought to be repealed, probably because it was becoming too heavy a drain on the treasury. At December term, 1804, "on petition of Thos. N. Gautier ordered that a mulatto named Philip Bazadare be emancipated." This man was for years the chief musician of the town, and his memory was preserved in an amusing sketch by the late Col. James G. Burr. He was also the fashionable barber, and the trumpeter of the Light Horse Company, whose bugle blasts as he dashed about the streets sounding the "Assembly," brought out every boy in the town.

SUPERIOR COURT—(ASHE AND SPENCER, JUDGES).

At the October term, 1765, the trial of a case which is mentioned in all the histories of the State, but in every one of them is differently, and in all of them is erroneously, described, took place. This was the case of Capt. Alexander Simpson, commander of the sloop of war, "Viper," charged with the murder of Lieutenant Whitehurst, of the same ship. The only correct account of the facts of this case that has ever been published, will be found in a foot note on page 127 of "A Colonial Officer and His Times,"* which is here reproduced, with the remark that since that note was published the latest and best history of the State, Ashe's, has appeared, but it also has the facts wrong by saying that the trial occurred at New Bern and

---
* By Alfred Moore Waddell.

HISTORY OF NEW HANOVER COUNTY. 223

that Simpson was acquitted, and that Judge Berry, believing he was going to be suspended, killed himself. The following is the note above referred to, as taken from "A Colonial Officer":

> NOTE.—As several of our historians have mentioned a certain duel fought by Capt. Alex. Simpson and Lieut. Thomas Whitehurst, of the ship "Viper," about the time of the Stamp Act excitement on the Cape Fear; and as not one of the statements given by these writers is correct, it may be well to give a true version of the affair as taken from the records. Wheeler, in his history, says that in February, 1766, a duel occurred between these parties; that Simpson sympathized with the colonists and Whitechurst (Whitehurst) favored Tryon; that Whitehurst being killed, Simpson was arrested, tried before Ch. J. Berry and acquitted; that Tryon insinuated connivance on the part of Judge Berry, summoned him before the Council, and the Judge, in a frenzy of apprehension, committed suicide, and Wheeler quotes Martin as authority for his statement. "Shocco" Jones, in his "Defense of North Carolina," says Simpson was condemned, but escaped and fled to England. Moore, in his History, says that Simpson (not Whitehurst) was killed, and that Whitehurst was convicted of murder, but that Judge Berry "granted him enough time before execution to enable him to escape," and that "Tryon was furious and so wrought upon the fears of Judge Berry that he committed suicide."
>
> In the first place, the duel occurred in Brunswick, March 18, 1765, and was caused not by the Stamp Act excitement but *by a woman*, according to Tryon's report to the Board of Trade. It was a brutal affair, in which Simpson not only broke Whitehurst's thigh with his shot, but broke his head with the butt of his pistol, breaking the butt and pan of the pistol at the same time. Simpson himself was shot behind the right shoulder, the ball coming out under his arm. The witnesses before the coroner's jury were Midshipmen James Brewster and James Mooringe. Simpson escaped the night before Governor Dobbs died, 28th March, and Tryon issued a proclamation offering £50 reward for his arrest, and wrote to Governor Fauquier, of Virginia, saying that as Simpson had some months previously married "Miss Annie Pierson, daughter of Mrs. Ramsberg, whose husband keeps a tavern in Norfolk," and as Mrs. Simpson had returned to Virginia he suspected Simpson had gone there; that "the weak state of his health and the dangerous condition of his wound, strengthened this conjecture, and it was "not probable that he should undertake a long voyage," and he characterized Simpson's conduct as "extraordinary." It certainly was extraordinary, and why the seconds or witnesses permitted it is incomprehensible. Simpson afterwards surrendered himself, was tried at Wilmington, October term, 1765, (a month before the stamp ship

arrived), was convicted of manslaughter, and branded with the letter M on the ball of the thumb of his left hand, in open court, and discharged, as appears by the record of the trial still preserved at the court-house in Wilmington. The allegation that Judge Berry's suicide was the result of his fright at the escape of Simpson, therefore, is wholly untrue.

In a letter to the Board of Trade, dated February 1, 1766, Tryon says: "Mr. Berry, Chief Justice of this Province, shot himself in the head the 21st December last, and died in Wilmington the 29th of the same month.* The coroner's inquest sat on the body and brought in a verdict of 'Lunacy.'" This was two months after Simpson's conviction, and nearly a year after the duel.

The following is a transcript of the record:

Wilmington, 23d October, 1765. Court met according to adjournment. Present, The Hon'ble Charles Berry, Esq., Chief Justice, Rob't. Howe, Esq., Associate Justice.

Evidence sworn,

Josh'a Grainger, Jr.,
Jon. Walker,
Wm. Lord,   The King
Jon. Eustice,   vs.
Jon. Fergus,   Alex'r. Simpson.
Wm. Hill.

On motion of the prisoner for counsel to be assigned him, Mr. Marmaduke Jones and Mr. Maurice Moore were admitted to speak to matters of Law, &c.

JURORS.

1. John Anderson,   7. George Parker,
2. John Daniel,   8. Wm. Campbell,
3. Uz. Williams,   9. Wm. Robeson,
4. Benj. Rhodes,   10. Rob't. Wails,
5. John Watson,   11. Benj'm. Stone,
6. Rob't. Walker,   12. John Gibbs.

Verdict—Jury find the Def't. not guilty of murder but guilty of manslaughter.

Court adjourned to Thursday morning.

Thursday, 24th Oct. 1765. Court met according to adjournment. Present, the Hon'ble Charles Berry, Esq., Chief Justice, Rob't. Howe, Esq., his associate Justice.

Alex. Simpson was brought to the Bar to receive sentence and prayed

---

*McRee (Vol. I, 175) speaks of Judge Berry as "that amiable gentleman and upright Judge Charles Berry, Chief Justice of the Province."

the benefit of his clergy—admitted. Ordered that he be branded on the ball of the thumb of the left hand with the letter M, which was executed in Court, and discharged by proclamation on paying the fees.

May, 1782. Alfred Moore, Esq., produced the Governor's commission appointing him Attorney-General pursuant to his election by joint ballot of both Houses of the General Assembly, and took the oath. Mr. Iredell (whom he succeeded as Attorney-General) appeared as one of the attorneys at this term.

November, 1782. At this term there were several indictments for murder and treason, and at the next term (May 1783) pardons were pleaded in these cases.

On the afternoon of the 11th of July, 1787, in rear of the original St. James church, and in what is now Fourth street near its intersection with Market street, a fatal duel was fought between Maj. Samuel Swann and Mr. John Bradley. The circumstances that led to the duel illustrated both a straining of the point of honor on one side, and the bitter hostility existing toward all Englishmen on the other.

A shipwrecked British officer who had lost all his belongings was brought into Wilmington, and his condition appealed so strongly to Maj. Swann, who was a highstrung gentlemen of fortune and distinguished lineage, that he invited him to become an inmate of his house. Mr. Bradley was a merchant, and the Englishman happening one day to be in Bradley's shop when some rings disappeared, Bradley charged him with stealing them. The stranger was helpless, and knew that if a personal encounter ensued and Bradley should be killed or even seriously injured, his own life would be the forfeit, but Swann immediately came to the rescue, and, asserting that the insult to his guest was an insult to himself, demanded an apology, which was peremptorily refused, whereupon he challenged Bradley. Swann, who had been an officer in the Revolution, was "a crack shot," and on the way to the meeting place told his second that he did not wish to kill his opponent and would only inflict a flesh wound upon him. This he did, wounding him in his hip; but as Bradley fell he fired, and his bullet struck Swann in the head killing him instantly. What became of the stranger is not known, but it is painful to reflect that he might have been an impostor, and really guilty of the theft with which he was charged.

At June term, 1788, of the Superior Court (Ashe, Spencer and Williams, Judges) Bradley filed a plea of pardon, which was demurred to, and the Court, after argument, took it under advisement and bound him over to the next term.

At the next term (in December) the court rendered its judgment, which was that the pardon appearing on its face to have been granted "by influence of a recommendation of the General Assembly and for no other reason," and being insufficient by the laws of the State, the demurrer was sustained—Judge Williams dissenting—and Bradley was bound over to the next term for trial, at which term he produced a second pardon and was discharged.

March, 1791. The Attorney-General (Moore) having resigned, John Louis Taylor, afterwards Chief Justice of North Carolina, was appointed Attorney-General *pro tem*, and Edward Jones, S. R. Jocelyn (a great lawyer), and Joshua G. Wright produced licenses, and qualified as attorneys.

March, 1792. Edward Jones produced his commission as *Solicitor-General*, (a new office the creation of which caused Moore to resign) and qualified.

May, 1796. Alfred Moore and Gen. Wm. R. Davie appeared as counsel on opposite sides, the two recognized leaders of the State bar. At this term a man from Onslow was indicted for murder, but the evidence showing that he had killed the deceased by a blow of his left fist given under the ear, the verdict was manslaughter, and the Governor pardoned him.

November, 1797. Johnston Blakely, son of John Blakely, deceased, appeared in court and chose Edward Jones, Esq., as his guardian. Bond given £4,000, with Peter and Daniel Mallett and John Hay as sureties. Blakely was the naval hero of the War of 1812, and a worthy successor of Paul Jones.

May, 1799. A man was sentenced to be hanged for grand larceny.

May, 1803. Wm. Gaston and John Haywood appeared as attorneys.

SHERIFFS OF NEW HANOVER COUNTY FROM 1739 TO 1804.

1739-41—Cornelius Harnett, Sr. (first sheriff).
1741-42—Thomas Clark.
1743-44—John Sampson.
1745-46—Robert Walker.
1747-48—Lewis DeRosset.
1749-52—Caleb Grainger.
1753-56—John Davis, Jr.
1756-59—William Walker.
1760-63—John Walker.
1764-65—Arthur Benning.
1766- —Obediah Holt.
1767- —James Moran.
1768-70—John Lyon.
1771-72—Arthur Benning (No courts from February, 1772, to April, 1773).
1774-75—Wm. Campbell.
1777- —James Bloodworth.
1779- —Thomas Jones.
1780- —Owen Kenan (British took possession and no courts from January, 1781, to January, 1782).
1782-1798—Thomas Wright (longest in office, 16 years).
1799- —William Nutt.
1800-01—David Jones.
1802-03—Wm. Bloodworth.
1804- —Roger Moore.

INDEX.

Albemarle 7
Allen, Eleazar 8, 12, 21, 23, 44
Anderson Fort 33
Armand, Colonel 182
Ashe, J. B. 12, 26, 46
Ashe, Col. J. 166, 167, 187, 221
Ashe, Samuel 210
Assup 24
Auburn 61

Bald Head 179
Barnett, Rev. J. 16, 31
Bartram 66
Bath County 7
Battle Moore's Creek 172
Battle Eliabethtown 189
Bear Inlet 7
Belfont 66
Belgrange 45, 68
Belvidere 48
Belville 48
Benning, A. 37
Bevis, Rev. C. 13, 67
Bishop 15
Bladen County 7
Blakeley, J. 226
Blanning, H. 194
Bloodworth 208, 209, 220
Blue Banks 20
Bluff, The 60
Borough of Wilmington 193
Boston 77
Boundary line 7, 8
Boyd, Rev. A. 102, 198
Bowlands 58
Braddock 22
Bridgen 72
Brown's Inlet 7
Brown, Col. T. 66, 189
Brown, Capt. J. 213

Brompton 67
Brunswick 9, 19, 23, 24, 25, 28
Burgaw Creek 218
Buchoi 47
Burgwin, J. 38, 98
Burr, J. G. 202
Burrington ... 8, 19, 21, 24, 39, 219

Calder, Lieutenant 30
Camp, Rev. J. 16
Carthagena 22
Carey, George 181
Castle Haynes 53
Caswell, R. 79
Caswell, W. 184
Charleston 15
Charming Peggy 28
Cedar Grove 51
Church, St. Philip's 12
Church, St. James's 200
Clarendon County 7
Clarendon Plantation 47
Clark, Gen. Thos., 41, 62, 63, 64, 65
Clayton, Francis 56, 181
Clinton, General 171, 179
Cobham 61
Collet, Captain 166
Convention 208
Corbett, Archd. 205
Cornwallis 171, 179, 182
Council of Safety 180
Cruizer Sloop .. 166, 173, 181, 213
Craig, Major 182

Dallison 61
Dalrymple 22, 46, 212
Davis, John 14, 21, 39, 46
Davis, Maj. Wm. 179
DeRosset, Mayor 27, 53, 196
DeRosset family 51, 52

INDEX

DeRosset, Louis 52, 201
DeKeyser, L. 56, 96, 199
Devane, Colonel 173, 210
Dick 14
Dickson, Wm. 183
Diligence Sloop 28
Dickinson, Colonel 189
Dobbs Sloop 28
Dorsey, L. 211
Dobbs, Gov.... 9, 11, 14, 23, 25, 46
Dram Tree 23
Dry, Wm....... 14, 15, 22, 29, 196
Ducking Stool 197
Dudley, C. 15
Dunbibin, D. 196
Duncan, A................... 196
Duplin 9, 12, 183
Dyer, M. 191, 205

Eagles 14, 15, 47
Education 203
Entry Book (note).......... 28
Evans 15

Female adventuress 73
Finian 71
Fire in Wilmington........ 73
Fisher, Fort 25
Forks, The 47
Fieldwork, Craig's 187

Gabourel 20
Gaston, Wm................ 227
Gause, Charles.............. 214
Gazette, N. C................ 198
Gazette, S. C........... 34, 187
Gillespie, Colonel 189
Godden, Colonel 189
Godfrey, Thos. 203
Gooch, Colonel 22
Gorman, Michael 182
Governor's Point 39
Graham, Maj. Jos........... 187
Grainger, Caleb 50, 196

Grainger, Joshua 191, 205
Gregg, F. 34, 196
Green Hill 57
Guerard 68

Halton, R........... 21, 22, 23, 50
Halton Lodge 49
Harnett, C. Sr....... 10, 11, 21, 28
Harnett, C. Jr., 34, 79, 81, 179,
              180, 185, 196
Hasell, Ch. J. 45, 68, 73
Haywood, John 227
Hellier, R. 195
Hermitage, The 53
Heron, B. 22, 186, 196
Higgins, M. 194, 201
Hilton 49
Hill, Wm................. 17, 87
Holt 72
Houston, Dr. 26
Hooper, Wm...... 64, 185, 197, 208
Hostler 202
Howe, Gen. Robt.... 23, 41, 65,
                166, 179
Howe's Point 40, 72
Hullfields 46
Huske, John 214
Hyrneham 55

Iredell, James 181
Irvine, Colonel 189
Innes, Colonel 192

Jocelyn, S. 202
Johnston, Gov... 11, 19, 23, 24, 191
Johnston, Fort.......... 22, 212
Jones, Edward............. 209
Jones, Marmaduke 196
Jones, R. J................. 217
Jones, Willie 208
Jumping Run 49

Kenan, Col. J....... 104, 168, 186
Kenan, Owen 96
Kendall 42

INDEX

Laurens 67
Lee, Light Horse Harry...... 190
Lee, Gen. Charles............ 181
Liberty Pond 180
Lillington, General.... 29, 59, 168, 186, 221
Lilliput 44
Lloyd, Thos. 29, 34
Lobb, Captain 29
London, J. 220
Lockwood's Folly 19
Love, Lieutenant 186
Lyon, John 196

Mabson, A. 91, 196
Maclaine, A....... 60, 92, 208, 209
Magnolia 61
Mallett, P. 199
Marion, General 67
Martin, Governor 73, 166
Martin, Colonel 181
Masonboro 70
Mason, Caleb 197
Masonic Lodge 199
Mass. Gazette 77
Maxwell, P. 68
McDonald 74
McLeod, A. 75
McRee family 43, 44
Mecklenburg Declaration 80
Mercury, Cape Fear... 37, 84, 198
Moore, Col. Maurice....... 18, 22
Moore, Roger 19, 20, 23, 41
Moore, Nathaniel 20, 21, 41
Moore, George 28, 57
Moore, Gen. Jas.... 23, 30, 34, 181
Moore, Judge Maurice....... 198
Moore, Judge Alfred. 47, 186, 209, 220
Moorefields 57
Morehead, Colonel 67, 189
Moseley, Edward 23, 55
Moseley Hall 57
McGallant 55
Mulberry 61

Murray, James........ 23, 62, 195
Nash, General 181
Neck, The 57
Negro Head Point.......... 48
New Inlet 25
Newton 23, 191

Oakland 66
Oak, The 54
Old Town 44, 47
Orton 42
Owen, Colonel 66, 189

Parry, Captain 175
Patience Sloop 28
Pennington 30
Person, Thos. 208
Pleasant Hall 55
Pleasant Oaks 44
Point Repose 62
Point Pleasant 54
Poplar Grove 50
Porter, John 39, 72
Potts, Joshua 213
Prospect 61
Purviance, Colonel 70, 171

Quince, Richard 37, 81
Quince, Parker 77, 78
Quincey, Josiah 76

Recorder 193
Regulators 32
Rice 23, 24, 45
Robeson, Col. Thos........ 67, 189
Robinson, Wm. 196
Rock Hill 51
Rocky Point 38
Rocky Run 51
Rose Hill 51
Rouse Tavern 186
Rowan, Matthew 23, 205
Ruby Sloop 28
Russellboro 42
Rutherford, John 58
Rutherford, General 168, 190

INDEX

Safety Committee...... 79 to 165
Sampson, John 196
Sans Souci 50
Schawfields 61
Scotch Highlanders 74
Sedgeley Abbey 68
Sheriffs of New Hanover..... 227
Slingsby, Colonel 189
Smallwood, J. 201
Smith, Landgrave 38
Smith, Benjamin........ 200, 214
Spring Garden 45, 55
Sprunt, James 40, 41
Stag Park 58
Stamp Act 25
Strawberry 56
Stewart, Andrew 198
Stevens "One"............... 31
Swain, Jo. 213
Swain, Governor 167
Swann Point 55
Swann, Samuel 54
Swann-Bradley duel 225
Swift, Lieutenant 216
Tabellion 218
Tapia 216
Tate, Rev. J............. 214, 209
Toomer, Lewis 20, 21
Tory Hole 190
Tryon, Governor 25, 73
Vats, The 56
Viper Sloop 28
Waddell, General....... 30, 51, 66
Waddell, John 48
Walker, Maj. Jack........ 69, 181
Walnut Grove 67
Washington's visit 210
Washington, Col. Wm........ 182
Watson, John 191
Webster, Lieutenant-Colonel.. 66
Wheat 39
Whitfield, Wm. 180
Whitehurst-Simpson duel 222
Wilmington 191
Wimble 191, 205
Wright, Colonel 189
Wright, Judge J. G.......... 210
York Plantation 41

www.ingramcontent.com/pod-product-compliance
Lightning Source LLC
Chambersburg PA
CBHW060116170426
43198CB00010B/918